3-

TALES *from the* ART CRYPT

TALES
from ART
the
CRYPT

THE PAINTERS,
THE MUSEUMS, THE
CURATORS, THE COLLECTORS,
THE AUCTIONS, THE ART

Richard Feigen

ALFRED A. KNOPF
NEW YORK
2000

THIS IS A BORZOI BOOK
PUBLISHED BY ALFRED A. KNOPF

Copyright © 2000 by Richard Feigen
All rights reserved under International and Pan-American
Copyright Conventions. Published in the United States
by Alfred A. Knopf, a division of Random
House, Inc., New York, and simultaneously in Canada by
Random House of Canada Limited, Toronto.
Distributed by Random House, Inc., New York.

www.aaknopf.com

Knopf, Borzoi Books, and the colophon are registered
trademarks of Random House, Inc.

ISBN 0-394-57169-X
LC 00-131136

Manufactured in the United States of America
Published June 23, 2000
Reprinted Once
Third Printing, September 2000

This book was set in Adobe Garamond.
Composed by North Market Street Graphics,
Lancaster, Pennsylvania
Printed and bound by Quebecor Printing,
Fairfield, Pennsylvania
Designed by Anthea Lingeman

For Sydney Freedberg

dernier des justes

Contents

Acknowledgments   IX

INTRODUCTION   3

DETECTIVE STORIES   5

THE JEFFERSON PORTRAIT   31

FRESH PAINT AND POSTAGE STAMPS   35

CHICAGO, NEW YORK, AND THE SAVING OF SOHO   39

THE STORM BEFORE THE CALM   66

DR. BARNES AND THE DEVIL   70

ROSE AND MORTON NEUMANN   92

THE WAR OF THE MUSEUMS   107

JULIEN LEVY   168

ARTISTS' VESTALS   175

THE BUTE "TRUMBULL"   196

BAKSHEESH   205

THE POWER OF THE PRESS   225

MARY AND LEIGH BLOCK   247

GERTRUDE STEIN: THE INHERITANCE   274

Notes   301

Acknowledgments

This started out as a collection of art-world memories, most of which were not extraordinary enough to record at the time but seemed worth recounting as the years passed. Some of the tales spun out easily, and to Vicky Wilson go my thanks for persuading me, notwithstanding a few false starts, that I could muster the discipline to actually get it done. Even so, I was surprised by her patience, and was left in no doubt about her storied skill as an editor. To Werner Muensterberger, who understands better than anyone the passion for objects, go my thanks for pressing me on.

As I stepped out, however, beyond anecdote, into waters treacherous for an art dealer, whenever I wavered there was always vital encouragement from Sydney Freedberg, for whom my respect and affection were profound. Sydney and I were of one mind on the subject, and he repeatedly admonished me to finish the museum chapter. Had this come from a less distinguished quarter, I might never have dared. If Sydney had still been around to have this chapter run by him, it would have been much improved. As it is, I am grateful to Catherine Freedberg for allowing me to dedicate this book to Sydney.

I am indebted to many old friends for refreshing my memories: Marilyn Alsdorf, Alice Albright Arlen, Robert Bernhard, William Bernhard, the late George Cohen, Edwin Eisendrath, the Earl of Elgin, Michael Findlay, Michel Fribourg, Chieko and Tokushichi Hasegawa, Scott Hodes, Jasper Johns, Burton Kanter, Werner Kramarsky, Stephan Lackner, Janice Levin, Susan and Richard Levy, William Lieberman, Sir Denis Mahon, Roger Mandle, Hubert Neumann, Analee Newman, Muriel Newman, Claes Oldenburg, Edmund Pillsbury, Cindy Pritzker, the Earl and Countess of Rosebery, James Rosenquist, Bernard Sahlins, W. Kelly Simpson, Saul Steinberg, Malcolm Wiener, and the late Claire Zeisler.

I am particularly grateful to busy colleagues and professionals who allowed me to intrude on their time for essential information, some on a number of occasions: Jane Alexander, the late E. Digby Baltzell, François Bergot, Arnauld Bréjon de Lavergnée, Coosje van Bruggen, Fred Camper, Timothy Clifford, Keith Christiansen, Anthony Crichton-Stuart, Charles Cunningham Jr., James Cuno, Irving Deal, Diane Dewey, Lawrence Feinberg, former President Gerald Ford, Anna Forlani Tempesta, Allen Frumkin, Frank Gehry, George Goldner, Irene Gordon, Marco Grassi, the late Francis Haskell, Catherine Hassell, David Jaffé, Lawrence Kantor, Richard Koch, Hilton Kramer, Bates Lowry, Malcolm MacKay, Souren Melikian, Lawrence Nichols, Anna Maria Petrioli Tofani, Rafael del Pino, the late Sir John Pope-Hennessy, Pierre Rosenberg, Bart Rykbosch, Samuel Sachs II, Alan Shestack, Susan Sontag, Ron Spronk, Eugene Thaw, Joseph Thompson, Nick Tinari, Roger Ward, the late Allen Wardwell, Bruce Weber, Shirley Williams, and Robert Wilson.

The book was the idea of my sister, Brenda Feigen; it was she who proposed it to Vicky Wilson. To Frances Beatty Adler, my friend and sidekick for over two decades, my thanks for reading the manuscript and steering me from some perilous shoals. Ann Milstein Guité followed through with tireless and boring research beneath her skills as a scholar, but with enthusiasm that was always encouraging. I also owe thanks to my other colleagues, Cynthia Boardman, Françoise Newman, Lance Thompson, Lance Kinz, Susan Reynolds, and Jeff Bailey, for their constant assistance; to my children, Philippa Feigen Malkin and Richard Feigen, for their encouragement; and finally, to my wife, Peggy, and my stepdaughters, Michaela and Christine, who entered my life with patience and understanding in the project's later stages, when they were especially welcome.

TALES *from the* ART CRYPT

INTRODUCTION

A rrows of barium nitrate pierce the black sky, tracings of invisible bullets aimed at the heart of what we have known as connoisseurship, the love and study of objects fashioned by man. Bit by bit, year by year, the ghostly missiles find their mark and the art crypt fills with casualties of the old order, museums, collectors, artists, those who already love art and those who could have. *Anciens combattants,* veterans of the culture wars, "elitists" who thus far dodged the bullets, still wander about in daylight hours as the legions of darkness sleep—hack political opportunists, affirmative culture activists, guardians of "family values," Bible-belting fundamentalists, strategic planners, management consultants, museum headhunters, box-office impresarios. The surviving veterans wander about, hoping for better days, lighting candles, trying not to curse the darkness, spinning vestigial myths from the crypt. . . .

At the dawn of the new millennium, things in the art world are not as they had always been. Dramatic changes started unfolding in the 1960s, triggered by Vietnam War inflation, the proliferation of money, the monetization of art, and the battle between the auction houses for hegemony in the marketplace.

During the last half of the century, there was still time for a ruthless buccaneer like Norton Simon to put together one of history's great collections, and for a scoundrel like Richard Glanton to break Albert Barnes's will and try to decimate his collection. Alice Toklas was still alive in the 1960s, clinging to the Picassos she had bought with Gertrude Stein in the early years of the century, and their paintings were still there in 1968 to be sold outside the auction rooms. There was still great twentieth-century art around for eccentric acquisitors like Rose and Mort Neumann, and for social climbers like Mary and Leigh Block. Art dealing did not yet seem like a dying profession, and there were still gentlemen dealers like Julien Levy and master salesmen like Sam Salz. There were art discoveries to be made. Countries were not yet provoked by the press and soaring prices into patrimonial protectionism. Although the American government had never placed a premium on culture, the Christian Coalition had yet to sight it in its cross-hairs as some blasphemous and lascivious beast lusting after its children. The corporate culture had not yet turned the museums into box-office palaces and mail-order houses, and transformed their directors from connoisseurs who proclaimed to the public their love of objects into administrators and fund-raisers who lured the crowds and spilled no red ink.

What will become in the new millennium of the kind of museum we had known for the last hundred years? Will the changes be reversed; will museums go back to surprising and exciting and teaching the public? Should they? Is the old way "elitist"? Should museums, like the entertainment industry, give the public what it wants to see—van Gogh, Monet, Renoir, Wyeth, Fabergé, more "multicultural" projects? Should finance and administration propel some young people into the museum field and others out? The questions are pressing.

DETECTIVE STORIES

For many art historians, some quite eminent, it would be convenient if a painting's paternity, like a person's, could be determined by a DNA test. This would obviate the need for an "eye" (of which, alas, many are deprived), it would save time, and it would prevent disputes, often ugly and personal, over authorship. For the few, however, born with the gift of connoisseurship—the ability to determine a painting's authorship through a sensitivity to its aesthetic qualities, like the recognition of a person's handwriting—life would be a lot less fun.

Nadine Effront was by no means a great sculptress, but she took herself seriously, must have had connections in her native Belgium, and had somehow obtained a commission for a big piece outside the Brussels airport terminal. She also had some good twentieth-century paintings in her Paris house, opposite Braque's studio. And she was also very chic. When she arrived in New York one day in the late sixties, I invited her to "21" for lunch. Not my favorite restaurant, but appropriate for a mondaine foreign visitor.

I arrived at the table holding the catalogue of a minor twentieth-century sale I was going to view at Parke-Bernet later that afternoon. Nadine took it from me and started thumbing through it. She stopped and started laughing. "Look at this," she said, and pointed at what looked like a bad late de Chirico, one of the usual later copies of the 1912–14 deserted plazas, a statue and its shadow. She asked me, "Have you ever seen a fake painting with a real signature?" "Well, voilà!" she said.

She explained how, in the 1930s, she had been living in Paris with the Spanish surrealist Oscar Domínguez. The surrealists operated as a tightly

Victor Brauner,
*Victor Victorach jette
au loin le coeur de la
culpabilité* (*Victor
Victorach Throws
Away the Heart of
Guilt*), 1949.
Inscribed "POUR
DICK SON AMI"

Gift of the artist to the
author, 1958

knit club, under the strict domination of André Breton. Of course I already knew the famous story of the evening in a bistro in 1938, when Domínguez had attacked Max Ernst, flung a bottle at him, and put out the left eye of Victor Brauner.

Domínguez was also unable to sell any of his own paintings, which may have contributed to his bad temper. He supported himself and Nadine by making and selling fakes of the work of his more successful friends. So Nadine explained her laughter at the Parke-Bernet catalogue entry. She and Domínguez had taken this same fake de Chirico to the artist. Domínguez explained that they had nothing to eat and asked de Chirico to sign the fake, which he did.

Years later, on New Year's Eve, 1957, Nadine was waiting for Domínguez at a bistro to celebrate with the surrealists. When he did not show up, she went with one of the artists to his studio. They found Domínguez, wrists slashed, blood gushing, painting a picture with his own blood. That's a painting, perhaps the only one, where a DNA test would work.

Victor Brauner, *La Porte*
(*The Door*), 1932

Los Angeles County Museum
of Art. Gift of Burt Kleiner

Usually, however, what works for humans does not work for paintings. Unless a painting is signed, or the artist is still alive to testify to authorship, or the documentation is complete, we have to guess who executed it. That is where connoisseurship comes in.

The most dependable way to figure out who painted a picture is to have an "eye"—to have taste, that ability to enter an artist's head, to see what he saw, to understand what he intended, as well as the intellectual climate of a period in history, to sense the age of materials like canvas or panel or pigment. Few people really have this flair. Although it has to be trained and honed, an "eye" seems to be born, not made. Many people become art historians, even well-known ones, without being so endowed. They try to remedy the deficiency by assimilating a lot of information, and with this information discover documents that purport to attest to a painting's authorship.

Since scholars of this stripe have difficulty recognizing an artist's "handwriting," they tend, in the course of their scholarly peregrinations, to run across important documents, and when they do they often try to find a painting that seems to fit the specifications in the document. They are unable to do it the other way around—that is, to recognize the artist's distinctive "handwriting" and then set about finding a document to prove the point.

Documents can indeed support an attribution. Someone with an "eye" can say, for instance, "This painting looks like a Poussin," based on its style, and then come across an inventory locating a picture of the same subject by Poussin in a contemporary collection, and thus tie the two together and establish the attribution. This is what happened in 1995.

Unusually, there were two quite separate old-master painting sales at Sotheby's in London on the same day, October 18, 1995: one quite unimportant, at ten-thirty in the morning, which, although it had 131 lots, Sotheby's squeezed into a thin catalogue by putting a number of illustrations on each page; and another, also supposedly minor sale, of the collection—really more the accumulation—of Ernest N. Onians, an eccentric Suffolk recluse. The Onians collection was divided into two parts: paintings, 283 lots, on the afternoon of the eighteenth; and furniture, objects, armor, and "curiosities," 245 lots, the next morning. This collection was given such short shrift that many of the items were not reproduced at all. Since the auctioneer usually sells about seventy lots an hour, he was obviously going to careen through the Onians paintings; Sotheby's never intends for sales to last much after five o'clock. The Onians catalogue looked more like a throwaway than a document demanding close attention. Most of the art trade, both in England and abroad, never received it at all. I, alas, cannot claim that excuse.

According to a memoir in the catalogue by Onians's nephew, the family had lost its Shropshire estates to gambling debts in the 1830s. Ernest rebuilt the fortune by recycling waste from hotel kitchens into pig swill, traveling sixteen hours a day, collected droves of girlfriends before he started collecting objects, married an "elegant" widow, and bought Baylham, a millhouse with a fifteen-foot spurting waterwheel, in 1940. He then spent the next fifty years, continuing after his wife's death, filling his "Medieval wing," "Georgian reception rooms," "Hall," and "Drawing room" with thousands of objects of every kind, locking them up in myriad rooms, carrying around rings of hundreds of keys, and protecting his treasures with wild security systems. Nothing was cleaned.

Everything was left as found. And it was in this condition that they came to Sotheby's in 1995.

This is exactly the kind of sale I would normally never miss. It seemed that Sotheby's had done nothing to check underneath the grime and had made no serious attempt at cataloguing, lazily calling almost everything "follower of," "manner of," "school of," "circle of," or "after" someone. A few paintings were "attributed to." It is lazy cataloguing that offers art sleuths their opportunities. Out of 283, only 13 paintings were reproduced in color, so parsimonious was Sotheby's with the catalogue of poor Ernest's treasures. Not only did the dirt on the paintings make the handful of tiny reproductions, as many as four to a page, unreadable, but the few in color were too red and of poor quality. Among those few reproductions, one caught my eye, but not enough to overcome my laziness that autumn Saturday night in the country and force me to rush to the airport to make the flight I had booked to London. The Onians collection was on view

Nicolas Poussin, *The Destruction and Sack of the Temple of Jerusalem*, 1626

Israel Museum, Jerusalem. © The Israel Museum, Jerusalem

at Sotheby's Sunday afternoon. The lot that made me pause, but barely, was number 49, "attributed to Pietro Testa," *The Sack of Carthage.*

Curiously, it was another discovery, in the catalogue of the morning sale that same day, that lulled me into remaining in New York: lot 50, catalogued as "Giovanni di Francesco Toscani." This painting was reproduced almost full-page in color. Toscani was a relatively minor Florentine follower of Lorenzo Monaco, working in the early fifteenth century. The saint's intense, almost ferocious gaze riveted me. It reminded me of *The Prophet Elijah* by Lorenzo Monaco in my own dining room. It still held something of the freshness, the excitement at the dawn of humanism, of these first forays into human emotions since ancient Greece. Yet this was not by Lorenzo Monaco. Nor, from reproductions in my library, did it seem to be Toscani. There was too much personality, too much power. Whatever it turned out to be, I was determined to buy the little painting. Finally, after showing a FedEx'd transparency to three of the most eminent authorities on early Italian painting, Lawrence Kantor and Keith Christiansen of the Metropolitan Museum and Carl Strehlke of the Philadelphia Museum, the answer emerged: the painting was by the young Fra Angelico, not long after 1418, probably a fragment of a Joseph from a lost *Adoration of the Magi,* influenced by Gentile da Fabriano's Strozzi altarpiece. The identification had been made without a trip to London. Sotheby's estimate was only £8,000 to £12,000. I was determined to buy the painting even if it cost me ten times the estimate, and for some reason I was overcome by laziness. I decided, as I was about to leave for the airport that Saturday night, to bid on the Fra Angelico on the telephone without physically seeing it. In the end, the Fra Angelico was knocked down to me for £26,000, a great bargain. But my complacency had kept me from ever seeing the Onians pictures.

Almost immediately after the Onians sale, rumors floated over that there was a lost Poussin in the auction. I grabbed my catalogue, of which none of my New York colleagues seemed to have received a copy. A quick look and it was obvious. Whoever had catalogued lot 49, "attributed to Pietro Testa," had even unwittingly inserted a clue: "In his choice of subject, Testa may have been inspired by Poussin's *Capture of Jerusalem by Titus* in the Kunsthistorisches Museum, Vienna." A glance at Jacques Thuillier's catalogue raisonné of Poussin's paintings revealed the answer, so elementary that it was amazing that the cataloguer had not

Fra Angelico, *Joseph*
(fragment), circa 1420

Collection Richard L. Feigen,
New York

even taken the trouble to look at Thuillier's new book. The Vienna picture is Poussin's copy commissioned by Cardinal Barberini in 1638–39 as a gift for Prince Egenberg, of his own earlier version, also painted for Barberini, in 1626, listed by Thuillier as lost and represented in his catalogue by a blank space. The painting, estimated at £10,000 to £15,000 and now, its identity established, worth some $10 million, sold in the Onians sale for £155,500 to a syndicate of dealers coached by the great scholar Sir Denis Mahon, with another London dealer as underbidder. Both dealers clearly thought that, even beneath the grime, they had a good chance of finding the lost Barberini Poussin. No one pays £155,500 for an autograph Pietro Testa, let alone a painting "attributed" to him. The Poussin, fully authenticated after cleaning, was sold in 1998 to Lord Rothschild, who donated it, most appropriately, to the Israel Museum in Jerusalem.

Discoveries like this are made only occasionally, and no one of us, regardless of an "eye," can spot them all, even after physically seeing them. No one's viscera reacts to every artist's "handwriting." But Poussin is an artist to whom I do respond, and on whose early work my teeth were cut in a previous episode.

Sometimes the execution of a painting of a certain subject by an artist is documented, like the lost Barberini picture, but multiple versions survive and the authorities disagree as to whether any of them is an autograph original. That is when forensics—scientific evidence—can sometimes help solve the problem. Scientific evidence, providing, for instance, the approximate date and place of origin, can, much like a pre-DNA paternity test, never establish authorship, but it can rule some possible authors out. So it was in the other Poussin case.

During a visit in 1975 to the scholar-dealer Malcolm Waddingham in London, I saw in his home a fascinating depiction of the horrendous scene of Saint Denis terrifying his own executioners by holding his decapitated head above his bloody torso. It was not just the bizarre subject and the drama that drew me to the painting; I found it beautiful, of extraordinary quality. I asked Malcolm who painted it, and he said, "Filippo Napolitano." Napolitano, a contemporary of Poussin whose real name was Filippo d'Angeli, was born in Rome between 1590 and 1596. He was primarily a landscape painter, working in Florence and Rome, and died in 1629. I bought the painting from Waddingham for £2,500, and it hung in my home for many years.

During those years, I had opportunities to see a number of Filippo Napolitanos. I had also become better acquainted with the work of Nicolas Poussin, particularly his peculiar dynamics—the tension between the figures in his paintings, the sense of suspended time and action—and his magisterial draftsmanship. First I became convinced that the *Saint Denis* was clearly not by Filippo Napolitano. Then I went through every artist I could think of who worked in Emilia, Tuscany, or Rome in the first half of the seventeenth century, which was the apparent place and time of origin of the painting. Nothing fit. And why, anyway, would an Italian artist paint this obscure legend which, according to Thuillier in *Poussin Before Rome,* had been "so intimately associated with Paris and the French monarchy" since the Middle Ages?

Furthermore, the composition of the decapitated Saint Denis frightening his executioners had, since the 1958 Paris Poussin symposium, been accepted as Poussin's. French revolutionary documents record one version, from the abbey of Saint-Denis, attributed to Poussin, and

Nicolas Poussin, *Saint Denis Frightening His Executioners with His Head*, circa 1618

Collection Richard L. Feigen, New York

another, from Saint-Jean-le-Rond, listed as a "copy after Poussin." What remained, of course, was to find the lost original.

It was clear that the former version from Saint-Denis, in Thuillier's opinion probably the one sent to the Trappist monastery of Notre-Dame at La Meilleraye in the reign of Louis XVIII and still in the convent there, is, despite the descriptions in 1795 and 1797 documents as "by Poussin" and "copy after Poussin," respectively, indeed an inferior copy. It has not been determined which, if any, of the other ten versions discovered so far is the ex-Saint-Jean-le-Rond version, referred to in the 1795 inventory as "copy made after Poussin." But the fact that eleven versions of this composition, more than of any other seventeenth-century French picture, as well as drawing copies in the Louvre and the Uffizi, have already turned up, leads inescapably to two conclusions: that the eighteenth-century ascriptions of the composition to Poussin are accurate; and that Poussin was already a celebrated painter by the time he painted the original. Copyists do not congregate around the work of minor artists. Yet the fact remained that the composition did not, at least superficially, look like Poussin's work that we know.

Meanwhile, as my interest in the painting increased, it gravitated from over my hall table to over my dining room fireplace. Over the years, as I saw more of Poussin's work, I was reminded more and more of the *Saint Denis*. What seemed to put one off from this ambitious attribution was the painting's small scale relative to the number of figures in it. But there seemed always to persist that powerful dynamic of tensions binding the figures to each other, and the way the players in the drama are caught in suspended action. Every time I looked at the painting, my mind turned to Poussin. At the same time, I knew of no Poussin with figures so small. And the painting had this dark and ominous atmosphere, alien to seventeenth-century French painting, which was usually more blond. Except for its French subject, the *Saint Denis* seemed to relate more to Emilian painters of the early seventeenth century—to the landscapes of Annibale Carracci and Masteletta, to Lodovico Carracci, Bartolomeo Schedone, and the young Guercino. And it did not remotely resemble the work of any French painter. Yet it must have been painted by a Frenchman. The answer finally came to me: a French painter who had visited Emilia and been influenced by Emilian painting. Could Poussin have painted the picture in Emilia, or shortly after his return from there to France, early in his career, before his style was fully formed? It was known from three of Poussin's contemporary biographers that Poussin had made a trip to Italy—it was assumed early in the 1620s—gotten as far as Florence, and suddenly returned to France without ever reaching Rome, the city of his dreams, before he made his permanent move there in April 1624. Most of the scholars who saw the painting in my home seemed to shrug off the Poussin attribution. But a few, like Edmund Pillsbury of the Kimbell Art Museum, a gifted connoisseur, did not.

The "Poussin Year," the 1994 quadricentenary of his birth, approached, and among the various exhibitions being planned, none, not

even the great retrospective at the Grand Palais, intended to deal with
Poussin's cloudy pre-Roman period. The neglect of the formative years
of perhaps France's greatest painter seemed strange indeed. I felt that
these years had to be explored. My attention shifted from my painting of
Saint Denis to the subject in general. If there was one attribute every
great painter seemed to share, it was that their genius revealed itself in
childhood and remained with them into old age. I had never heard of a
great painter who suddenly bloomed at thirty. There had to be early
work by Poussin, and from the documentary evidence of lost works, his
commissions—such as the altarpiece of *The Death of the Virgin* from
Notre-Dame de Paris, last recorded in Brussels in 1815—were substantial
enough to suggest that Poussin was a celebrated painter well before he
decamped to Rome. I decided that the subject merited an exhibition in
our London gallery, concurrent with the Poussin retrospective's London
venue at the Royal Academy and the exhibition at the Dulwich Picture
Gallery of the sixty-five Poussin drawings from the Royal Collection at
Windsor Castle. This latter group included, incidentally and fortu-
itously, the fifteen "Marino" drawings, of only nineteen drawings, and,
at that time, no paintings, ascribed to Poussin's pre-Roman period.

To have an exhibition, *Poussin Before Rome,* we needed something to
exhibit. A hunch about a body of work was not enough. I was intrigued
not only by my *Saint Denis Frightening His Executioners* but also, from
reproductions, by the *Saint Denis Crowned by an Angel* in Rouen, despite
its rejection in 1966 by Sir Anthony Blunt, the leading Poussin authority,
and by all subsequent scholars except Jacques Thuillier. In April 1993 I
took my painting and boarded a plane for London's Gatwick, the only
access to Rouen's airport from a major city. I changed to a small plane at
Gatwick, into which the painting barely fit, and arrived in Rouen in a
rainstorm. I was greeted at the museum by François Bergot, the director,
whose interest in the project had encouraged me from the outset and
who had invited me to come with the painting. I set it up on the floor
next to the *Saint Denis Crowned.* I studied the larger painting for a long
time, and drew two conclusions: that it was indeed by Poussin; and that,
although my smaller, horizontal picture was different in some ways, the
two paintings were by the same hand. The major difference was in the

palette—dark, "Emilian" in the smaller picture, blond and "French" in the larger. One positive factor was that in the left background of the Rouen picture Poussin painted, sketchily and in reverse position, the scene of Saint Denis beheaded. Given Poussin's authorship, it seemed impossible that an artist important in his own time would have adopted a rare scene from a lesser artist and then, instead of copying it laboriously, sketch it into his larger work, and in reverse at that. Only the author himself would have taken such a liberty.

Rouen offered the additional opportunity to examine one of the other versions of the *Saint Denis Frightening His Executioners.* I took my version over and set it against the wall. There was no question that the Rouen picture was a copy. The groups of figures were slavishly conceived, with no tension between them. Irrelevant details had been added to the landscape. I put my picture back in the carrying case, bade Monsieur Bergot goodbye, and took off by train for Paris. I left the painting at our shippers to be examined by Jacques Thuillier. Pierre Rosenberg invited me to his home to see his own version, which he knew to be a copy. Interestingly, and I think misleadingly, it was inscribed in French "faict a Rome 1641." It may well have been this inscription and the poor quality of Pierre Rosenberg's own copy that put this distinguished scholar, now director of the Louvre, off the scent of the lost original. The inscription implied a Roman origin for the composition and a date in the middle of Poussin's career. It was Rosenberg's belief, as it was of most of the scholars, that my *Saint Denis* was painted in Italy. Since I had come to believe more firmly than ever that Poussin had painted it, either during that first, aborted trip to Italy or just after his return to Paris, the only thing that remained unresolved was the dramatic difference in palette between my picture and the Rouen *Saint Denis Crowned.* If Poussin's first Italian trip had to be squeezed into a short period before the summer of 1622, when he apparently arrived in Paris from Lyons, met the Cavaliere Marino, and became involved in making drawings for Marino's poems, it would be difficult to resolve this stylistic change. But then, at dinner one night in a Paris café, Thuillier informed me that a document had surfaced in the National Archives dated June 10, 1619, placing Poussin in Paris by September 1618, four years earlier than anyone had thought. The document, a bill for rent from a master goldsmith, implied that Poussin was already affluent at the age of twenty-four, and since he had inherited nothing, he must already have been successful enough to have made the money from painting.

I now had a plausible scenario. Thuillier postulates that Poussin made his way to Italy in 1617 or early 1618, most probably traveling to Venice and from there to Bologna, where he undoubtedly encountered some of the leading artists, before going to Florence, from whence he suddenly, for reasons that his biographers leave unclear, returned to Paris by September 1618. Among the works he executed in Paris would have been the *Saint Denis Frightening His Executioners,* which I assume was done soon after his return and his exposure to Emilian painting, and, later, the Rouen *Saint Denis Crowned,* commissioned for the church of Saint-Germain-l'Auxerrois. I speculate that when he left for Rome in 1624, he took with him the small and portable Saint Denis beheaded. Although it would require testing the fabric supports of nine inferior copies and one fragment, my hunch is that at least some of these were painted by artists who saw the original in the celebrated French artist's Rome studio between 1624 and at least 1641, the date of the Rosenberg copy. As for the fragment of the composition that Bréjon de Lavergnée discovered in Lille in 1993, if it is, as Thuillier speculates it may have been, from an autograph Poussin, Poussin himself may have painted an enlarged version, in Rome, of the smaller French original. It remains to test the fragment's fabric support.

Sir Denis Mahon, the other great Poussin scholar who was inclined to accept Poussin's authorship for my painting, had told me that he remembered seeing in the Gabinetto di Disegni of the Uffizi almost forty years before, during his research for the 1958 Paris Poussin colloquium, a copy of the subject of my painting. But despite his extraordinary memory in his ninth decade, he could not remember in which portfolio he had seen it. So, during a week in Florence in July 1993, I went every morning to the Uffizi Gabinetto di Disegni to go through every possible folder. I never found the drawing, which Thuillier later located in preparation for his book *Poussin Before Rome,* which, much to my amazement and joy, he wrote for my exhibition.

But one day in the Gabinetto di Disegni I was introduced to Dottoressa Anna Forlani Tempesta, the scholar who had catalogued the Lehman Collection drawings for the Metropolitan Museum. Hoping she might have run across the missing Poussin copy in the Uffizi folders,

I showed her the photograph of my painting. She said she recalled a drawing in the Lehman Collection that reminded her of the painting. I got hold of a Lehman catalogue, and there, catalogued by Forlani Tempesta as early seventeenth-century Emilian—later attributed by Arnauld Bréjon de Lavergnée, director of the Musée des Beaux-Arts in Lille, to Filippo Napolitano—was a discovery much more important than the missing Uffizi copy. It was clearly a red chalk preparatory study for the decapitated figure on the right side of my painting. I confirmed this to my satisfaction when I went over to see the drawing at the Metropolitan on my return to New York. The Emilian attribution of course made sense. The drawing was clearly indebted to the work of Lodovico Carracci, and closely resembled what Guercino was doing when Poussin most probably passed through Bologna in 1617 or early 1618, the dates Thuillier now ascribes to the Italian trip. It may well have been brought back, perhaps with others, by Poussin to France from Italy. I asked Linda Wolk-Simon, curator of the Lehman drawings, if she could find a French or Italian watermark. The drawing could not be safely removed from its mount to be examined. In any event, I was certain this was the earliest known Poussin drawing.

There remained, as far as I was concerned, one final step toward convincing the dissenting scholars who still believed that my version—as well as the other ten that had surfaced by the opening of the *Poussin Before Rome* exhibition in January 1994—was just an Italian copy of a lost Poussin composition. That step was the forensics, still only an adjunct to connoisseurship: Is the canvas Italian or French? And are the pigments and their application consistent with Poussin's? A tiny canvas sample was removed from the edge and submitted to the French Textile Institute. The results came back: French. Catherine Hassell of Painting Analysis, University College, London, tested tiny samples of each pigment. None of the results was inconsistent with Thuillier's speculation that Poussin had painted the picture between 1618 and 1620.

No DNA test exists for paintings—except perhaps for that single bloody Domínguez—and, like paternity tests, there can be no scientific or documentary proof of authorship, only disproof. But in the presence of stylistic evidence, science is a powerful ally.

The *Poussin Before Rome* exhibition opened in London in January 1994 to critical acclaim, due largely to Jacques Thuillier's groundbreaking

text. Every Poussin ascribed to the pre-Roman period was in the exhibition, with the exceptions only of the queen's fifteen "Marino" drawings—which were concurrently on view in the area, at Dulwich—and one other drawing. Couriers brought loans from the Rouen, Budapest, and Munich museums and from the Metropolitan. Rouen had kept its promise to lend the *Saint Denis Crowned* even after Pierre Rosenberg had changed his mind and finally accepted Poussin's authorship in the autumn of 1993. The owners graciously sent the watercolor study for the lost *Death of the Virgin.* In addition to ten of the eleven known versions of *Saint Denis Frightening His Executioners* (the eleventh, at the Fondazione Cini in Venice, was committed to the exhibition but was held up by the Italian cultural authorities just long enough to miss the London opening. Its quality, Thuillier agreed, was so inferior that the catalogue reproduction was allowed to suffice).

Of the nineteen works on paper and the single Rouen paintings universally accepted as authentic works by Poussin in his pre-1624 period, all were in London for the scholarly activities celebrating the artist's four hundredth birthday. All, that is, except one small battle drawing. The Louvre was the only museum to refuse to lend.

One more detective story, still in progress. In March 1973 my wife and I were on a buying trip in the Cotswolds for her Bedford, New York, antique shop. The rolling green hills, networked by narrow winding roads through ancient villages, at the outskirts of which one usually came upon an endless stone wall and then the august gates of a great country house, and, in the center, on the green, the old church, with its ancient graveyard seemed to me what the countryside is all about.

Again I digress from the story. I was reminded of this English countryside on Thanksgiving Day, 1996, driving with my son near Upperville, Virginia. Later, at the holiday table, I heard how Disney had almost succeeded in building a "theme park" on thousands of acres in the area, and I realized how threatened is the little we have left of our early history, and how few Americans care about it. That night I slept in Dolley Madison's four-poster in James Monroe's "Oak Hill," designed by Thomas Jefferson, one of America's great houses, and sat the next day in George Washington's and James Madison's chairs in front of the white marble mantels given to President Monroe for his new house by his Revolutionary colleague, the Marquis de Lafayette. Seeing the difficulty the owners have in keeping the place up, what with confiscatory inheritance taxes, I was hardly surprised that our host, my children's uncle, had favored the Disney theme park proposal, while their aunt had opposed it. The community was riven on the subject, and still was, months after Disney had abandoned the project in the face of all the controversy. It crossed my mind that my children's children might never celebrate Thanksgiving in that historic house, set in that rolling Virginia horse country. And how many Americans would have gotten there in time before it disappeared? Should the government in some way compensate these owner-caretakers for spending their lives caring for these national shrines? If not, will they all be abandoned? Might there not, in compensation, be some mitigation of inheritance taxes on national monuments and their surrounding property?

Back in March 1973, my then-wife and I pulled onto the green of the Cotswolds village of Stowe-on-the-Wold at dusk, as lights were being turned off in the antique shops around the green. She said, "Let's get

back to our hotel," in the nearby village of Tetbury. "Everything's closing. This place is a tourist trap." "We're here," I said. "Let's give it a shot
for a few minutes anyway." Sandra went into one shop and I another.
There were paintings scattered around the room. I was suddenly
brought up short by a landscape in an early eighteenth-century frame
painted bright yellow. I asked the girl standing near the door, "Are you
the proprietor?" "I'm sorry, sir. They're at the Chelsea Antiques Fair. I'm
afraid most of our stock is there." "Well, you might give me your trade
prices on a few of these pictures here." I waved at four or five paintings,
among which was my little "landscape with travelers and a hermit."
"How much is this one?" "£175." "What's your best trade price?" Just
then my wife walked in the door. "Let's go," she said. "I found a few
pieces of brass, but really not worth the stop. There's nothing in this
town." I motioned to her with my hand. Seeing that I was holding a
painting and not an antique, she gathered it was serious. "£160, trade
price," said the shopgirl. "Well, I don't want to leave empty-handed, so
I'll take this one." I wrote a check. "Should we give this to your truckers?" My wife was having her brass picked up from across the square. "If
you have some newspaper or a bag, I'll just take it along. And can you
give me a bill of sale for customs?" As we walked out onto the village
green, my wife whispered, "What is it?" "I'll tell you in the car." I was
not in fact sure what it was, except that it was painted in Rome in the
first quarter of the seventeenth century. It was clearly someone close to
Domenichino, someone earlier than Claude Lorrain.

Back in New York, I had the yellow paint taken off the period frame.
And I gave the painting, which was filthy, to a conservator to clean. He
removed the old lining canvas and on the back of the original canvas
found the inscription "Jabach/no. 582." This was of considerable importance, since Jabach was the greatest collector in seventeenth-century
France, and one of the biggest buyers at the sale in the 1640s, after
Cromwell's revolution, of King Charles I's legendary collection. Jabach
later sold the bulk of his collection to Louis XIV in 1671, and this formed
the original nucleus of the Louvre. The inventory of the remainder of
Jabach's collection was taken in 1695 after his death, and was published
in 1894. I checked this inventory, and there, under number 582, was the
description: "un aveugle assis au pied d'un arbre ou il y a une chapelle
avec des signes de miracles et deux paisans passans devant. 80 liv. [a blind
man seated at the foot of a tree where there is a chapel with emblems of

miracles and two peasants passing before it. 80 livres.]" But as with many pictures in this inventory, no artist's name was listed.

The conservator was a disciple of Caroline and Sheldon Keck, who had developed conservation techniques that were still popular in the 1970s but that have since been largely discredited. These techniques included relining pictures, even if they did not immediately need relining, as a preventative against future cracking rather than as a cure for damage already suffered; relining with wax rather than glue, or a combination of glue and wax; and using nonorganic rather than organic varnishes.

Both the lining and the varnishing theories indeed had a basis in logic. The traditional lining technique, used through some three hundred years, required great pressure to bind together the original canvas and the new support. This pressure resulted in squashing the painting's impasto. Some of the artist's handwriting, his vigor, was lost. The new wax lining technique used heat, which melted the wax, to bind the two canvases together. In theory, the painting's surface would not be affected. In practice, it turned out that the wax often seeped through to the surface, altering the painting's aesthetic. This depended to some extent on how porous a fabric the artist used. I remember one case of a famous Miró that came into my hands in the 1960s, in which the artist used a rough, porous burlap, which, when Miró retrieved the painting years later, even he could not rescue from the effects of its wax relining. As for the traditional organic varnishes, they yellow with age, and nonorganic varnishes theoretically remain clear.

So it was that the conservator, after taking the old lining canvas off my picture, applied a new wax lining, in this case a transparent one to reveal the Jabach inscription through it. I have no idea now whether the painting really needed to be lined at all. I was less sophisticated about conservation in those days. I have learned to trust my common sense more and the word of "professionals" less, whether an airlines desk agent telling me a flight has already left the gate when I doubt that it has, or a conservator telling me a painting should be relined when it looks sound to me.

Nicolas Poussin, *Saint Denis Crowned by an Angel,* circa 1620–21

Musée des Beaux-Arts, Rouen. © Musée des Beaux-Arts de Rouen. Photograph: Didier Tragin/Catherine Lancien

After my landscape was cleaned those nonorganic varnishes were applied. As the grime came off, the painting's quality emerged. After it was taken to London and Rome for inspection and comparison by the leading authorities in the field, Denis Mahon and Luigi Salerno, who later published it in his book *Landscape Painters of the Seventeenth Century in Rome* as an autograph work by the great Bolognese painter Domenico Zampieri, called Domenichino. But Richard Spear, a professor at Oberlin College, was about to stake his claim on the artist with the catalogue raisonné he was preparing, and published in 1982. When a scholar publishes the only modern monograph on an artist, whatever the sensitivity of his connoisseurship, he considers himself and sometimes comes to be considered the authority on the artist. Sometimes, however, if his "eye" is not highly regarded, he is not. In the case, for instance, of Annibale Carracci, Domenichino's master, it is not Donald Posner, author of the standard catalogue raisonné, who is consulted on authorship, but Sir Denis Mahon, an octogenarian "gentleman scholar," without academic affiliation, so distinguished for his connoisseurship that he was knighted by the queen. Mahon is also considered the authority on Domenichino. But while Posner has absented himself from scholarly debate on Annibale Carracci since publication of his book, Spear continues as a presence in Domenichino scholarship.

After discovery of the Domenichino, Spear asked me for photographs of various details of the painting. In due course he informed me that he did not consider the painting to be by Domenichino and was omitting it from the list of autograph works in his book but including it as a copy. Although I did not agree with him, nor at the time did Denis Mahon, who wrote to me quite adamantly on the subject, this was Spear's privilege, although not with my photographs, to which I held the copyright. Further, I discovered quite by chance some months after publication of his book that Spear had deposited, in a file of Domenichino copies in the Witt Library in London, all the detail photographs I had lent him for his private examination.

There are certain unwritten rules of the scholarly game. One of them limits use of borrowed material, like photographs, to the purpose for which it was borrowed, and dictates return to the lender. Another— for instance, in the case of works borrowed for an exhibition, or photographs borrowed for a book or article—is to adhere to the lender's understanding of the work's attribution unless he is alerted to a change in attribution and agrees, in the first case, to lend it under the changed name, and, in the second, to having his photograph used for the changed attribution. Often, however, an institution, usually Italian, but in at least one case I recall, German, borrows a painting, and then months later the owner, having been given no notice at all, opens the exhibition catalogue and finds his painting with a new name.

This happened to the Earl of Elgin in 1967. His family had, for almost two centuries, owned what they always believed was a *Liberation of Saint Peter* by the rare early seventeenth-century German painter Adam Elsheimer, and it had always been catalogued as such, as late as 1952 in Weizäcker's catalogue raisonné. Lord Elgin was asked to lend it to the Elsheimer exhibition in Frankfurt, and he agreed. When the catalogue reached him at his home in Scotland, he found his painting ascribed to Pieter Lastman, a follower of Elsheimer. The organizers had a right to reattribute the painting. But they did not have the right to change its name without giving Lord Elgin the option of withdrawing it from the exhibition.

In 1989 I received a request for the loan from my collection of an *Adoration of the Child,* by the strange early sixteenth-century Sienese mannerist Girolamo Genga, to the *Domenico Beccafumi* exhibition at the church of San Agostino in Siena. For years I had admired this crazy painting on the London sitting room wall of the legendary dealer Julius Weitzner—with its bizarre distortions and lemon-green and raspberry palette. Julius would never sell it to me because it belonged to his daughter Margie, who lived in Rome. When, in 1979, Margie tragically predeceased her father, Julius sadly sold me the painting. He knew it was for my own collection, and that I would not sell it. Although Julius called the painting "Sodoma," I had no idea who had really painted it. I think he gave it the name "Sodoma," the nickname of Giovantonio Bazzi, a foppish Sienese contemporary of Genga and pupil of Leonardo da Vinci, because the weirdness of Sodoma's life—he kept a menagerie of young boys and exotic animals, with the former of which, and possibly the latter, he conducted his extravagant sex life, hence the nickname—seemed to fit the weird distortions of form and palette of my *Adoration*. My first clue to the authorship of my painting, which hangs in my dining room, came at lunch there one day with Sir John Pope-Hennessy and Keith Christiansen, consultive chairman and curator, respectively, of the Euro-

Domenichino,
Landscape with Shrine and Figures, circa 1615

Collection Richard L. Feigen,
New York

pean paintings department at the Metropolitan Museum. Pope-Hennessy asked me if I would sell him the painting. Though he repeated the question several times over the ensuing months, I never knew whether he was asking for himself or for the museum. Each time he asked, I said, "John, I'm flattered by your interest, but I love the painting, and, incidentally, when Julius Weitzner sold it to me from Margie's estate, I told him I wouldn't sell it." And each time I asked Pope-Hennessy who had painted the picture, he coyly demurred, and Christiansen kept his confidence. Then one day, when "the Pope" finally came to believe I would indeed never sell it, he gave me the name: Girolamo Genga. Keith Christiansen concurred. So the painting had been baptized by two of the most eminent scholars in the field of early sixteenth-century Italian painting.

Then, in 1989, came the loan request from Siena. On the loan form, "Girolamo Genga" was carefully typed in. I signed the form, it went off to Siena with a transparency, and in due course the painting left for

Siena. The next summer, while walking through the Beccafumi exhibition, I came upon my painting. There on the wall was the label "Maestro dell'Adorazione Feigen [Master of the Feigen Adoration]"! I opened the telephone-book-sized catalogue, and there again was this attribution to the newly minted, nonexistent artist, with a catalogue entry relating it to a copy in a Milanese collection. There are those, I suppose, who would be amused to have an artist named after them. I was not.

Shortly afterward, I found myself sitting next to Dottoressa Anna Maria Petrioli Tofani, director of the Uffizi, at a dinner at I Tatti, the wonderful home that Bernard Berenson left to Harvard University. It happens that Petrioli Tofani was not only a member of the scientific committee for the Beccafumi exhibition, she had written her doctoral dissertation on Genga and is considered the authority on this rare artist. I asked Petrioli Tofani, "Who do you think painted my picture?" "There is no question. It is by Genga. The version in Milan is a copy of your picture." "Then what is this attribution to the 'Master of the Feigen Adoration'? On what authority do they change these attributions? When the catalogue entry was written, my painting hadn't even arrived in Siena, and whoever wrote the entry hadn't even seen it. And what do they use this 'scientific committee' for? You are the authority on the artist, you are a member of the committee, you are firm about the attribution to Genga, and yet they fly in your face with this absurd attribution." Petrioli Tofani explained it. "There is in Italy a confrontation between the universities and the museums. These entries are written by university students. They pay no attention to us." So there it was. I had seen it in other cases but never knew why. The point here was not bad scholarship. A scholar has the right to be bad, or good. The point is that you can't make an agreement on one basis and then change the terms without alerting the other party and giving him the chance to rescind the agreement.

As to Spear's confusion about the Domenichino, and to the doubts that he has been able to sow with others over the past twenty-odd years about the painting's authorship, the clue lies, I think, in his description in his book: "pasty in execution, heavy and airless." The problem with these nonorganic varnishes is that while they indeed do not yellow with age, in the two decades since these varnishes were widely used, instead of remaining clear, they have become rather milky and opaque. This, I sus-

Girolamo Genga,
Adoration of the Child,
circa 1505

Collection Richard L. Feigen,
New York

pect, was the reason for Spear's initial assessment. At this writing, the suspect varnish and wax lining are in the process of being removed, and I wonder if Spear will revisit the subject after the cleaning.

Spear's refusal to accept the painting has caused other scholars to seek an alternative attribution, and the Louvre to revive a Domenichino attribution for a painting of the same subject which had been relegated for generations to its basement as a copy. The Louvre version had, interestingly, been among the pictures sold by Jabach to Louis XIV in 1671. The question now of course is, did Jabach sell the king a copy painted in France, and keep the original; or did he sell the original and have a copy painted for himself? By the autumn of 1996, Pierre Rosenberg and Stéphane Loire of the Louvre believed in the latter theory, I in the former. They were convinced that Jabach had sold the king the Domenichino original and had a copy painted for himself in France some forty or fifty years later.

I examined my picture again very carefully, as I had done for over twenty years, and I could not bring myself to believe a Frenchman could have painted it. As far as I was concerned, it had to have been painted in Rome, and by an Italian, in the first twenty years of the seventeenth century. The style told me this. And I remained convinced that the Louvre version, considerably "blonder," smaller, more French in feeling, was indeed a French copy. Furthermore, the Louvre picture is on a wood panel, notwithstanding that the Louvre records show it on canvas, whereas mine is on canvas. Spear in his book lists only three paintings by Domenichino on panel. Wood was not Domenichino's usual support.

By the time I discussed my thoughts with Sir Denis Mahon on the eve of the 1996 Domenichino exhibition at the Palazzo Venezia in Rome, organized by Richard Spear, Sir Denis had been swayed by the long controversy over the picture and the Louvre's new conclusions about their own version. He now had his own doubts. Salerno, who had died some four years earlier, never abandoned his conviction that my painting is by Domenichino.

I recalled the forensics on the Poussin *Saint Denis Frightening His Executioners.* "Denis," I suggested, "why don't I have the Institut Textile de France in Lyons test the fabric for its origin, France or Italy?" In the case of the Poussin, the tests had proved that the canvas was French, and therefore unlikely to have been painted by an Italian. If the Louvre was right, my Domenichinesque canvas would most likely have to be French as well. "Good idea," said Sir Denis, "and could you let me know the result as quickly as possible? I'm writing an article on the exhibition."

The painting was taken down to a conservator, Marco Grassi. Grassi carefully removed from the edge of the original canvas a thin strip sufficient for scientific testing, and it was rushed by DHL to Lyons. The results, for which Sir Denis telephoned daily from Rome, Bologna, and London, unfortunately arrived too late for his article, in which, in light of the new investigations, he deferred addressing the debate between the two versions of the *Landscape with Shrine and Figures.* Just a few days too late for Mahon's article, the answer came from Lyons: the canvas, a form of burlap, was Italian.

What remains to resolve the question is, first, for the Louvre, which has finally acknowledged that its version is indeed painted on wood, to check whether the wood is poplar, generally used in Italy in the early seventeenth century, or oak, common in France. Of course the Italian origin of the canvas does not prove Domenichino painted my picture, nor does French wood, if such it be, prove that he did not, any more than blood tests prove paternity. Sensitive connoisseurship, the handwriting analysis to which the painting will be subjected after its veil of milky varnish is lifted, should prove the "DNA test" of authorship.

THE JEFFERSON PORTRAIT

One of the attractive things about art dealing is that it can, from time to time, be done almost anywhere. I was sitting on a beach in Grenada in 1975 when I came across an interesting footnote in Fawn Brodie's new biography of Thomas Jefferson. The book had achieved a certain notoriety with its revelations of Jefferson's love affair with his slave, Sally Hemings, and the mulatto family they spawned. And it went into great detail about his other relationship, with Maria Cosway, wife of the British miniaturist Richard Cosway. Both of these affairs bloomed during Jefferson's years as American minister to Paris from 1785 to 1789. Brodie made no discoveries here; both of these relationships were history, though the Hemings affair had usually been swept under the rug and Jefferson's black descendants marshaled out of the genealogy. But buried there in the footnote at the back of the paperback was a piece of information that was a discovery for me, a discovery particularly exciting to an art dealer sitting in the sand in a place where art dealing was supposedly impossible.

The book itself told how Maria commissioned from John Trumbull a portrait of her lover. Trumbull had been in Paris taking portraits of the French officers for his *Surrender at Yorktown,* and of Jefferson for *The Declaration of Independence.* What the footnote revealed was that this painting, surely one of the most romantic relics of American history, apparently still existed. Brodie knew of its discovery in 1952 in the Convent of Maria SS. Bambini in the town of Lodi, south of Milan, from its publication by Elizabeth Cometti that year in the *William and Mary Quarterly.* In 1812, Maria, born in Florence, always devout, had founded the convent school in Lodi and returned there with the relics of her romance—her portrait of Jefferson and his love letters to her—after

Cosway's death in 1821. It was there that she spent the last seventeen years of her life. Her lover, Jefferson, had died in 1826. The footnote gave no details about the portrait, not even whether it had remained at the convent over the twenty-two years that had elapsed between its discovery and the publication of Brodie's biography.

During those years, Clement Conger, curator of the art and furniture collections of both the State Department and the White House, was actively looking for portraits of the key figures in the history of American foreign policy. Fortunately for the country, Conger was determinedly acquisitive and persuasive with an affluent constituency of donors across the country. I could think of nothing he would covet more for the State Department than a Trumbull portrait of Jefferson, painted from life during Jefferson's tenure as the first minister to France from what was then the world's only republic, a republic that Jefferson's French friends had sacrificed so much to help bring into existence. As I sat there watching my one-year-old son playing in the sand, I hatched a plan to try to buy the portrait and give it to Clem for the State Department.

The first thing I did when I got back to New York was to phone a colleague in Turin, Mario Tazzoli, with whom I was doing a lot of business at the time. He had, it seemed, heard of Jefferson but not of Trumbull. I explained the importance of this object to our history and asked him to track it down and see if it could be bought. For months I phoned and telexed him. Nothing happened, and I got the feeling that I wasn't being taken seriously. Then one day I picked up the phone and called an old friend from my Harvard Business School days, an enterprising Milan businessman, Piero Ottolenghi. Piero lost little time in running down to Lodi, and reported back to me that the sisters of Maria SS. Bambini were very cloistered and he was having a lot of trouble making contact.

He finally succeeded, exactly how I don't know, except that it was through the mayor of Lodi. The Jefferson portrait was still there, though Piero had never seen it; the sisters needed money and were disposed to sell it. The prefect of Milan would have to approve the sale, and Piero needed a telex containing a formal offer. I still didn't know what the painting looked like, and Trumbull was, after all, not a great painter. I asked Ottolenghi what he thought I should offer. He had no idea. I suggested $100,000. He said it was too much. Then $50,000; again too much. He suggested $30,000, and I telexed accordingly. The next day

Piero telephoned and said the offer was accepted, and that all that had to be done was to formalize it with a telex, which I did immediately. I was waiting for instructions on cabling the money when suddenly Piero telexed that the deal had been called off. Neither of us could figure out what had gone wrong.

John Trumbull, *Portrait of Thomas Jefferson,* 1787–88

I opened the *International Herald Tribune* on September 8, and there on the front page was a photograph of President Giovanni Leone and President Ford in the Oval Office. The president of Italy was shown celebrating his state visit by presenting, as a gift from the people of Italy to the people of the United States, the miniature portrait of our third president by the American patriot painter John Trumbull. Italian officials had apparently been made aware of the object during the export formalities and decided that $30,000 to the sisters was a bargain for such a significant gift for President Ford. That summer the miniature was unveiled to the American public in the National Gallery's bicentennial celebratory exhibition, *The Eye of Thomas Jefferson.*

A dozen years later, my son and I were sitting at a table next to the Fords in a restaurant in Vail. On our way out, I stopped and thanked them for their hospitality to my ex-wife and me at a 1975 White House dinner, and particularly for Mrs. Ford's kindness in showing us around the White House paintings that evening. Then I asked, "President Ford, whatever became of the Trumbull miniature of Thomas Jefferson that Leone handed to you in the Oval Office in 1975?" He said, "When I left, it was sitting on my desk." I wonder if it is still there four administrations later.

FRESH PAINT AND POSTAGE STAMPS

The last time I was at the National Gallery, walking through the tunnel from the East to the West Building, through the vast gift boutique, I came upon an entire little shop dedicated to adaptations and copies of a single painting by one artist, Monet's celebrated *The Artist's Garden at Argenteuil*. The scene is of Monet's own garden. During a visit with Monet in 1873, the year before the first impressionist exhibition, Renoir painted a picture, now in the Wadsworth Atheneum in Hartford, Connecticut (*Monet Painting in His Garden at Argenteuil,* 1873), of Monet at his easel in the garden, painting the very picture now in the National Gallery. These two paintings' subjects and their treatment seem to define impressionism, and John Rewald so treated them in facing color reproductions in his volume *The History of Impressionism.* The National Gallery shop was selling everything from framed reproductions of various sizes for as much as $200 to postcards. The painting happened to be one that I had sold in 1971 to Janice and Phillip Levin, and Janice had donated it to the National Gallery for its fiftieth anniversary in 1991. The singular popularity of the Monet painting called to mind an anecdote.

Two of the legendary art dealers had at least one thing in common: neither could stand to see a colleague sell a painting. One of them, Lord Duveen, died when I was a child. But there is the famous story of an important client proudly inviting Duveen to his New York palazzo to see a painting he had bought from another dealer. The collector asks Duveen his opinion of his new acquisition. Duveen starts sniffing the air. "I smell fresh paint!" The client sends the painting back and never again strays from Duveen's fold. My story, however, concerns the other legend, Sam Salz.

Claude Monet, *The Artist's Garden at Argenteuil*, 1873

Collection Janice Levin, New York; partial gift to the National Gallery, Washington

I did not encounter Salz until 1968. My first nine years in the art business had been spent in Chicago, and I did not arrive in New York until 1966. I had been largely preoccupied in those Chicago years with expressionism, surrealism, and the twentieth century, not much yet with impressionism. Salz, in New York, limited himself to impressionism and the School of Paris. So our paths never crossed.

A Yale classmate of mine, an actor and theatrical producer, Konrad Matthaei, and his beautiful wife, both endowed with taste, had in the 1960s bought and furnished with fine French furniture a town house on Seventy-first Street between Park and Madison Avenues. In a single visit to Sam Salz, they had bought a small collection of fine French impressionists sufficient to cover the walls. The best of the pictures was a large Renoir, *Young Girls and a Lad in a Landscape,* the beautiful Monet, *The Artist's Garden at Argenteuil,* and a large Monet *Nymphéas.* And then they stopped collecting. Suddenly, in 1970, Konrad, after losing money

Pierre-Auguste Renoir,
*Monet Painting in His
Garden at Argenteuil,*
1873

Wadsworth Atheneum,
Hartford. Bequest of Anne
Parrish Titzell

financing a Broadway theater, asked me to sell his pictures. He had put their house on the market and the paintings in the Morgan Manhattan warehouse at Eightieth and Third Avenue.

Phillip Levin was a successful New Jersey real estate developer who had recently bought and sold to Edgar Bronfman a controlling block of MGM shares, on which Levin made a fortune and Bronfman lost one. Levin had then bought control of Madison Square Garden. The Levins had recently started collecting art and had moved to an apartment in the Pierre Hotel. They were eager to buy first-rate impressionist paintings, so I rushed them over to Morgan Manhattan to see the Matthaei pictures. They fell in love with the Monet and the Renoir. Negotiations commenced.

The warehouse was dark. The only way to see anything was to request a wire-covered bulb on a long cord. It was not the way to look at impressionists, painted in natural light. I told Matthaei that I had some clients seriously interested in two of his paintings, but that I simply could not sell them out of that dank prison. He finally let me take the paintings to my gallery, where my office was daylit from a skylight I had had the architect Hans Hollein construct specifically for impressionist pictures. The Levins came again to see the paintings, and this time made an offer. Matthaei wanted time to think it over.

Over the next few weeks, there were offers, meditations, and refusals. Meanwhile, Matthaei would intermittently ride over on his motorcycle, stride into my office, helmet in hand, and ask to have the Monet and Renoir returned immediately to his house for some dinner party. I would tell him that the Levins were still negotiating for the pictures and that I thought it unwise to move them around lest the Levins drop in unannounced. He said we could have them back in a couple of days, and off they went. I would coax them back, and then a week later the same thing happened again. I was in some kind of mortal tug-of-war. Even by then I had enough battle scars in the business to know that these were no dinner parties. I had a tenacious competitor. I finally persuaded Matthaei to accept the Levins' offer for the Renoir. But the mysterious competitor kept battling me for the Monet, the motorcycle visits went on, and it took me six more months to get the Monet for the Levins. Matthaei later admitted that the competitor had been Sam Salz.

By late spring of 1971, Janice and Phillip's paintings had all been hung, and they gave a festive cocktail party to welcome their friends to the completed apartment. In the midst of the party, Janice came over to me in the living room and repeated a conversation she had just had with Sam Salz, who was in the library. He had waved dismissively at the Monet and the Renoir and said, "Vair ya got dese pustidge stemps?" I did recall hearing that any painting Salz did not sell was a "postage stamp." But he himself had sold these paintings, just not this time around. "From Richard Feigen." "Vot's Feigen?" Not even "Who's Feigen?" "Vot's Feigen?" So I strolled up to Salz in the library. "Mr. Salz, I'm Richard Feigen." "Aha, Feigen! I hoid ya solt sum pentings ladely." Not a single rope burn on his hands from that interminable tug-of-war. "Mr. Salz, I'm flattered you think they're paintings." Given Sam Salz's fame for stomping the competition, no offense was taken, and I hope none given.

CHICAGO, NEW YORK, AND
THE SAVING OF SOHO

Most of the thousands of people who stream through SoHo every day know that it is the arty, trendy, chic neighborhood of New York. Some are aware of all the press about how the galleries are being priced out by fancy boutiques and moving to Chelsea, the galleries that made SoHo trendy in the first place. A few even remember when it was still a desolate area of run-down rag and button factories just twenty years ago, and have witnessed its extraordinary transformation in a very short time. But I suspect that no one knows how close SoHo came to never happening.

This is a story of preservation, in this case almost accidental. As a child, I was never given a sense of history—the history of my family or the history of where I lived. This may be the reason I feel so palpably the romance of places where great things have happened and great people have been, and so bereaved when any facet of them has been destroyed. I am as depressed by the neon Martini sign in Florence beyond the Duomo as by the removal of an original frame from a painting. I am even a bit saddened when a new scaffolding goes up in the Place des Vosges; I love the three houses that remain unrestored, at this writing, more than all the rest of the beautiful square. Almost everywhere I look, some of life's flavor has gone, and often what is left is flavorless.

Chicago, where I grew up, had its particular flavor. Louis Sullivan's Garrick Theater and Stock Exchange are now needlessly gone, and where the Potter Palmer and Edith Rockefeller McCormick castles once stood on Lake Shore Drive, tacky, tasteless jerry-built high-rises are already crumbling onto one of the most beautiful waterfront drives in the world. The fine Federal Court of Appeals building on Lake Shore

U.S. Court of Appeals, 1212 North Lake Shore Drive, Chicago, 1921–23 (demolished 1966)

Chicago Historical Society. Photograph: Dr. Frank E. Rice, 1950

Drive, no longer needed when the Mies van der Rohe Federal building opened downtown, was destroyed because my old client, Suzette Morton, of the powerful Morton Salt clan—which had donated the Morton wing to the Art Institute—opposed its use for the new Museum of Contemporary Art.

The Contemporary Museum, born of the antagonism of the Art Institute to contemporary art and to the Jews who by then composed most of Chicago's collectors—an antagonism supported to no small degree by Leigh Block, who, along with the architect Samuel Marx, was a token Jew on the Art Institute board—had held its organizational meeting in my apartment in 1958. Joseph Randall Shapiro, the dean of the city's surrealist and contemporary art collectors, who would become the father of the Contemporary Museum several years later, did not attend. By 1958 Joe had been put on the Art Institute's drawings committee, and was not about to risk alienating the establishment.

Several years later, after consulting with the architect Phyllis Bronfman Lambert, at the time working in Chicago with Mies van der Rohe, we decided to go after the handsome, now redundant Court of Appeals building at 1212 Lake Shore Drive, and I made a trip to the General Services Administration in Washington. The government's price was one dollar, conditional on the city's acceptance. But we crashed into a wall: the unwritten pact between the city's financial and political powers. Our request and the government's offer were turned down by the city at the establishment's insistence, the beautiful building was torn down, and a ghastly apartment tower with a white stucco facade went up in its place— another irreversible blemish on Lake Shore Drive. The sad fact is that those with the power to effect change are usually those with the worst taste.

Notwithstanding some destruction, and the construction of some bad buildings—as examples, every post-Mies apartment building on Lake Shore Drive, the Prudential and Standard Oil of Indiana buildings, and, perhaps saddest of all, the new Museum of Contemporary Art— Chicago has managed to retain much of its architectural character. Manhattan had less to begin with, and, as an island, suffered from chronic destruction and reconstruction.

As for the assault on taste by financial and political power, I remember an encounter with Roger Stevens at a party in Washington in 1961 at the home of my friends Carmen and David Kreeger. Plans had just been announced for the new Kennedy Center for the Performing Arts. Stevens had total control, as chairman of what was then known as the National Cultural Center. He had chosen Edward Durell Stone as the architect. As usual when faced with impending aesthetic disaster, I panicked. But having learned the hard way that no one is convinced by confrontation, I asked, gently, I thought, "Mr. Stevens, how did you come to choose Edward Durell Stone?" I was quite unprepared for the furious reply: "Mr. Feigen, Mr. Stone is a great architect!" Subject closed. Ten years; myriad mistakes; $39 million in budget excess as of the building's completion, and still climbing as the building's acoustics fail; the monstrously ugly building is falling apart. While New York's Lincoln Center is not exactly disintegrating, $6.4 million was spent in 1976 correcting faulty acoustics at Avery Fisher Hall alone, and the whole complex stands as a glitzy, overembellished testimonial to bad official architecture, the kind of taste that holds that "more is more." It is not a surprise to find trinket stands in the lobbies peddling T-shirts, or people in jeans

Josef Kleihues, Museum
of Contemporary Art,
Chicago, 1996,
looking east

Photograph: Steve Hall.
© Hedrich Blessing

and black tie mingling at concerts. Unlike Carnegie Hall, there is no sense that one should get dressed up for a special evening. It's not elegant, and it's not really populist. What goes on in the outdoor plaza is fun—the music, the performers, the food, the people enjoying themselves in nice weather—but this could just as easily, maybe more easily, have happened in front of a great building. Bad architecture, the offspring of powerful, arrogant, tasteless people, has not only created a tacky atmosphere, like most bad choices it has proved more expensive than good choices. I suspect the same thing will prove true with the new Museum of Contemporary Art in Chicago, which resembles a cheap imitation of an Albert Speer confection for the Third Reich, except that it wasn't cheap.

I came to New York from Harvard in 1954 and lived in a narrow, charming place on Fifty-first Street, facing Rockefeller Center, called the Hotel

14. I worked at Lehman Brothers, down on William Street. I recall on a few occasions being invited by "Bobby" Lehman up to lunch in the partners' dining room, and what I remember about those lunches were the early Italian paintings on the wall. But usually I wandered up Front Street, past Coenties Slip, for lunch at Sloppy Louie's, or sometimes past the Lorillard building, which then was still standing, and the Brooklyn Bridge and the old Jewish cemetery to Chinatown. And what I remember of those lunchtime walks is the strong flavor of lower New York, which was the whole length and breadth of the city in the eighteenth century, the old sail factories and Greek Revival buildings, redolent of the city's maritime history. Now all that remains is a small fly trapped in amber, the South Street Seaport. A lot of the half-empty office buildings that rose from the destruction finally filled up in the prosperous nineties.

I moved out to Los Angeles in 1955, back to New York in 1956, then to Chicago to open a gallery in 1957. I have often since been asked why I chose Chicago. Well, apart from its being my hometown, I was operating, I suppose, on the "big fish in a small pond" theory. So it took me about five years longer than it would have in a city where nobody knew me, or if I had arrived in Chicago with a beard and a funny accent. Those were the days when Chicago's "Second City" problem was in full feather. It still is, for that matter. Chicagoans thought that nothing significant could happen in Chicago, ignoring all that had already happened. Children went East to school and never came back. To get a decent meal, you had to know the ethnic neighborhoods, belong to a club, or eat at home. Chicagoans were oblivious to the occasional out-of-town tryout of a great play like *The Glass Menagerie,* which almost closed in Chicago, but for the daily harping of a critic named Claudia Cassidy. Chicagoans were barely aware of their great orchestra—I remember being taken as a child to hear Rachmaninoff play his Second Piano Concerto under Frederick Stock—and as for the Art Institute, it rested on its impressionist laurels, more an attraction for tourists than for the locals. The Second City— founded at the University of Chicago as the Compass Players, among whom were Mike Nichols and Elaine May—opened in a former Chinese laundry on December 16, 1959, its facade implanted with elements lovingly salvaged from Sullivan's Garrick Theater by its founder, Bernie Sahlins. Notwithstanding a galaxy of future stars like Alan Arkin, Barbara Harris, Severn Darden, Bill Murray, Joan Rivers, John Belushi,

Gilda Radner, and John Candy, Chicagoans paid scant attention until the world came in droves for the new improvisational political humor. Only a handful of the intelligentsia grieved over the destruction of the great Sullivan buildings—the Garrick Theater in January 1961, and the Stock Exchange in March 1972—certainly not the financial and social Brahmins who could have saved them.

The battles to save Lake Shore Drive and the Sullivan buildings were much on my mind when I married in 1966 and moved to New York to run what had been until then a branch of my Chicago gallery. Oblivious to politics until the McCarthy hearings politicized me in 1953, by 1963 I was in torment over Vietnam. I became politically active, in the McCarthy and Allard Lowenstein campaigns, in 1968 in the Howard Samuels gubernatorial campaign, and in 1969 with John Lindsay. It was the summer of that mayoral campaign, 1969, that this story is all about.

I had been captivated by the old areas of lower Manhattan when I worked in Wall Street in the early 1950s. By the early sixties, artist friends like Jim Rosenquist, Robert Indiana, Barnett Newman, Jasper Johns, Bob Rauschenberg, and Ellsworth Kelly were working or living, illegally, in the old sail factories on Front Street and Coenties Slip. Many of the walls were hung with copper sail stencils they found lying around on the floors, and the roofs were supported by old schooner masts. By nightfall, down there for dinner, there was nothing but silence. You could hear your footsteps on the cobbled streets, smell the salt air, and almost sense the maritime bustle of the eighteenth century. The area south of the Brooklyn Bridge was, of course, the whole of Manhattan in the seventeenth and eighteenth centuries. The "Jews' Burying Ground," now just a stone's throw away up in Chinatown, had been relegated to what was in 1683 the far-off countryside. The older European cities, much more thoughtfully planned, had not been confined to islands, had been laid out by monarchs, and had had centuries to grow.

Now, by night, Wall Street went to sleep. It was like the transformation of a stage set between acts. The massive towers, only yards away, were barely visible in the darkness. I could not imagine a more dramatic contrast, not only between centuries but between ways of life, between the work that was sustaining the area by day and the work of the artists at night. This seemed a precious balance, unique to New York, something to be cherished and protected.

Louis Sullivan, Garrick
Theater, 64 West Randolph
Street, Chicago, 1890–92
(demolished 1961)

Chicago Historical Society.
Photograph: Clarence W. Hines,
1960

Not long after my move to New York in 1966, during the first Lindsay administration, it became apparent that all this was threatened. Harassment of the artists living illegally downtown had intensified. Beds had to fold into walls on short notice. Vietnam had begun to cause rising inflation, business was booming, and with it, pressure from the developers. There was no Landmarks Commission in those days. Fragile zoning ordinances were the only barrier to rampant destruction. If a developer included a little plaza in front of his project, he was allowed to build to the sky, almost without restriction. This only meant, after all, higher property taxes for the city. Public zoning hearings were held, and I remember at one of them the issue under discussion was the fate of the remaining Greek Revival commercial structures just south of the Brooklyn Bridge, which architects crossed oceans to see. Much of the area had by the late sixties already been demolished, the 1837 Lorillard building in 1962. The proposal from a developer was to destroy the area and in its place put up, not skyscrapers, but two-story apartments. This made no sense at all. I stood up and asked, "Why not restore the old buildings, fill them with

Louis Sullivan, Chicago
Stock Exchange
Building, 30 North
LaSalle Street, Chicago,
1893–94 (demolished
1972)

Chicago Historical Society.
Photograph: Barnes-Crosby,
circa 1905–10

architects' and designers' offices, businesses that
relate to them and would pay a premium for such
space, and protect the character of lower Manhattan?" Back shot the reply from some arrogant
politico: "Mr. Feigen, if that were feasible, Mr.
Tishman would have thought of it." So on Sun-

days, on the eve of the wreckers' balls, my wife and children would pile into the old Lincoln convertible, drop the top on the way to Chinatown, and drive down for a farewell look.

Back in my Wall Street days in the 1950s, whenever I found myself on a high skyscraper floor, I noticed a strange phenomenon. There was a valley in Manhattan. Towers at the lower tip, towers in midtown, and a valley of low buildings in between. Even before moving to New York, I became fascinated, in the early sixties, with this area of wonderful cast-iron buildings, interrupted by an occasional pitch-roofed relic of the Federal era. By 1963, when I opened a New York branch of my Chicago gallery on Eighty-first Street, the cast-iron area was blighted. Almost every building had a "For Sale" sign. The rag merchants and button factories had fled from taxes and wages to Brooklyn and New Jersey. Many floors of the buildings were now occupied, again illegally, by artists chased by the developers up from lower Manhattan. A 2,500-square-foot loft rented for $100 a month. Buildings were for sale for $50,000—$5,000 down, the balance a purchase-money mortgage at 6 percent.

I had become increasingly involved with contemporary art in Chicago since I started there in 1957 with the twentieth-century classics. The first exhibition, in the autumn of 1957, was *Masterpieces of 20th Century German Art.* It is easy to use a term like "masterpieces," but in the case of that show the terminology was no exaggeration. Most of the paintings and the one sculpture in it are now in museums, mainly in Europe. The Kirchner painted wood sculpture, *Dancing Woman,* 1908–12, for instance, is in the Stedelijk Museum, Amsterdam; the Grosz, *The Lovesick One,* 1916, in the Kunstsammlung Nordrhein-Westfalen, Düsseldorf; and Kirchner's *The Masked Ball,* 1911, in the Staatsgalerie Moderner Kunst, Munich. When I started, I did not have a lot of money to invest in inventory—just what remained from the sale of my New York Stock Exchange seat, which I had held for only six months and had just broken even on when I sold it in the spring of 1957 for $86,000. My own collection of German expressionists had to serve as the first show. It had at least been exhibited and catalogued intact the previous spring, at the instance of the great émigré German dealer J. B. Neumann, at the World House Gallery in New York, to which Neumann was acting as advisor.

The collection, largely accumulated from the early 1950s on but begun around 1940 with Isaac Cruikshank's *The Meat Market Evacuated,*

Ernst Ludwig Kirchner,
Masked Ball, 1911

Staatsgalerie Moderner Kunst,
Munich

or The Sans-culottes in Possession, also included some earlier works like Fuseli's *Sin Separating Death from Satan* (Los Angeles County Museum), a Lodovico Carracci drawing, and Puvis de Chavannes's *Euterpe,* which I still own. I bought the first thing, the Cruikshank, for $100 from the legendary Chicago bookseller and curmudgeon Walter Hill. I had been collecting old books as a child, and I used to hang out on the periphery of Hill's famous bibliophilic Saturday afternoon kaffeeklatsches. What interested me, practically since childhood, was essentially imagistic and emotional. I owned nothing formal or abstract. This fitted Chicago's mood, both in terms of what was being collected and what was being made by the artists there.

It's difficult to trace the origins of the "Chicago School," but that the city spawned an imagery of its own there is no doubt. The earliest traces

George Grosz, *The Lovesick One*, 1916

Kunstsammlung Nordrhein-Westfalen, Düsseldorf

I can detect are in the work of Ivan Albright in the late 1920s. Although Albright is little known outside Chicago, he is certainly one of this country's great painters. His imagery of decayed flesh and crumbling still life was briefly revealed to the public in the final, shocking portrait (at the Art Institute of Chicago) in the movie *The Picture of Dorian Gray*. Albright agreed to this project with Metro-Goldwyn-Mayer in 1943. He received $100,000,

Ernst Ludwig Kirchner, *Dancing Woman,* 1908–12

Stedelijk Museum, Amsterdam

a fortune at the time, but insisted on keeping the painting after the filming. They also gave him a dressing room on the lot, like the star he was. The painting was, after all, an essential element in the film. I will always remember the frightening moment when, as a teenager, I saw George Sanders pull away the velvet attic curtain to reveal, in brilliant colors in the midst of a black-and-white film, Albright's depiction of Dorian's horrendous crimes and dissipations. Albright and I were next-door neighbors at 55 and 53 East Division Street, respectively, from my purchase of the house in 1959 until 1963, when the Albrights moved to Woodstock, Vermont, and we became close friends. Ivan had *Dorian Gray* at Division Street, along with almost all of his other major works.

In retrospect, Albright was certainly the leading artistic presence in Chicago in the 1930s and 1940s. It seems likely that his work had an influence on what the students were doing at the Museum School of the

Art Institute of Chicago, where he taught and most of the later generations of Chicago artists studied, among them the founders of the "Monster School" and the "Hairy Who." But evidence of Albright's influence
is shadowy, for several reasons. First, as George Cohen, an important
artist of the postwar generation who attended the school during
Albright's tenure, recently explained (oral interview, January 20, 1997),
Albright's work, and his teaching, stressed a "meticulousness" that was
out of step with the younger artists' commitment to *art brut* and infor-
mality. The artists respected Albright but tended to minimize any influence he may have had. George Cohen told me of a party where he found
himself standing with Albright and Franz Kline. Kline said, "Ivan, if I
didn't drink so much, my work would look just like yours." Albright's
reply was, "Franz, if I drank a little more, my work
might look like yours." The fact is that Kline, even in
his soberer years, couldn't paint like Albright. And if
Albright had drunk any more than he already did, his
liver would have looked like his paintings.

Isaac Cruikshank, *The
Meat Market Evacuated,
or The Sans-culottes in
Possession,* 1792

Collection Richard L. Feigen,
New York

The Chicago artists returned from the war tired of "the emptiness of French formalism." Their interest lay in the rougher images of psychotics, the art of New Guinea, New Caledonia, New Ireland, and the Native Americans they saw at Chicago's Field Museum of Natural History; in Jean Dubuffet, to whom they had been exposed through the early Chicago collector Maurice Culberg and Dubuffet's seminal talk at the Arts Club in December 1951 ("Anticultural Positions"); and in German expressionism.

Further, Albright was older and a "loner," and did not socialize with the other artists. Because of his wife's great fortune and lofty social status, the Albrights did not fit the image of a hungry artist's family. Also, Albright did not look or act like an artist. He resembled a short, round, florid Santa Claus without a beard, his bald head framed by white tufts, punctuated by bushy white eyebrows. He looked a bit like Mickey Rooney in old age. And Albright never talked about art.

Chicago also had a strong vanguard tradition, if not particularly in the art that was being made there between the two world wars, then in what was being collected and shown, largely at the Arts Club, by enlightened matrons like Rue Winterbotham Carpenter and "Bobsy" Goodspeed. Albright, although very advanced in his ideas, anticipating "neoexpressionists" of the 1970s like Anselm Kiefer and Julian Schnabel, worked in none of the current European styles, was deceptively imagistic, and, worst for Chicago's vanguard Brahmins—who always looked eastward and never believed in their own—was a native son from their own social set.

Finally, Albright did not, until shortly before his death, see any reason to disperse his work. Most of his paintings were worked on over many years, he was not prolific, and what with Josephine's vast Patterson newspaper fortune, he had no need to sell anything. He preferred to keep the work rather than lose it and pay massive taxes on the proceeds. Like his friend and admirer Dubuffet, he had no need to work *sur commande*. If he painted a portrait, it was because the subject interested him and fit his imagery. Mary Block, with whom I deal separately, obviously had no notion of why Albright agreed to the only portrait commission he ever accepted. She may have thought it was because she was so important, or maybe because Albright needed the money. Neither was the case. Albright was not impressed with anyone, certainly not the self-anointed empress of the Chicago art world. And as for the money, the Albrights

Ivan Albright, *Self-portrait in Georgia*, 1967–68

The Butler Institute of American Art, Youngstown, Ohio

were richer than the Blocks. Albright was apparently fascinated by Mary's terrifying personality and captured it brilliantly. He seated her in a Directoire chair in a spooky room, swathed in crimson and black brocades—the devil's colors—bedecked in jewels, surrounded by her baubles and trinkets, two white roses lying on the table beside her. Mary's fierce eyes impale anyone who crosses her. Albright began work in 1955, and when the portrait was finished in 1957, Mary so hated it that she immediately gave it to the Art Institute.

I used to ring the next-door bell in the afternoons and have a drink with Ivan. One day a Western Union messenger appeared at his door with a telegram. Ivan opened it, read it, and showed it to me: IVAN ALBRIGHT/55 E. DIVISION STREET, CHICAGO, ILLINOIS/I LIKE 'THAT WHICH I SHOULD HAVE DONE I DID NOT DO.' HOW MUCH IS IT/HUNTINGTON HARTFORD. Ivan took a form and wrote, HUNTINGTON HARTFORD/1 BEEKMAN PLACE, NEW YORK, NEW YORK/SO DO I. ONE MILLION DOLLARS/ALBRIGHT. I said, "Ivan, the guy's an idiot. I know him. But he's serious about the painting." This was before Hartford had somehow succeeded in throwing away his whole $100 million A&P fortune on mad projects. "Why blow him off?" "I worked on that painting for ten years. At plumber's wages, a million dollars is a bargain." Albright proceeded to show me the arithmetic. Nothing more was heard from Huntington Hartford. Albright's greatest paintings were still stored at 55 East Division when he moved away in 1963.

In 1976, seven years before Albright died, he phoned me in New York from Woodstock and asked me to meet him for lunch at the Century the following week. At lunch that day he said, "Dick, you always told me to disperse my work. You were right. Can you do it for me now?" And he handed me what I considered a historic project. The problem was that by that time I had no public gallery to exhibit the work. I had sold my Hans Hollein building in 1973, largely because the artists I represented found Hollein's statement too sculptural and too strong, and his Wiener Werkstätte colors were also inhospitable to the old masters I had begun to show. For the ten years from 1973 to 1983, we occupied small offices, with no public exhibition space, at 900 Park Avenue. I had hesitated to buy another building after I sold the Seventy-ninth Street building and the three in SoHo because I thought the prospects for New York City were gloomy. I was convinced that New York real estate was a bad investment. And for a time it seemed I had been prescient. The city defaulted on the interest payments on its bonds in October 1975, and the real estate market crashed to its nadir in 1977. By 1981 the real estate market had turned around and I was afraid of missing the chance of buying a building, but the lease at 900 Park, which I had signed in 1973, still had two years to run and I could not envision a sublessor for that dreary space.

Without a gallery to show Albright's work, I went down to see Leo Castelli. Not only did I have a great deal of respect and affection for Leo, he seemed like the right partner for the project. It was Leo whom I had called in in 1975 to represent the Joseph Cornell estate with me, and our collaboration had been a happy one. By the 1970s, the art scene had become snobbish. Certain galleries were on the menu, and Leo's was one of them. The "neoexpressionists" were coming into vogue, and I felt that if Albright's work were shown at Castelli, he might well be accepted by the younger artists as a precursor. After all his years in the shadows, I wanted instant recognition for Ivan. At seventy-nine, he did not have that much longer to wait. Leo was not receptive, despite the fact that it was rare to find a major artist who still owned almost all of his important paintings, executed over a span of half a century. Leo seemed to know the work only vaguely, and thought of it as being somewhat old-fashioned. So he demurred. About a year later, Leo phoned me. "Richard, I think you were right about Albright." Had he been talking to someone? An artist? "Let's do it." I phoned Ivan immediately in Woodstock. Just one week before, he had donated his life's work to the Art Institute. I was brokenhearted, because, knowing Chicago's patronizing attitude

Ivan Albright, *That Which I Should Have Done I Did Not Do (The Door)*, 1931–41

The Art Institute of Chicago, Mary and Leigh Block Charitable Fund (1955.645). Photograph: © 1999 The Art Institute of Chicago. All Rights Reserved

toward its own, I was sure this would condemn Albright to years more, perhaps an eternity, of obscurity. But the museum had promised him a permanent display of the work in a room of its own. When the institute's report for that year arrived, I was shocked to find Albright's entire benefaction, worth perhaps $15 to $20 million even in those days, listed in the category of $500,000–$1,000,000 donations. I urgently wrote the board chairman, Arthur Wood, pleading with him to contact

Albright immediately, explaining the "typographical error." I heard nothing further.

Although the director, James Wood, and the curator at the time, Richard Bretell, finally, in 1981, made a trip to Woodstock to make amends, the Albright donations have never been given their promised separate space. And the 1997 Albright retrospective was a small, half-hearted effort, with only one other venue, the Metropolitan Museum. During the months of its preparation, the big Monet exhibition, much more promising as a box-office smash, was given precedence and the full attention of the curator, Charles Stuckey, who left for the curatorship at Minneapolis after the unchallenging Monet project. No arrangements were made for European venues, where Albright's work remains completely unknown and might be most meaningful to the current generation of artists. European art is, after all, only now in the process of being revived after the Nazis asphyxiated it over sixty years ago, and might well respond to these American images.

Whether Albright was an influence on or simply a precursor of Chicago's expressionist and surreal imagery, my new gallery's program fitted what was going on in Chicago. It was primarily the artists who came to see the first exhibition of German art. The active collectors of the period—the Leigh Blocks, Arnold Maremonts, Nathan Cummings, Florene Marx Schoenborn, even the James Alsdorfs and Morton Neumanns—concentrated on French painting. The Joseph Shapiros collected surrealism. There were a few sales from the German show: the apocalyptic paintings of Ludwig Meidner to Gerhard Strauss, a Milwaukee collector; and Nolde's *Three Russians,* 1914, to a pair of colorful Beverly Hills financial buccaneers, Burt Kleiner and Eugene Klein, who bought it in partnership and somehow sorted out ownership later. I had discovered Meidner, completely forgotten and living in penury in a Prussian barn, and was fascinated by his early paintings. We corresponded, he was effusively grateful that someone appreciated his work, and he sent me his photograph.

The 1959 Francis Bacon exhibition was even more popular with Chicago artists like George Cohen, Leon Golub, Seymour Rosofsky and Cosmo Campoli, though not particularly with the collectors. Bacon's work had been exhibited only once before in the United States, in a small exhibition at Durlacher Brothers in New York in 1953. I had never met Bacon, but on trips to London I accumulated fourteen of his best works, dating from 1948 to 1956. I told Bacon's dealer, Erica Brausen of the Hanover Gallery in London, about the exhibition. She phoned me and said that Bacon wanted to attend the opening. I thought that was a great idea. A bit later, however, I was told that Bacon was eagerly antici-pating his Chicago visit, that I was expected to line up some young boys for him, and that I should be a bit wary lest he use a little knife he carried around to slash any earlier paintings he felt like disowning. Whether any of this was true or not, I panicked. There were already three Bacons in Chicago, including one of his masterpieces, *Figure with Meat,* 1954, in the Art Institute, and I didn't want any of them slashed. As for the young boys, I had not, nor have I still, reached that level of sophistication. As the weeks passed before the opening, I was getting less and less sleep. In the end I managed, how diplomatically I was never sure, to have Brausen discourage Bacon from coming. The Bacon exhibition was a magnificent Grand Guignol of trapped, choking, screaming men and beasts. The artists returned again and again to see it. But of the fourteen paintings, and despite the fact that they were priced from $900 to $1,300, only one was sold, *Study for Portrait VI,* 1953, for $1,300 to the Minneapolis Insti-tute of Arts, though Jory and Joe Shapiro later bought two important Bacons from me, *Study for Portrait,* 1949, for $1,900 (Museum of Con-temporary Art, Chicago) and *Study for Portrait,* 1957, for $1,600.

In addition to one year's international representation of Victor Brauner, from 1958 to 1959, godfathered by Matta and heralded by all of the more pecunious surrealists (a tale told in another chapter), I became very much involved with Joseph Cornell, whose hermetic fairy-tale world captured my imagination. Cornell's imagery already had a foothold among Chicago's artists, and with the pioneer surrealist collec-tor Joseph Shapiro. Allan Frumkin had shown Cornell's work in Chicago as early as 1953. I began to stop at Cornell's little house at 3708 Utopia Parkway on taxi rides to and from La Guardia Airport, close by. I needed patient drivers because I never knew how long a trip Cornell would take me on, through thimble forests, into nineteenth-century ballets, crum-bling French seaside hotels, voyages to the bottom of the sea and up into starry nights of the interplanetary system, and back down to Renaissance palaces. Sometimes I came away with a box or two, sometimes nothing. I never knew whether to ask Cornell if I could buy something, whether he

Ludwig Meidner, circa 1957

Collection of Richard L. Feigen (gift of
the artist, 1958)

wanted me to ask or he wanted me not to. Once, when I dared ask and he agreed to part with a box, he wrote telling me he appreciated the "crisp" manner in which I had handled our encounter.

I learned much about Cornell's early days from Julien Levy, with whom I became close friends. Julien had closed his seminal New York gallery in 1949 after Arshile Gorky's suicide the previous year. Gorky had suffered a disastrous studio fire, which destroyed much of his work, a broken neck in an auto accident while driving with Julien, and finally the defection of his wife with Matta, whom he had more or less adopted on the New York scene in the 1940s. Julien himself had some years earlier suffered the usual rupture with Cornell, an artist with whom almost no one could sustain a relationship, over some long-forgotten contretemps. The only Cornells Julien still had, apart from several of his films that had been shown in his gallery, were *L'Égypte de Mlle. Cléo de Mérode . . .* , which Julien had been bought out of one of his own Cornell shows, and a box Cornell had given Jean and Julien as a wedding present.

In addition to the expressionists, surrealists, and younger Chicago artists, others I had begun in 1960 to show were some of the younger generation of New Yorkers and Californians who were also in revolt against the cult of abstraction preached and practiced in New York. My attention was particularly captured by Claes Oldenburg, himself a former Chicagoan, James Rosenquist, and Jasper Johns. We had a show of Oldenburg's work in 1961 and helped to stage his 1963 performance, *Gayety,* at the University of Chicago, handling ticket sales at my Division Street gallery. The gallery basement had, incidentally, also served in 1962 and 1963 as headquarters for Lenny Bruce's defense against the police bust of his nightclub act for obscenity in December 1962. He was convicted in June 1963. The judgment was reversed in July.

As for California, I had bought a number of Edward Kienholz's pieces in California and showed them in 1960, though I soon decided they were

Francis Bacon, *Study for Portrait VI,* 1953

The Minneapolis Institute of Arts

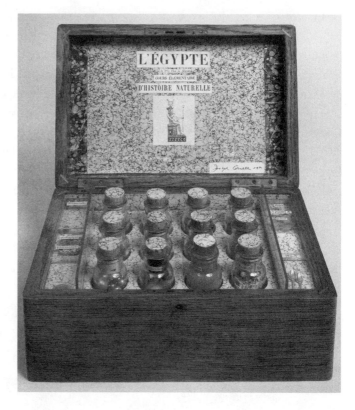

Joseph Cornell,
*L'Égypte de Mlle.
Cléo de Mérode . . . ,*
1940

Collection Robert
Lehrman, Washington,
D.C.

too topical and not beautiful enough to ever be really consequential. Though Oldenburg was dubbed a "Pop" artist—like his colleagues Johns and Rosenquist, largely because their work was imagistic and because of where it was being shown in that crucial year of 1961—his Chicago origins seem obvious. He never denied the influence of George Cohen's 1954 constructions, one of which, *Anybody's Self-portrait,* has long been in the Museum of Modern Art, and though Oldenburg, then a reporter on the *Chicago's American,* did not attend Dubuffet's 1951 Arts Club lecture, the analogy between Dubuffet and Oldenburg is remarkable.

When I was preparing our 1969 New York exhibition, *Dubuffet and the Anticulture,* in the catalogue of which we reproduced the 1951 Chicago Arts Club lecture with Dubuffet's cabled permission, I was careful to send Dubuffet photographs of everything in the exhibition. I wanted the entire concept, every artist being included, to have Dubuffet's stamp of approval. The theme of the exhibition was, after all,

Dubuffet's own. A number of the Oldenburgs were from his *The Street,* which had been shown at the Reuben Gallery in May 1960. I also included some of Dubuffet's *Hourloupe* sculptures of 1964 and 1965. The 1964 Dubuffets and 1959 Oldenburgs looked like they were conceived by the same imagination. Yet the Oldenburgs antedated the Dubuffets by some five years. Before our exhibition opened, actually before our catalogue had been printed, I got a call from William Lieberman at the Museum of Modern Art. The Oldenburg retrospective was in progress at the time. Bill told me that Dubuffet was in New York, hiding out as usual at the One Fifth Avenue Hotel, and that he had covertly gone through the Oldenburg show, written out a moving tribute to Oldenburg, and given it to Lieberman to pass on to Claes, whose work he had not known until my photographs reached him. Now Bill was asking me to give it to Oldenburg. The envelope was open, so I read it, and only because it was so personal did I not stop the presses and ask Oldenburg, and of course Dubuffet, if I could print it in the catalogue. Oldenburg told me that Dubuffet stopped at his studio on a later visit to New York and, while talking to Oldenburg, started tampering with one of the wet plaster pieces.

In those years that we showed Oldenburg in Chicago, I always wanted to place a large outdoor piece in his hometown. When the Chicago Latin School, of whose 1946 football team Oldenburg had been a star, moved to its new location on North Avenue, I talked to the architect, Harry Weese, about placing an Oldenburg outside, but there was apparently no way to get it funded. Several years later, I was approached by Skidmore, Owings & Merrill about an Oldenburg commission on the plaza in front of the new Sears Roebuck building, at the time the tallest building in the world. Both Oldenburg and I were excited by the prospect. Then the directive came from the Sears CEO. "Tell Oldenburg to make us a soft Sears catalogue." I passed this on to Claes, and the answer was as I expected. "Tell them to make it themselves."

The Chicago artists were always jealous and angry at the public success of their New York contemporaries and the hegemony of abstract painting. They kept badgering for New York exposure. In the end, New York exposure meant nothing to any of them except Leon Golub, and that was because Leon and his wife, Nancy Spero, actually moved to New York and entered the "scene." But in 1963 I decided, misguidedly, it seems in retrospect, to open a gallery in New York, primarily to show the Chicago artists' work. Though the gallery at 24 East Eighty-first Street was designed for this purpose, by 1965 the area between Houston and Canal streets seemed a more natural area to show contemporary art—big, high-ceilinged, inexpensive spaces, close to where the artists lived, close to excitement like Oldenburg's performances in his "Store" not far away at 107 East Second Street, which he called the Ray Gun Theater.

In 1965, I started shopping for a building and ended up with three: 139 Greene Street, a Federal house of around 1815—across the street from the spot where Isabella Stewart Gardner's birthplace used to stand—which I intended for a weekend retreat, so peaceful was the area at night and on weekends (I found the original carved pine mantel behind the rubble and rusty machinery of the rag dealer from whom I had bought the building, later stolen during some work I was having done, and under the loading platform, the old marble front steps); 141 Greene; and 135 Wooster. I even had a contract for a while, later dropped, on St. Joseph's Mission and its chapel, to the north on Lafayette Street. The price was $55,000, $5,000 down. It was later bought by Bob Rauschenberg. Later, in 1967, Jasper Johns bought the Provident Loan Society at Houston and Essex streets.

Leo Castelli was still in his cramped space at 4 East Seventy-seventh Street. Representing artists who worked on a large scale, like Jim Rosenquist, whose 86-foot-long classic, *F-III,* was shown that year, wrapped around the four walls of the Seventy-seventh Street gallery, and Lee Bontecou, Leo clearly needed more space. He agreed to join me in the building at 141 Greene Street, three floors, two of exhibition space and the top floor an apartment for the director. Leo and I each took a floor. Leo didn't have the cash available to buy the building with me, so I agreed to rent his half to him, and we ran it that way for a year, the first art gallery in what was later to be called SoHo. Paula Cooper already had a gallery in the area, but it was on LaGuardia Place, just north of Houston, not technically in SoHo.

After that first year, Leo rather timidly approached me and asked to be released from his commitment. It turned out that his sidekick, Ivan Karp, who lived just across Houston Street in one of the New York University apartment buildings, had told him that no one would ever come to look at art in that remote area. It was later reported to me on good

Richard Feigen Gallery,
141 Greene Street,
New York, 1965

authority that Ivan didn't want to be disturbed when he was absorbed in his television football games by having to work on Saturdays. Ivan later left Leo and opened one of the pioneer SoHo galleries. As for Leo, before later moving his own gallery to West Broadway, he had taken a large storage space on the Upper West Side. My own SoHo gallery continued under the direction of Michael Findlay, whom I had hired fresh from England, via Toronto, at the age of eighteen. Michael, now director of impressionist pictures at Christie's, did some historic things down there, including the first American show of Joseph Beuys, the first New York representation of John Baldessari, an exhibition of Frank Lloyd Wright windows and drawings, the New York venue of my 1968 Chicago Richard J. Daley show, which had protested the police brutality during that year's Democratic Convention, and soon it was a lively place.

Then, in 1973, fearing a New York real estate crash and the demise of the city in some form or other—a few years later, with New York's bond default, it looked like such a collapse had actually happened—and as usual overly impatient, I sold my building on Seventy-ninth Street—designed for me by Hans Hollein, and to date his only project in America—and my three buildings in SoHo. I got $250,000 for all three SoHo buildings, and $750,000 for Seventy-ninth Street, in which I had invested $1,100,000. The SoHo boom took off a scant three years later. As for Seventy-ninth Street, I made one condition of its sale to the Japanese couturiere Hanae Mori, sponsored by my friend Stanley Marcus: that she not disturb Hollein's design, inside or out. Much to Hollein's pleasure and mine, she has scrupulously stuck to that promise, with a single exception: she installed a protective gate across the front. I drove Hollein past the building on one of his visits, and he found the gate quite consistent with his design.

Meanwhile, in the early months of Lindsay's 1969 mayoral campaign, there had been rumors of plans for a cross-Manhattan expressway for truck traffic from New Jersey to Brooklyn. I had become involved in the campaign, and early that summer I found that these were not just rumors. The expressway was the dream of Constantine Sidamon-Eristoff, Lindsay's transportation administrator. Eristoff pursued the project with extraordinary determination, like Ahab his white whale—I have never figured out why. The Lindsay team plan was to wait for the improvident but extremely vocal artists to leave their illegal lofts for the summer, then, before their return in September, have the buildings destroyed to make way for the access roads on either side of the Canal Street route. This would have included a number of the great cast-iron monuments. With the desecration well under way, and with the commercial incentives provided by the expressway, it is unlikely that anything could have stopped the development of the rest of the Cast Iron District.

I recruited some friends—I did not want my name mentioned for fear of compromising any influence I might have on the Lindsay people—to organize a protest meeting. The Museum of Modern Art agreed to let us use its auditorium. I confided in Grace Glueck of the *New York Times*. A date was set, and the other media were alerted. Then suddenly, just before the meeting, MoMA withdrew the offer of its auditorium. I always suspected powerful financial and real estate interests. I went to see David Solinger, then president of the Whitney Museum, and David courageously arranged for the use of the Whitney auditorium. The meeting turned out to be boisterous, and Grace Glueck gave it prominent—and, as it turned out, important—coverage in the *New York Times.*

The day the *Times* article appeared, I rushed over with it to Richard Aurelio, Lindsay's campaign manager. I said, "Dick, this is a disaster!" "What are you talking about?" "Look at this. This is going to kill Chinatown and Little Italy. We're dead with the Chinese, the Italians, and the Jews on the Upper West Side!" "Are you serious?" "Absolutely. This is only the beginning of the bad press." And somehow the Cross-Manhattan Expressway died that summer. I got the feeling that Eristoff suspected a Trojan horse but could never be sure. In 1970, Nixon cut the money supply, liquidity suddenly dried up, and by the time New York's economy revived from the recession in 1978, a Landmarks Preservation Commission was in place and SoHo was no longer in danger.

THE STORM BEFORE THE CALM

The last room in the 1995 Royal Academy Poussin exhibition, the room of the great landscapes, had a stillness about it: the calm of the Roman Campagna—not Claude's naïf wonderment of dawn or dusk, but a sophisticated commitment to the grandeur and formalism of the antique. And in this room, there was no picture more beautiful than the Sudeley Castle *Landscape with a Calm,* with its pendant, the Rouen *Landscape with a Storm,* both occupying places of honor on the end wall. Seeing those two pictures there together called to mind the story of how the *Calm* came within half an hour of being lost to Sudeley Castle.

The old-master trade convened in London in March 1974 for its thrice-annual trolling of the auctions. The Sotheby sale was, as usual, at eleven o'clock on the Wednesday morning, the twenty-seventh. A palpable buzz had started—perhaps not through the whole crowd, but at least among the four or five of us involved in seventeenth-century Roman painting—almost from the moment the sale went on view on Monday morning. Six pictures had been consigned by the trustees of the Morrison Settlement at Sudeley Castle: four landscapes by Gaspard Dughet and two by Jan Both, all obscured by dirt and yellow varnish, difficult to decipher except by specialist professionals, to whom the dirt and grand Morrison-Sudeley provenance made them singularly appealing. But one of the Dughets, lot 14, was more than appealing; it was the cause of all the excitement. The painting was catalogued as *An Italian Landscape with a Palace by a Lake,* estimated at £4,000 to £6,000. But even under the grime, the picture was too blond, too authoritative, too stately for Dughet. It was clearly by his brother-in-law, Nicolas Poussin.

Nicolas Poussin,
Landscape with a Calm,
1650–51

The J. Paul Getty Museum,
Los Angeles

The reigning Poussin authority at the time was Sir Anthony Blunt, later to be shorn, as a spy, of all but his academic credentials. In 1979 they took away his knighthood, and along with it even his Cambridge fellowship, though his scholarship largely stands firm, as does Berenson's despite his involvement with the art trade. The subject of Blunt leads me to digress on patriotism and treason.

The problem is in the definition. Certainly Blunt, in accepting access to state secrets and then violating that trust—whatever his reasons—committed treason as I define it. So does a butler or valet in accepting access to an employer's life and then selling confidences—whether because of some grievance or for money—commit, if not treason, then theft, which I think should be prosecuted. But then we have others' definition of treason. Some would, I suppose, find treasonable my inability to rise for "The Star-Spangled Banner" during ten years of the Vietnam atrocity, just as they did Jane Fonda's peace pilgrimages to Hanoi. But I was privy to no confidences, nor, I presume, was she—only public disinformation. I obviously do not subscribe to "my country, right or wrong." Nor, in his way, did Anthony Blunt.

Blunt was the product of exactly the kind of society that produces mutants: rigid yet permissive of eccentricity. Ours, fluid but intolerant of eccentricity, does so more seldom. Blunt's apostasy has been written about too often to discuss here at any length. What happened to Blunt, a sensitive romantic, and his band of Cambridge communists, might be at least partially explained by their birth into a rigid class structure, several notches from the top, yet almost within grasp of it; the entrenched subordinacy of the British underclasses; and the rise of the Nazis in Germany. But none of this had anything to do with his scholarly accomplishments, and of one thing I feel sure: Blunt should never have been stripped of his honorary fellowship at Trinity College, Cambridge.

In any event, on the Tuesday before that sale in 1974, I was curious as to Blunt's thoughts about the Sudeley

Nicolas Poussin,
Landscape with a Storm,
1651

Musée des Beaux-Arts, Rouen.
© Musée des Beaux-Arts de
Rouen. Photograph: Didier
Tragin/Catherine Lancien

picture, if he was even aware of it, so I rang him at the Courtauld and went over to see him at his apartment in Portman Square that afternoon. We sat in the darkness of his study over a glass of sherry, and I asked him if he had seen the Sudeley pictures. He had not. There was speculation about one of them being not a Dughet but a Poussin. Of this he was aware, because the Morrison trustees, apparently having gotten wind of the buzz, alerted the Sotheby old-master department, which had rushed a photograph of the suspect picture over to Blunt that morning. He assured me, though, that it was indeed a Dughet. A photograph was lying on his table. I asked if that was the photograph from Sotheby's. It was. Except that it was of the wrong Dughet.

I usually get to auctions at the last minute, but the next morning I sprinted from the Connaught through Bloomfield Place and up the stairs. Gloom had now replaced the buzz. At ten-thirty a notice had gone up on the wall that lot 14 had been withdrawn from the sale. I bought from the Sudeley group the other three Dughets, lots 13, 15, and 16, and the two Boths, lots 11 and 12, but Poussin's *Calm* remained, frankly through no fault of mine, at Sudeley, where it belonged, and the storm of a Sotheby blunder was averted by just half an hour.

In 1997 it was announced that the trustees of Sudeley Castle had sold Poussin's *Calm* to the J. Paul Getty Museum. No United Kingdom purchaser could be found to meet the price and when the export license was finally granted in October 1997, the amount was £16 million.

DR. BARNES AND THE DEVIL

I n the summer of 1960, I made my first trip to the Deep South. Passing through New Orleans, I met a young art-collecting couple, a
leading neurosurgeon and his wife, Richard and Susan Levy. I had
gone down there out of curiosity. Social and political systems, like those
that existed in South Africa and our own South, that run economies on
apartheid and cheap labor, had always appalled me. What I had seen in
the press had barely prepared me for the relegation of blacks to the back
of buses, nor for separate public drinking fountains, and certainly not
for separate windows at roadside vegetable stands. Twenty-eight years
later, in 1988, Richard Levy, knowing my feelings about civil rights,
asked me if I was interested in joining the board of trustees of Lincoln
University in Pennsylvania. A friend of his, Franklin Williams, had
recently become chairman.

Lincoln, the oldest black university in the country, was originally
called the Ashmun Institute, until 1866, when it was renamed after the
assassinated president. The university was founded in 1854 by a Presby-
terian minister, John Miller Dickey, to educate young black men, who at
that time had no place to go for an education. It also served before the
Civil War as a safe house for runaway slaves on the Underground Rail-
way.

Lincoln had always attempted to attract some white students, and
until 1945 its presidents were white. The first women were admitted
in 1952, and in 1987 Lincoln elected its first female president, Niara
Sudarkasa.

Lincoln's reputation quietly grew through its first century, along with
the distinction of its alumni body, which included Langston Hughes,

Kwame Nkrumah, and Thurgood Marshall. Then events not so quiet catapulted Lincoln out of the obscurity of the Pennsylvania mushroom country.

Albert Barnes was born in Philadelphia in 1872. While working for a Philadelphia pharmaceutical manufacturer, H. K. Mulford and Company, Barnes went to Germany in 1900 to find a research chemist, and while taking courses at the University of Heidelberg, he met Hermann Hille. He talked Hille into immigrating to the United States. Hille and Barnes discovered a formula for a silver nitrate substitute which became the product Argyrol, an antiseptic for the eyes of newborn infants. This was the basis for Barnes's fortune, and ultimately his art collection. Barnes and Hille formed a partnership in 1902, which by 1907 had disintegrated, and Barnes succeeded in forcing Hille out of the business. Barnes always claimed credit for Argyrol's discovery. The product may indeed have been his idea, but it was Hille who developed the product and Barnes who merely sold it.

By 1910 Barnes had become rich, and turned his attention to art. He had previously tried painting and come to realize that he had no talent. He started collecting minor Barbizon paintings, but from 1910, when Barnes was thirty-eight, he came under the guidance of his high school friend the painter William Glackens. The great Barnes collection was launched by Glackens in Paris in 1912 with the purchase of a Degas. Initially under Glackens's guidance, Barnes continued collecting presciently and voraciously from 1920 until his death in 1951.

Barnes, however, always thought of himself as an educator, not a collector. He established the Barnes Foundation in 1922 as an educational institution. The paintings were intended as teaching tools. When Barnes started amassing the Cézannes, Matisses, Renoirs, Picassos, and Seurats, he was virtually alone. When he first allowed them to be exhibited at the Pennsylvania Academy in 1923, they were ridiculed in the press, and by both the public and the Philadelphia establishment.

For the remainder of Barnes's life and for some eighteen years after his death, the Philadelphia establishment was to wage a war against Barnes's foundation. The early public rejection of his pictures had transformed Barnes into a curmudgeon. He became irascible, hurling epithets at the Philadelphia Museum, writing poison-pen letters, posing as a janitor and refusing entry to whomever he pleased.

Further, the fame the collection was soon to achieve made it impossible for the world to see it as Barnes did, as a "teaching collection" rather than a museum. Barnes's educational theories were idiosyncratic, rejecting art history as irrelevant, and were disavowed by responsible educators. The final coffin nail was the foundation's tax exemption, which made it vulnerable to carping and the various lawsuits that followed.

There are many institutions whose agendas are much more unpopular than the Barnes's, and whose tax exemptions remain unchallenged. One example is Bob Jones University, rigidly fundamentalist and discriminatory, whose significant collection of Italian baroque paintings has never been encumbered with official museum status. Another is the Church of Scientology, whose tax-exempt status was reaffirmed by the Internal Revenue Service on March 10, 1997.

Dr. Barnes's trust indenture stipulated that upon the death of his wife, Laura, her successor trustee be nominated by the Girard Bank (which later merged into the Mellon Bank). The remaining four trustees were to be nominated by the board of trustees of Lincoln University. When Richard Levy brought the Barnes-Lincoln relationship to my attention, I sensed that the responsibility vested in Lincoln presented a historic opportunity.

Black academic institutions were barely involved in the visual arts. They had trained few black art historians or museum officials. The black colleges were more concerned with the basics—training lawyers, doctors, clergymen, and social workers. Here, then, was a niche. The Barnes connection could give Lincoln instant status in the world of the visual arts and access to academic alliances. The Barnes could also become more accessible to the black community, and to the community at large, without the social and bureaucratic baggage of a mainstream institution. And the connection—the Barnes, with the mystery and romance of its legendary collection; Lincoln, with its mission and history—could, if exploited with dignity, result in a fund-raising bonanza for both institutions.

Franklin Williams, to whom Richard Levy had introduced me in 1988, judicious and reserved, experienced as to what he could and could not push through his suspicious faculty and board, nonetheless subscribed to my ideas. Williams was an impressive man, lean, craggy and lined of face, serious, cultivated, someone clearly to be reckoned with, a "man of stature." He was a lawyer, a former U.S. ambassador to Ghana, governor of the American Stock Exchange, director of the Council on Foreign Relations, the New York City Center Opera, and of companies like Consolidated Edison, Chemical Bank, and Borden. The list goes on, as do his honorary degrees. Williams was also a devoted Lincoln alumnus. He told me that but for his education at Lincoln on a scholarship, he would have ended up "at best a postman, at worst in jail."

I was flattered to be accepted by Franklin, not only as a professional but as a friend. He was convinced that my interest in Lincoln was rooted in a commitment to civil rights and went beyond the Barnes connection, and I accepted his invitation to join the board. He explained his plan to gently open Lincoln to some limited white involvement. I later came to understand how delicately Williams had to deal with his more scarred and less urbane colleagues. Those Saturday mornings when there was a Lincoln board meeting, I found myself rising at five-thirty to meet Franklin at Penn Station for the monthly trip to Wilmington. A car would take us to the Lincoln campus, about forty-five minutes away.

At the outset, Williams knew little about the Barnes Foundation. He was astonished at my description of the wealth of its collection. As the custodian of one of the greatest concentrations of late nineteenth- and early twentieth-century paintings—including some 180 Renoirs, 69 Cézannes, 60 Matisses, 44 Picassos, and 6 of the handful of finished Seurats—I wanted him to be wary not only of those who would try to poach this responsibility from Lincoln but of those who would try to exploit the relationship. To this end, I gave him an idea of the monetary values involved. At one Lincoln meeting, he asked me to tell the board the value of the collection, which I then estimated in the range of $3 billion to $4 billion.

I had envisioned my role on the Lincoln board as advisor on eventual control of the Barnes, which would come as three more Barnes trusteeships opened up: how to conduct its affairs so as to command the art community's respect and thwart attempts to litigate control away from Lincoln, as the *Philadelphia Inquirer* had done in 1959, and the Pennsylvania attorney general in 1969; and how to use the Barnes connection to develop an art history department at Lincoln. As discussed during our long train trips and car rides to and from the board meetings, this was exactly the role Franklin seemed to envision for me, but always cautioning me not to rock the boat too hard. I had never before been in the minority, but on the Lincoln board I learned what it felt like.

Franklin Williams, 1978

Photograph courtesy Mrs. Franklin Williams

When Laura Barnes died in 1966 at the age of ninety-two, she was replaced as president of the Barnes Foundation by Nellie Mullen, who died in 1967 at eighty-three. Mrs. Barnes was replaced as a Barnes trustee by Lincoln's first nominee, Benjamin F. Amos. The next board seat opened up in 1988 on the death of Violette de Mazia, Barnes's disciple, literary collaborator, rumored companion, and finally Barnes's director of education. Williams and I discussed prospective candidates for her seat. I urged selection of an academic so distinguished as to thwart any allegations of provincialism or inexperience. Franklin explained that he wanted to fill Barnes vacancies only with Lincoln trustees. He feared, probably with good reason, that after years of Barnes inaccessibility, a known art-world personality would immediately become a lightning rod for press, academic, and museum access, would become in fact synonymous with the Barnes, and Lincoln would be lost in the shuffle. Franklin wanted to hold control of this vast resource in the Lincoln family. His decision was to take the first seat himself, and that seemed to me credible, considering his national and international credentials and the general respect in which he was held.

I understood Williams's decision not to name an art-world personality to the Barnes board, and respected Williams's own credentials, yet I felt strongly that to avoid future attacks, Lincoln nonetheless had to demonstrate a high level of sophistication. I recommended that we form an art advisory committee, consisting of instantly recognizable names upon whose expertise the Barnes could call. Franklin welcomed the suggestion and asked me to draw up a list of candidates. As we left Penn Station that Saturday afternoon, he took leave with a caveat: "Richard, make sure you have some black people on your list. I have to deal with our faculty."

I set about compiling a massive list of museum and academic dignitaries for the proposed committee. I telephoned Dewey Mosby, a black art historian and director of the Picker Art Gallery at Colgate University. Dewey gave me a few names, I added them to my list, and, per Franklin Williams's request, submitted the list to Niara Sudarkasa. In fairly short order, the Barnes art advisory committee was announced. Though all the names were well known and eminently qualified, they seemed to have been taken from my list almost at random. Apparently these were the people who could be reached on short notice. Among them were Anne d'Harnoncourt, director of the Philadelphia Museum; Roger Mandle, deputy director of the National Gallery; Gary Tinterow, curator of nineteenth-century paintings at the Metropolitan Museum; Kirk Varnedoe, director of collections at the Museum of Modern Art; and Tom Freudenheim, head of museums for the Smithsonian. A few more African-Americans had been added to my list, apparently at the suggestion of the Lincoln art faculty, which at the time consisted of one person. Notwithstanding the hasty, almost ad hoc way in which the committee had been composed, the prestige of the board's membership would certainly accomplish its purpose: to allay potential accusations that Lincoln lacked the sophistication to run the Barnes Foundation.

During the next year, on our trips back and forth to Lincoln meetings, Franklin and I discussed plans for the Barnes. The first thing he made absolutely clear was his determination to honor both the letter and the spirit of Dr. Barnes's legacy. There had developed over the years considerable confusion in the academic world between the letter and the spirit. It was assumed, for instance, that there was a restriction in Barnes's will against color reproductions of the paintings. This was not the case. The restriction was simply a result of Violette de Mazia's interpretation of Barnes's theories, and the rule she imposed, which was carried on by her staff even after her death.

No sooner did Lincoln take up its Barnes responsibilities, Franklin Williams assume the chairmanship, and my involvement become known than I was besieged by a museum community long starved for color transparencies of some of the Barnes masterpieces. Judi Freeman, the twentieth-century curator, wanted a color reproduction of the Matisse *Le Bonheur de vivre* for the Los Angeles County Museum's *Fauve Landscape* exhibition catalogue. Gary Tinterow, the nineteenth-century paintings curator, wanted color reproductions of the Barnes Seurats, particularly the *Grandes Poseuses,* for the Metropolitan Museum's *Seurat* catalogue. Both of these were worthy projects, and I promised the curators I would try. I reread the Barnes trust indenture several times, and there was no restriction against color photography. The famous policy had clearly been imposed by de Mazia and carried on by Esther van Zant, her deputy, who was still administering the foundation when the Lincoln nominees took control in late 1989. Furthermore, the foundation was being funded by income from de Mazia's $8.5 million bequest, in van Zant's charge.

Franklin would not be rushed by my pleas for the color transparencies. He was the kind of man who rushed into nothing. First of all, he was uncertain of Barnes's intentions. Second, in light of the foundation's dependency on the de Mazia trust, he did not want to suddenly force van Zant into changing her policies. Williams suggested I present the suggestion at the next meeting of the Barnes board. David Driskell, a fellow Lincoln trustee, professor of art and art history at the University of Maryland, and an African-American, was also invited to attend. We were there as advisors to the Barnes board. Van Zant was also present. At that next meeting of the Barnes board, I presented the case for cooperating with the museums. I stressed the educational implications. I assured van Zant that advances in photographic technology since Barnes's day would make a change in policy consistent with his educational objectives. Van Zant strenuously argued the infidelity of color reproductions. In the end, no decision was taken, and on the trip back to New York Franklin told me that for the time being he did not want to confront van Zant, custodian of the de Mazia trust, the Barnes's sole source of funding.

Williams also wanted to take no action on another proposal. The Barnes paintings were generally in fine condition. Although very dirty, over all those years they had never been subjected to conservation. Fortunately, the Barnes Foundation had no conservation facilities of its own and no money to have the paintings worked on elsewhere. When they asked for color transparencies, both museums made an offer: if the Barnes Foundation would allow a painting to leave for cleaning just before the opening of an exhibition like Los Angeles' *Fauve Landscape* or the Metropolitan's *Seurat,* the museum would pay for cleaning it in its own laboratory. I did not feel that this violated the spirit of Dr. Barnes's will. Franklin, ever cautious and conservative, was of no mind to take at this juncture a step even more radical than the authorization of color transparencies. He had more immediate concerns.

There was a dangerous roof leak in the main Barnes building. There was no inventory of the important collection of early American antiques at Ker-Feal, the Barnes's eighteenth-century farm some thirty miles away, and no security system there at all. With no security system, no one in residence, and no inventory, a thief could enter the place at will and empty it, and no one would have a clue as to what was missing. The contents had never even been listed. And Williams wanted a professional survey of the security and climate-control facilities at Barnes's main building in Merion. These were the things to be dealt with first, funding for which the de Mazia trust was to be approached. Williams would not permit van Zant to be alienated by a confrontation over old de Mazia policies like color photography, and certainly not over unnecessary conservation projects. And throughout all these discussions, Franklin Williams's attitudes were governed by his determination to honor Dr. Barnes's wishes, explicit and implicit.

Franklin agreed to my suggestion that we proceed with surveys of the security and climate-control systems at the Barnes. I contacted several of the leading museum directors, got the names of the outstanding firms in each field, and had the surveys done. There was general agreement that the Barnes building was in fine condition, having been constructed to the highest standards in 1926. The roof leak had already been fixed with de Mazia funds. The estimate to bring the security system to state-of-the-art level was $324,650. The feasibility study for a climate-control system would cost $18,000. The study was not contracted before Williams's death, but the implication was that the final cost of the system would not exceed $7 million. As for an inventory of Ker-Feal, I suggested that we contact the decorative arts departments of several of the leading museums and graduate schools to locate a doctoral candidate in the American ceramics field who might catalogue the collection without charge as part of his or her academic project.

Williams announced at the September 23, 1989, Lincoln board meeting that the Barnes president, Sidney Frick, and trustee Benjamin Amos had resigned, and that Julius Rosenwald had been elected to the Barnes board at their meeting on the twenty-second. The board now consisted of Franklin Williams, Richard C. Torbert (the Mellon Bank representative), and Julius Rosenwald. Williams also announced that he would assume the Barnes presidency on September 26. That left two vacancies, and Williams felt it was imperative to fill them. At this point, Williams took the position that only one vacancy should be filled at that meeting.

Williams had not envisioned so sudden a transition, leaving Lincoln unprepared. He took Frick's resignation in stride but saw it as an unfriendly gesture, which in fact it was. Frick had seen the handwriting on the wall and Lincoln as an interloper. He seemed uninterested in an orderly and constructive transition, thus dishonoring Barnes's wishes, and for this the Barnes, and Lincoln, would pay a price in the months to come. As for Amos, his resignation may have been urged privately by Williams, or it may have been the result of lack of interest on Amos's part. In any event, he had been a mute trustee for twenty-two years.

On the trip down to that board meeting, Franklin raised the question of my taking the second Barnes board seat. I advised him against it. I felt that, notwithstanding what seemed to be the Barnes's impregnable indentures against buying, selling, lending, or borrowing, my profession as a dealer might leave us vulnerable to criticism. Also, I was the new white boy on the Lincoln block. There were others far ahead in the old-boy queue, which was as long at Lincoln as at Yale or Princeton.

As we were milling around at the Franklin Institute before the meeting convened, Richard Glanton, a forty-three-year-old lawyer, Lincoln's general counsel, and a trustee, came up to Williams, who was chatting with me, and said, "Franklin, I'd like that seat on the Barnes board." Glanton, polished and slick, a power in the Pennsylvania Republican party, had previously served as deputy counsel for the incumbent governor, Richard Thornburgh, and later under him at the Justice Department. For reasons no one seemed to know, Glanton and Thornburgh had had an acrimonious falling-out. They were now Pennsylvania Republican party adversaries. I knew little of this at the time, and I do not know how much of it Williams knew, but I suspect a good deal. I later learned that Glanton had his own eye on the governorship. He was also later mentioned in the press as a potential Philadelphia mayoral candidate to replace the hard-hat incumbent Frank Rizzo, and for the U.S. Senate nomination. When, three years later, a reporter asked Glanton about his political ambitions, he grinned and said, "Look at Clinton. I'm forty-six, he's forty-six, and I've got more sense than he does. If I ran for office, it would be the Senate. It's remote, but it is a possibility."

In any event, Williams's rejoinder to Glanton's proposal at the Lincoln board meeting was, "Richard, I don't think that would be a good idea. We want to keep Lincoln and Barnes separate. You're general counsel of Lincoln. You shouldn't serve on the Barnes board." That ended it. No one argued with Franklin Williams. Glanton was not happy. Williams then proposed Niara Sudarkasa, the Lincoln president, for the vacant Barnes seat, and the nomination was approved by the board. I was convinced that he had deferred the second board nomination because it would have been politically difficult to seat the other Lincoln trustee who had been proposed, Cuyler Walker, a white man, over Glanton, who Williams did not want on the Barnes board.

On the train back to New York that afternoon, Franklin told me of his distrust of Glanton, and of Glanton's blind political ambition. With Williams in firm control of the Lincoln and Barnes boards and only two more Barnes seats to fill, I sensed no threat to Williams's control or to my continued input. Shortly thereafter, the remaining Barnes trustee announced his decision to resign, also by year-end. Williams proposed for the two vacancies Cuyler Walker, the white Lincoln trustee who had worked at the Justice Department with Glanton, and Shirley Jackson, a Rutgers physicist.

Before the art advisory committee could hold its first meeting, Franklin told me that he had been diagnosed with throat cancer. The first art advisory meeting had been called for April 27, 1990, at the Barnes Foundation in Merion. As the date approached, Franklin's health had deteriorated and the venue was changed to his office at the Phelps Stokes

Richard H. Glanton, 1991

Photograph: Sal di Marco, Jr. NYT Pictures

Fund in New York. As we convened, we were told that Franklin could not even make it to his office from his home on the West Side, and that he would be with us on the speakerphone. In addition to the affection I had developed for Franklin, almost as a surrogate father, and the grief I felt, I had a sinking feeling about my dreams for the Barnes and Lincoln. But I could not possibly have imagined the calamity that was about to befall both institutions.

The meeting was merely introductory. There were no substantive matters to be discussed. Franklin, ever deliberate and careful not to alarm the incumbent Barnes staff, wanted to introduce van Zant, the Barnes administrator, to the art advisory committee and convince her that there would be no disturbance of the foundation's educational program. In my dream of a combined Barnes-Lincoln art history department, training black art historians, I had from the outset envisioned an eventual shift away from Dr. Barnes's idiosyncratic, anti-art-historical program. But Franklin had no knowledge of these matters, and so intense was his determination to honor Dr. Barnes's wishes that in my discussions with him I had barely alluded to the educational program. I had previously mentioned that I thought we should convene an educational advisory committee as well, to help develop an effective program. This was for the future. Right now there were more pressing matters, like a Ker-Feal inventory, the lack of which was kept a secret between Franklin and me lest it leak that there was none, and invite a theft. Barnes procedures had historically been kept so mysterious, however, that some questions did come up. I asked van Zant, for instance, how the paintings were secured to the walls. I have intermittent nightmares of aging, corroded picture wires breaking, of screw eyes pulling out of frames and picture hooks popping from walls.

I was startled when van Zant said, "Of course we take pictures down for classes." I asked, "Who takes them down? Where are they put?" "The guard takes them down and puts them on a bench, or on the floor." I imagined a guard dropping a Cézanne, or a Matisse impaled on a bench corner. I let it drop.

Franklin Williams died not long after that meeting, on May 20. Although he was much respected at Lincoln, I doubted that the president or anyone on the board comprehended the magnitude of the loss, nor do they still, or the tragic consequences for both Lincoln and the Barnes.

My concern for civil rights had blinded me to the gulf between the races that had become apparent and so troubled me during my tenure on the Lincoln board. Bridging that gulf would have been impossible without Franklin's sponsorship, and even with it, breaking down my colleagues' suspicion and gaining their confidence would have taken a long time. And this, after all, was a group of educated men—ministers, judges, lawyers, doctors. I could only imagine the hostility of a less educated group. Franklin was indispensable in this respect because he had a foot in both worlds. His background was not in the liberal arts, but he valued them. He respected the establishment's institutions and the importance of preserving them and building bridges to them, whereas his colleagues seemed to treat them as alien entities, to be ignored or taken advantage of. Only now do I understand the pain of the historic wounds that permitted even enlightened African Americans to accept the use of the "race card," to acknowledge O. J. Simpson's guilt yet condone his acquittal; that acknowledged Clarence Thomas's mediocrity yet supported his appointment.

Franklin Williams had, as an example, understood the availability of funding from private sources, whereas his colleagues thought all bounty flowed from foundations. This gulf between the black and white worlds became graphically apparent in 1991 as I watched Niara Sudarkasa testify at the televised Senate hearings for Clarence Thomas and against Anita Hill, without, I would suppose, a word of admonition from the Lincoln board. Had I been on the board at that time, I could never have raised my voice on this issue, as I suspect Franklin Williams would have done had he lived. I felt, in short, that Franklin was "one of us," and this may have been the very reason why he treaded so softly, moved so slowly, and restrained me so sternly, and perhaps why his loss did not seem to affect his fellow board members as much as I thought it would.

I had believed from the outset that the establishment was wrong and Dr. Barnes right, that Lincoln was perfectly capable of discharging the responsibilities with which Barnes had vested it. Now, with Franklin gone, I was led, by events that were about to unfold, to the painful suspicion that the establishment might have been right all along, and Dr. Barnes wrong.

Four days after Franklin's death, a notice arrived of a special Saturday board meeting, called for June 2, 1990, to elect a successor to the Lincoln chairmanship. I was scheduled to appear on a panel at the Los Angeles County Museum that day, a meeting that had been widely publicized, so despite my commitment to attend Lincoln meetings, I felt compelled to show up in Los Angeles. I telephoned Niara Sudarkasa's office not once but twice to make absolutely certain that the Barnes vacancy would not come up at the meeting. If it were, I intended to miss Los Angeles, whatever the consequences. I was assured that the Barnes was not on the agenda and would not be discussed.

When I returned from Los Angeles on Monday, I discovered that Dr. Bernard Anderson had been elected Lincoln chairman, that he had immediately appointed a nominating committee for the Barnes seat, and that the committee had nominated Richard Glanton as its only candidate. Ballots went out to the board members that week. I had two curious phone calls. The first was from Glanton, who was contacting every trustee. "Richard," he said, "I want your vote. I don't need it, but I want it." I told him, "Richard, I'm sorry. It's nothing personal. I can't give it to you. I think we should have one art person on the Barnes board. I'm nominating David Driskell." Glanton meant business. "I've got enough votes without you. The train's pulling out of the station." Shades of Mayor Daley. Franklin Williams was right.

Apparently viewing me as Williams's spiritual heir, they had to get me out of town. I found out later, when I checked the Lincoln bylaws, that all trustees must be furnished with the full agenda of a special board meeting with adequate notice; nothing can be added or deleted. The second call, from Niara Sudarkasa, was even more curious. She asked me to rally opposition to Glanton. She never told me her reasons. It's possible that Williams had confided in her as well. I got the feeling that despite Franklin's being an alumnus, he was not particularly close to anyone on the board. But I was aware that, as chairman, he was in frequent contact with his president. Glanton was elected with only a small minority opposing him, myself included.

No sooner did Glanton force himself onto the Barnes board than he had himself elected chairman by his four captive colleagues. Charles Frank of course wanted to keep the Barnes–de Mazia account at the Mellon Bank. With Anderson under Glanton's thumb, Sudarkasa wanted to keep her job as Lincoln president. Shirley Jackson, a physicist who had only accepted the Barnes seat reluctantly and with the warning that she could not give it any time, always seemed to depend on Sudarkasa, and not really to care what was going on. As for Cuyler Walker, I never could figure him out. He seemed to have opinions on nothing. He would say one thing and do something else. Maybe he suffered from the old white man's guilt. Or perhaps, being in government, he did not want to appear to oppose the black majority. Later, when Glanton's actions became so blatant that I couldn't understand how any responsible person could remain on the Barnes board and expose himself, legally if not morally, Walker claimed he could oppose Glanton better from the inside. Yet I never heard a hint of opposition, before or after I left the board.

The second meeting of the art advisory committee and the Barnes trustees did not take place until February 28, 1991, at the Barnes Foundation. Glanton had no questions for the distinguished museum officials. He needed no advice on operations, the budget, the educational program, cataloguing the collection, the humidity and climate controls and security system for which Franklin Williams had requested reports, conservation of the paintings, authenticity of the old masters, which had been called into question—even advice on inventorying the valuable and unprotected antiques collection at Ker-Feal, a matter that had so worried Williams and was his first priority. Glanton said only that he had filed a petition with the Montgomery County Orphans' Court to sell $15 million worth of paintings from the collection, a collection supposedly protected by the donor's trust indenture from any incursions whatsoever, a trust indenture that would not even allow paintings to be shifted from one place to another on the walls. He had filed a petition to break Dr. Barnes's will. Glanton didn't even know the artists' names, and had not a clue as to what money was necessary for what, or where or how the money could be raised without plundering the collection. Glanton had even boasted to committee member Roger Mandle that this was only the first stage of a bigger plan to sell not $15 million worth of pictures but $200 million worth, ostensibly to make the Lincoln-Barnes combination a "force" in the Philadelphia educational scene, but really to give himself political "clout."

While we were sitting there speechless, before the meeting exploded, Glanton said three other things. His power with the state attorney general and the court ensured that his petition would be granted. He had invited Walter Annenberg to serve as honorary chairman of the art advisory committee, Annenberg had accepted, and he supported Glanton's deaccessioning plan. This of course panicked the officials of the National Gallery, the Philadelphia Museum, and the Metropolitan, because of the American Association of Museums stricture against deaccessioning and because all three thought they were in contention for Annenberg's great collection, which had not yet been bequeathed to the Metropolitan. And finally Glanton announced that he was inclined to award the contract to publish the Barnes Collection to Alfred A. Knopf, whose owner, S. I. Newhouse, had donated $2 million to Lincoln University.

Then, after the shock, came the explosion. I lay back, since I thought I might still be able to convince the Lincoln board of the destructiveness to Lincoln's image and fund-raising potential of this deaccessioning program. My colleagues were venting our anger well enough. Shortly after the meeting, Roger Mandle and Tom Freudenheim drafted an open letter of protest, which they intended to publish but then called off. Walter Annenberg's involvement posed too great a risk to the museums.

On March 18 Glanton filed his petition with the Orphans' Court to sell Barnes paintings. At the Lincoln board meeting on April 13, presided over by Bernard Anderson, I waited for the agenda to be covered. Anderson called on Glanton to report on the Barnes, which he did in a cursory way. Then, just as Anderson was about to gavel the meeting closed, I asked to be recognized and made my plea. I mentioned the petition to the Orphans' Court, explained the American Association of Museums rule against deaccessioning objects except to replace them with other objects, and how damaging this activity, undertaken under Lincoln's stewardship, would be to the university's image. On a practical level, it couldn't help the university, or the Barnes, in future fund-raising to have these multimillion-dollar figures bandied about in the press. Only one trustee asked a question. Anderson gaveled me down. He said, "If you have any questions about the Barnes Foundation, ask Richard Glanton after the meeting." The meeting was adjourned. The hostility in the room was palpable. From that moment on, I knew I was a pariah, useless to Lincoln and to the Barnes. The only thing left to do was to try to stop Glanton from selling the paintings. This had to be done not only for the Barnes but for Franklin Williams, whose primary concern had been the preservation of Dr. Barnes's legacy.

I had no desire to alienate a billionaire art collector, the Annenbergs had always been nice to me, their extended family were friends of mine, but somebody had to do this, and between me and the museum directors, I was the more expendable. I phoned Grace Glueck of the *New York Times* and gave her the story.

Glanton's petition hit the press like a bombshell, the *Philadelphia Inquirer* on March 26, 1991, and the *New York Times* on the twenty-ninth. It was national news for four months. Roger Mandle's protest letter had gone out on April 9 to the individual members of the art advisory committee, interestingly, in light of how events later unfolded, on National Gallery letterhead. Glanton stuck to his plan. Glueck's article presented me as Glanton's primary adversary in the plan to sell the Barnes paintings. As a player of the "race card," Glanton had no equal, before or since, including Clarence Thomas and Johnnie Cochran. So I was not particularly pleased to see our pictures juxtaposed in the *Times*. What I most definitely did not want was to have this painted as a case of white versus black, or of the haves versus the have-nots, which it wasn't.

On July 23 I received by Federal Express a letter on Barnes Foundation letterhead:

July 22, 1991
Mr. Richard L. Feigen
49 East 68th Street
New York, NY 10021

Dear Mr. Feigen:

The Barnes Foundation's Board of Trustees hereby informs you that your membership on the Arts Advisory Committee to the Board has been terminated, effective immediately.

The Board firmly believes your service on the Committee has not been constructive.

The invitation which you have received to attend a meeting scheduled on July 31, 1991, is hereby rescinded.

Sincerely,
Board of Trustees [signed]
Board of Trustees/The Barnes Foundation.

The letter was signed, in ink, "Board of Trustees." In the lower left corner, above the notation FEDERAL EXPRESS, was "/deg." Not only were other Barnes trustees not made aware of my firing, but Glanton did not sign the letter, which bore only the initials "deg." Shortly thereafter, Anderson phoned and said that if I did not resign from the Lincoln University board by the following Friday meeting, he would ask the board to vote to dismiss me. I still harbored a fragile hope that the Lincoln board might wake up to the damage Glanton and his ally Anderson were doing, and that I might still be useful. So I checked the Lincoln bylaws and found that a trustee could not be dismissed until the end of his term. Mine did not expire until the following spring. I wrote the Lincoln board on July 24, giving my decision not to resign from the board, indicating the harmful effects that Glanton's conduct of Barnes affairs was having on both institutions, and stressing my loyalty to Lincoln and my feeling that I still had a constructive role to play on the Lincoln board.

In writing her story, Grace Glueck had contacted Anderson about my dismissals, and when she put the question, he had backtracked and said he wouldn't ask the board to fire me, that I was "still a board member and [would] be invited to the next meeting," but that if I was "a man of honor," I would "leave . . . and then," he hoped, they could "get beyond this and get on with the business of administering Lincoln." What more important business Lincoln had to get on with than discharging its responsibilities to the Barnes, I could not have imagined.

It became apparent, however, that with Franklin Williams gone, and in light of what had transpired, with Glanton and Anderson arrayed against me, I had no credibility left with the Lincoln board and there was nothing further I could do for the university. So on February 11, 1992, I resigned from the board. I held on to memories of my partnership with Franklin, and commencement photographs, in which I appear proud in my blue and orange academic robes, three stripes on my sleeve as a trustee, quite frankly tearful at the graduation of all those eager young people, so vital to the future of their communities.

As the date approached for the hearing of Glanton's petition before the Orphans' Court, the national press picked up on the *Times* story. The publicity became so intense and the opposition so vocal that Glanton was forced to drop his petition. He then amended it to request permission to rent out the collection, ostensibly only while the building was undergoing renovation, and for the alleged purpose of generating funds for his vastly overblown construction program. What Glanton had discovered was another "cash cow," rental fees running an average of $3 million per venue, with Glanton apparently charging each what he thought the traffic would bear.

Whereas the museums in contention for Annenberg's collection had been pitched on the horns of a dilemma by the deaccessioning proposal—either to honor American Association of Museums rules or risk alienating Annenberg—with the National Gallery taking the lead, the rent-a-Barnes petition presented them with no problem at all, Barnes's will notwithstanding.

I had introduced the National Gallery into the equation by putting both J. Carter Brown, the director, and Roger Mandle, the deputy director, on my list of candidates for the art advisory committee and discussing with Mandle, their designee, various Barnes conservation and cataloguing projects. Now Carter Brown, ever the master showman, threw the massive prestige of the National Gallery behind Glanton's petition. In this new era of the museum blockbuster, Glanton would now have the hit show of the century to peddle. The deal Carter Brown cut was for the National Gallery to help push the project through, act as advisors, and clean the paintings to be exhibited in return for getting the show for free. And in charge of the project he put the author of the erstwhile protest letter, Roger Mandle.

With the National Gallery's backing, the American Association of Museums' and College Art Association's combined legal counsel's retirement from the fray after withdrawal of the deaccessioning petition, and Glanton's political clout, the Orphans' Court approved the plan to loan Barnes paintings to just four museums, but strictly limited the loans to the period projected for the completion of the Barnes renovations. The collection was then to be returned permanently to its home, never again to leave. Nobody believed that would be the end of the story, any more than that the "crumbling building" was the reason for the renovations, protecting the paintings the reason for removing them, or that renting the collection was the only way to pay for the work.

Glanton's opposition—counsel for the Barnes's students, and scattered grumbling from the academic community—was no match for Carter Brown's benediction and Glanton's populist rhetoric and political muscle. This notwithstanding Glanton's much publicized loss of a sexual harassment suit, which had apparently snuffed out his political career. A white female associate in his law firm, Kathleen A. Frederick, had sued Glanton and his law firm, Reed Smith Shaw & McClay, in federal court for sexual harassment, accusing Glanton of forcing her to have sex with him in return for advancing her career. Despite Glanton's political power, the jury found that his harassment was "pervasive and regular" and created a "hostile work environment." The jury did not award Frederick damages, but did award her $125,000 for a remark Glanton made about her. Despite all this, Glanton held tightly to the reins of the Barnes.

Glanton had hit the jackpot as producer of the glitziest of all hit shows at just the moment when the museums were mutating into pleasure palaces. This was to be the era of the box-office bottom line and the director-impresario, and Carter Brown had taken Glanton under his wing and Glanton's show on the road. Every museum wanted to book it, even the stuffiest, like the Kimbell, or those that had seemed to stand firmest against Glanton's deaccessioning program, like the Philadelphia Museum.

Glanton, deprived by the publicity of the huge art slush fund he had envisioned from selling off Barnes paintings, and effectively burning his bridges, now decided to grab his full measure of art-world power. Every museum courted the proprietor of the biggest box-office smash of them all. He might as well have been Elton John's or Andrew Lloyd Webber's manager. There was barely a black-tie museum dinner where Glanton wasn't holding forth, treated as an august personage, presenting himself as director of the Barnes Foundation. Albert Barnes, Franklin Williams, even Lincoln University had long since been lost in the shuffle.

The original tour authorized by the court comprised the National Gallery, Washington; the Musée d'Orsay, Paris; the Museum of Western Art, Tokyo; and the Philadelphia Museum of Art. Then, in October 1993, although the court had decreed that there were to be no extensions, Glanton petitioned it to add the Kimbell Art Museum, Fort Worth, and the Art Gallery of Ontario to the itinerary before its scheduled closing at the Philadelphia Museum on May 4, 1995. There was a hearing in December and Glanton's request was granted in February.

The Barnes paintings were exhibited everywhere to sellout crowds. Despite the astronomic rental fees, the museums made big profits. Now the paintings were finally to return home to the Barnes. The entire tour had been controversial with professionals all over the world. Museums are increasingly reluctant to lend even a single masterpiece to a single venue, let alone an entire collection of such unique importance to so many places, each requiring crating, uncrating, shipping, hanging, and involving all the attendant risks of disaster and human error. The Paris venue caused special concern. Not only have several loans, like the famous fauve Matisse, *Femme au Chapeau,* suffered damage from negligence while on loan to French museums, but the huge Barnes Matisse, *La Danse,* which was not even scheduled to be exhibited at the Musée d'Orsay because of its size, was shown across the city at the Musée d'Art Moderne de la Ville de Paris, a building hardly staffed or equipped to handle a loan of this significance.

The court had twice decreed that the tour could not be extended, but the art world had not counted on Glanton's gall. He was not going to put his cash cow out to pasture, let alone into retirement, without a fight. Glanton allegedly agreed to send the show to the Museo Capitolino in Rome, and then succeeded, over opposition hardly equal to his political power, in extending the tour to the Haus der Kunst in Munich. It was alleged in Rome's lawsuit against the Barnes that Glanton, in changing the venue, accepted less money for the Barnes in exchange for personal gain in the form of law-firm business. The action by the city of Rome for breach of contract was eventually dismissed.

By the time of the Barnes's reopening in November 1995, with its collection back in place, the worldwide publicity resulting from the tour advertising and from Glanton's antics had dramatically increased traffic in the Barnes's quiet residential neighborhood. Chartered as an educational institution, not a museum, open to the public two and a half days a week, traffic had never before been a problem. Now the street was glutted with giant tour buses. Meanwhile, Glanton planned a parking lot for one and a half acres of Mrs. Barnes's cherished Arboretum, an integral part of Barnes's bequest. The citizens of Lower Merion asked their board of commissioners to limit traffic, and the commissioners responded to their concerns. Glanton filed a lawsuit against the township of Lower Merion, and the commissioners as individuals, under Title VII of the Federal Civil Rights Act, claiming that the zoning regulations were being enforced only because the plaintiffs were black and the defendants white. The township countersued. Even the Barnes's pliant trustees could not sit back and watch this blatant play of the "race card," and Charles Frank, Shirley Jackson, and Cuyler Walker resigned from the Barnes board. That left only Glanton and the captive Sudarkasa. After a long delay, the resignees were replaced by two Lincoln trustees, Dr. Kenneth Sadler, the Lincoln chairman who succeeded Anderson, Randolph Kinder, and Sherman White, the new Mellon Bank representative.

Finally, after catapulting the Barnes Foundation out of obscurity into international notoriety, after trying to sell paintings from the collection and then breaking Dr. Barnes's will by renting it out, after years of strutting around museum dinners brandishing his blockbuster exhibition, Richard Glanton was ousted by the Barnes trustees on February 9, 1998, amid allegations of a conflict of interest. When Niara Sudarkasa, Lincoln president and Barnes trustee, turned against him, Glanton retaliated by triggering a Pennsylvania State investigation into Sudarkasa's handling of Lincoln's finances, and into charges that she and her husband had renovated their residence at the university's expense. About to be fired as Lincoln counsel, Glanton resigned on March 20, 1998. Sudarkasa then filed a lawsuit against him, accusing him, as Lincoln counsel, of violating a lawyer-client relationship and operating the Barnes as a "private slush fund." The Lincoln trustees finally fired Sudarkasa herself, effective October 7, 1998.

Glanton eventually settled the defamation suit filed against him by the Commissioners of Lower Merion Township, paying $400,000 in legal fees and a forced "conditional retraction" in which he apologized for any "misunderstanding" caused by his words. Unsurprisingly, the Barnes Foundation's insurance had to cover these legal fees, as well as the fees Glanton's own firm charged in his frivolous litigation.

Franklin Williams's death had many unfortunate consequences, as is so often the case with uncommon men, none more tragic than the irreparable damage inflicted on Lincoln University and the Barnes Foundation by Richard Glanton, the man Williams had tried so hard to keep at bay.

ROSE AND MORTON NEUMANN

The Art Institute of Chicago finally announced, for 1997, a retrospective of the work of the city's greatest native son, Ivan Albright, the lion's share of whose life work he had donated to the museum shortly before his death in 1983. Oblivious of Albright's international importance and the treasure the Art Institute housed, the museum's powers that be paid scant curatorial attention to the project; even, with their skewed priorities, misjudged its box-office potential; and treated the whole effort as a bone thrown to a local artist's prominent family.

Had the Albright exhibition been mounted on the scale his coterie of sophisticated fans had anticipated, art historians, curators, and groupies would undoubtedly have made their way to East Division Street, spotted the number "55" on a neat, white-pillared red brick neo-Georgian house, and "53" next door on what appeared to be a grimy yellow brick, completely blanketed by untrimmed ivy, the front lawn overgrown with weeds, tattered curtains barely visible behind the ivy and unwashed windows, and would have sworn the Albright catalogue had gotten it wrong, that "53," not "55," had housed the master of decay and decadence, and his *The Picture of Dorian Gray.*

The house at 53 East Division was my home and gallery from 1959 to 1965, and Jo and Ivan Albright were my next-door neighbors. When I married and moved to New York, I sold the house to old family friends from the South Side, Rose and Mort Neumann. I had been badgering the Neumanns for years to follow everybody north, closer to the art action to which they had long since become a fulcrum.

I had grown up a block away from their old apartment at 5555 South

Morton Neumann,
Pilar Juncosa de Miró,
Rose Neumann, Joan
Miró, and Joan Prats
aboard the SS *Liberté*,
June 1, 1959

Photograph courtesy Hubert
Neumann

Everett. The neighborhood was in its last throes. The important German Jewish families had in the 1920s left this area around the University of Chicago, where they had built their rusticated castles in the late nineteenth century, for the Near North Side and the northern sub-urbs, Glencoe and Highland Park, leaving only their wid-owed grandmothers at the Windermere East Hotel, which is where my family lived.

The Neumanns lived in a duplex apartment with a two-story living room. The walls were stippled beige stucco. The rounded wall above the front door was emblazoned with a fantasy armorial shield. The din-ing room was separated from the living room by wrought-iron Spanish gates. The furniture came from Marshall Field's, and so did what art there was, mainly beaux arts Austrian genre scenes of ermine-trimmed cardinals downing steins of beer, though the Neumanns' elder son, Hubert, claims there was a sprinkling of Utrillos and Vlamincks among them. But then, if anyone in the Neumanns' circle during the war years, people like my parents, had noticed, they would have thought all this quite elegant. If Rose and Mort Neumann weren't art collectors yet, at least they had a collection of antique silver.

In the mornings, they went to work together at their mail-order cosmetics company, Valmor Products, in a big old Cadillac limousine. To the day they closed the business after Mort died in 1985, Rosie would pretend to be the switchboard operator and answer, "Good morning, Valmor Products," and I would say, "Come on, Rosie, I know it's you," and it would take her a while to unwind and admit it was indeed she. Valmor's factory was in the South Side ghetto into which Mayor Daley had herded Chicago's vast black population, on South Michigan Avenue, at the northern end of the valley between the vestigially affluent neighborhood where the Neumanns lived and the downtown "Loop."

Sometime around 1948 Rose and Mort went to Europe, and here, as the saga passes into legend, versions differ. One way or another, whether they were influenced by more sophisticated critiques of their ermine-trimmed cardinals or became disenchanted on their own, they found their way to Paris and Pierre Loeb's gallery, one of the cradles of

Rose and Morton Neumann with Picasso, circa 1955. The artist's watch, with the twelve letters PABLO PICASSO in place of the numbers on the dial, was a gift of the Neumanns.

Photograph courtesy Hubert Neumann

twentieth-century art. The version of the story that was long given credence had it that Loeb was in the process of hanging a show, and the paintings were on the floor around the gallery. A bearded man in a black suit and pince-nez was immersed in the paintings. Mort was said to have interrupted the man's reverie, in the broken French he retained, even after countless visits to France, to the end of his life: "Monsieur, ces tableaux, est ce qu'ils sont bons?" As the bearded man dropped his pince-nez and turned, he joined his right forefinger and thumb, placed them on his lips, and loudly kissed them, exclaiming, "Monsieur, ils sont des merveilles!" whereupon Mort turned to Rosie: "Look, Rosie, look what he did! He kissed his fingers! In French that means they're good!" The bearded man, it turned out, was Henri-Pierre Roché, legendary critic, the man who inspired and guided, among others, John Quinn.

Mort approached Loeb, who by this time was dashing across the room, visitors in those lean postwar days being a rarity, and said, "Monsieur, ces tableaux," waving his hand around the room, "ces tableaux, ils sont combien?" Loeb, with understandable excitement, fetched a pad and started quoting prices for each painting, whereupon Mort interrupted, "Non, monsieur, pour tous les tableaux." Loeb then toted up the prices and quoted the total. Mort had by this time apparently become quite frightened and was wondering how he had gotten himself into this mess and how he could get out of it. Rosie was, as usual, saying nothing. In an effort to terminate the whole thing and flee, Mort offered half. He was shocked when Loeb said, "d'accord."

The story goes on, and though Hubert Neumann claims it is apocryphal, or at least partially and chronologically so, at least some of it must be true because I have recollections from my own youth, not from art-world legend. Sometime after the Neumanns' rather panicked return to 5555 South Everett, the crates arrived, and not long after that, the calls started coming in from the likes of Alfred Barr and James Johnson Sweeney asking whether Mort did indeed have this or that Picasso or Giacometti, and might the Museum of Modern Art or the Guggenheim borrow it for this or that exhibition. And it is said that Mort on one of these occasions called out to Rosie, "Rosie, Rosie, Mr. Barr is on the phone! He says we have Picasso's *Femme nue assise*," and then asked Barr to spell the title. Now it may be that Hubert is right and all this has been romanticized in light of future events, that by the time Rose and Mort

Pablo Picasso, *Femme nue assise* (*Seated Nude*), 1909

Private collection, New York

had their Picassos and Giacomettis they knew full well what they were. But it is relevant here to mention the central facet of Mort's personality that makes believable all this and much that follows.

Mort Neumann, despite his shaggy gray hair and bushy eyebrows, and notwithstanding his birth date of 1898, was in one respect like a child of about six: out of his mouth came absolutely everything that

entered his head. He was incapable of dissembling. Unlike anyone else I
have ever known, he was also incapable of an *arrière-pensée*. Like a child,
he never had a bad word to say about anyone. He trusted everyone, and
everything he was told. Rosie, whose year of birth she never revealed to
anyone, not even her two sons, just stood by with a knowing smile, saying nothing, giving the distinct impression that she knew very well what
was going on and was fooled by none of it. She stood guard over Mort
lest anyone take advantage of him. Over the span of some forty-five years
that I knew Rose and Mort before he died, I cannot once remember seeing one of them without the other.

Sometime in the late 1940s or early 1950s—and here recollections differ as to whether it was before or after the advent of the Picassos—a lady,
by then in her nineties, suddenly became disenchanted with a pair of
high-button lace-up boots she had bought at Marshall Field's around the
turn of the century and had been wearing ever since. Marshall Field's had
made itself famous over the years for its policy of standing behind its
merchandise and taking things back from dissatisfied customers. So the
lady brought back her boots, and the store gave her a new pair and
promptly put the old ones in the Wabash Avenue window.

It was at this moment that Rosie and Mort happened down Wabash
Avenue, and Mort pulled up short in front of Marshall Field's window.
"Look, Rosie, look!" he shouted. "They took back the shoes! They took
back the shoes!" And so it was that Mort and Rosie piled all the ermine-
tipped cardinals into the big Cadillac and headed back to Marshall
Field's art gallery. Apparently, however, Marshall Field's policy did not
extend to its art gallery, and Mort experienced one of his few disenchant-
ments with human nature. To no avail, Rosie and Mort rushed up to the
executive floor, and were dispatched to South Everett Avenue without
satisfaction and with their collection of cardinals intact. I had thought
the paintings long gone by 1997, but their son Hubert tells me they are
still around somewhere.

Naïfs they may have been, but Rose and Mort soon raced far ahead of
their local coaches. It was not merely that they were fast studies. Their
world and their passion quickly became the art world—the artists, writers, scholars, and collectors. They still went down to Valmor to work
every day in a succession of vehicles, ranging from Cadillac limousines,
driven by a chauffeur called Edgar (later purloined by Leigh Block), to

an old Rolls-Royce (Mort's boyhood dream), and finally, after many summers in France, to a series of big Citroëns that raised and lowered themselves hydraulically, much to Mort's glee. Rose and Mort lunched together every day at the Standard Club, the old Jewish city club. But Valmor's wigs and hair cream receded into the background of their lives.

Rosie and Mort's immersion in the art world was quick and total. By November 1951 they were already entertaining Jean Dubuffet and his wife, Lilly, at Thanksgiving dinner at 5555 Everett. Dubuffet, most comfortable anyway with naïfs, children, and the insane, was mainly astonished by the huge turkey. The Dubuffets were in Chicago for his Arts Club exhibition and his revolutionary talk, "Anticultural Positions." By early 1952 the Neumanns were in New York at the Plaza's Persian Room with the Dubuffets and Willem de Kooning. When the maître d'hôtel tried to turn the tieless de Kooning away, Mort raised such hell that he backed down. Jean and Lilly Dubuffet then performed an Apache dance so wild that it would have wrung sight and a "Hoo-ha!" from Colonel Frank Slade himself.

Even in the 1950s and early 1960s, when there were few buyers of Picassos, Mirós, and Giacomettis, art collecting required funding, and Valmor provided it. Although never consciously, Mort had been an early beneficiary of the black self-hatred fueled by a bigoted society, the desire of African Americans to be more white, to dekink hair with ointments and wigs. Valmor's mail-order advertisements, composed by Mort himself, were visionary. When one of his wig ads was used by the Rolling Stones on the *Some Girls* album cover, though Mort had never even heard of the Rolling Stones, he filed a lawsuit for copyright infringement and won a large settlement. Later, Oldenburg included one of Mort's catalogues in his "Mouse Museum," another took its place in the Andy Warhol Museum, and one was recently included in the Museum of Modern Art's *High-Low* exhibition. To the artists, Mort had become a sort of cult figure.

When the era of "black pride" dawned and Malcolm X started preaching about Jewish exploitation of the blacks, Mort got defensive about his business. One afternoon in Paris in the early sixties, I was sitting with a group of colleagues at Heinz Berggruen's gallery on the rue de l'Université, a few blocks from the Hôtel Pont-Royal, the hotel of choice of the art world at the time, and where the Neumanns were then in residence.

Rose and Mort had already become internationally known for their art collection, and the presence of collectors this active, in an era when there were barely any buyers, was cause for heated discussion among the assembled dealers. One of them exclaimed, to no one in particular, "Ce Neumann, comment est-ce qu'il a gagné la fortune pour ramasser tous ces Picassos? [This Neumann, how did he earn the fortune to amass all these Picassos?]." Another dealer ventured, "Moi, je sais, il fait des médicaments pour défriser les noirs! [I know, he makes medicines to dekink blacks' hair!]." When I got back to the Pont-Royal for dinner with Rosie and Mort, I told them of the conversation at Heinz's that day. Mort wheeled around in terror. "Rosie, I never said it took the kinks out! I didn't say that!" I never knew, until a discussion with their son Hubert in 1997, of Mort's fear of a black anti-Jewish backlash.

Unlike most collectors advancing into their fifties, Mort had a childishly eccentric personality that kept his energies and interests out on the cutting edge. In the autumn of 1951, he had been at the Cedar Bar, hangout of the abstract expressionists, with Rosie and his twenty-one-year-old son, Hubert. He was at the first Rauschenberg show in 1954 at Charles Egan's gallery and tried to buy one of the "combine" paintings. Egan, who was talented but perpetually drunk, was asking $10,000, which was what Curt Valentin had quoted Mort for an important cubist Picasso, and was an absurd price for a young artist's work. Mort finally bought Rauschenberg's *Factum 2* from Leo Castelli in 1962, along with Lichtenstein's *Live Ammo* and Twombly's *View,* one of the artist's first four Roman paintings. Leo couldn't sell Twombly's work at all at the time, and the sale to Rose and Mort was cause for Leo and Ivan Karp, his sidekick, to celebrate. Mort had tried to buy Jasper Johns's *Target with Plaster Casts* from Leo in 1958, the year after he opened his gallery. It was priced at $900, but Leo had already sold *Green Target* and *Target with Four Faces* to Alfred Barr for the Museum of Modern Art during Johns's first solo show in January and was keeping *Target with Plaster Casts* for himself.

Mort had a tough time getting a Rosenquist from Dick Bellamy at the Green Gallery because Bob Scull, who was such a big client of the improvident gallery that he was rumored to be its backer, was grabbing them all. Mort finally got a Rosenquist in 1962. That same year, I remember Mort frequenting Claes Oldenburg's "Store" and the "Happenings" there, down on East Second Street. The window was filled with outsized painted plaster shirts, appliances, and plates of food, with outsized price tags dangling from them: $79.95, $129.95, $249.95. . . . Although clearly understandable to the plugged-in art world, there was always a cluster of puzzled neighbors at the storefront window.

Mort and Hubert were lunching one day at their favorite place, the Stage Delicatessen, when Mort, as he was leaving, spotted the last slice of a sumptuous cherry cheesecake sitting on a tin plate. "Sir," he said to the waiter, "I want that cheesecake." As the waiter put the cake on a plate, Mort said, "No, I want the tin plate. I want the tin plate, too." Mort and Hubert rushed down to Second Street with the cheesecake and tin plate. Oldenburg loved it, and it was not long before a box from Oldenburg arrived at 5555 Everett with a painted plaster cheesecake slice on the same tin plate, complete with plaster crumbs.

To Mort, who like a child wouldn't have understood "elegance" at all, the Stage Delicatessen was the greatest restaurant in the world. On one of their European trips, Jan Krugier, a vastly refined art dealer who knew all about fine food and who ran with a very grand crowd, told Mort that he was imminently arriving in New York, and asked him what was the best restaurant in town. Without hesitation, Mort told him "the Stage Delicatessen." Soon after he landed in New York, Krugier arranged a black-tie dinner party and, grateful for the sophisticated recommendation of so eminent a collector, booked the whole Stage Delicatessen without so much as a visit. The guests, bejeweled and betitled, were flown in from all over the world, and what transpired when they piled out of the flotilla of hired limousines onto Seventh Avenue has also passed into legend. To his credit, it still brings tears, of one sort or another, to Krugier's eyes some thirty years after the event.

By 1959 Rosie and Mort's dining room had become known for its wall-to-wall Mirós. Strolling down Madison Avenue one day after the opening of the Museum of Modern Art Miró exhibition that year, Mort encountered the artist. In his ever-fractured French, he discovered that Miró was also sailing on the *Liberté* the next day. In high excitement, Mort ran up Madison Avenue to George Wittenborn's art bookstore and grabbed every Miró book on the shelf. As he was carrying the load to the counter to pay, he passed the table with new and forthcoming titles, and there Mort spotted a new Miró book, which he added to his pile. But when he presented it at the cash register, George Wittenborn said it was not for sale, and when Mort protested, Wittenborn showed him that, despite the dust jacket, all the pages were blank and it was only a dummy. Mort refused to leave without the book, so Wittenborn had no choice but to confect a price and sell it to him.

The first day at sea, Mort spotted Miró sitting on the deck. He ran to his stateroom, grabbed the pile of books, ran back on deck, and found Miró still sitting there. He thrust them all at Miró and asked him to sign them, which Miró, who was in good spirits and who in some ways was almost as childlike as Mort, cheerfully did. When he got to the dummy book and saw all the blank pages, he said, "Monsieur Neumann, donnez-moi des crayons en couleurs." Mort raced around looking for Rosie. When he finally found her, he cried, "Rose! Rose! Miró wants colored crayons! Miró wants colored crayons!" Then he took off all over the ship looking for crayons. Finally he found a steward, who showed him the nursery. Mort ran inside, where a nanny was sitting on the floor with a little boy drawing with crayons. "Little boy," Mort said, "Mort wants to borrow your crayons." The little boy clutched his crayons, and the nurse, by now alarmed, looked for help. Mort cried, "Little boy, Miró wants to draw with your crayons!" The boy burst into tears. Mort said, "You naughty little boy! Miró wants to draw with your crayons!" grabbed the crayons, and ran out onto the deck looking for Miró. He found him still sitting there and handed the crayons to Miró, who proceeded to fill the blank book with drawings. What the terrified nanny didn't understand was that this was a squabble between two six-year-olds.

Just as Mort was free of guile, he lacked the ability to selfishly guard even coveted relationships. Dubuffet was notoriously perverse and inaccessible. Few collectors who had managed to develop a relationship with him would have invited an unannounced guest to come along on a visit, least of all an art dealer. In the late 1950s and 1960s, I used to spend several weeks every summer at the Hôtel du Cap d'Antibes. These visits followed the annual June stay at the Pont-Royal in Paris, where I stocked up on surrealist pictures for my Chicago clients, at a time when Breton and Tzara and myriad ex-wives and girlfriends were living off intermittent sales, and the artists were still alive and painting. Rosie and Mort were lunching with me one day in early August 1961, and after lunch they asked if I wanted to drive up to Vence with them to visit Dubuffet. I was touched, and still am, by their generosity. To them, of course, I wasn't an art dealer but an old friend and the son of friends. But had I not been, they would not have had the guile to keep their postlunch plans a secret and not invite their lunch companion, whoever it was.

So off I went to Dubuffet's house in the death seat of the big black Citroën, Mort at the wheel, Rosie in back, around the hairpin turns of the Corniche, hanging over the precipice. It was only when Mort was driving along madly and merrily like this that Rosie would emerge from her knowing silence and try vainly to intervene. As for me, with knuckles blanched, my thoughts, when I could gather them, were on this visit to the artist I considered the most important of the second half of the century.

Picasso, Matisse, Beckmann, Miró, Braque, Ernst, Léger, Brancusi—their major contributions were clearly in the first half. As for Giacometti and Bacon, I had held a Bacon show in 1959 and by 1961 had handled many Giacomettis, but I felt that both artists' imagery was too narrow in range to quite grant them a place in the pantheon with Dubuffet. Dubuffet did indeed work during the 1920s and 1930s, but his pre-1942 work was tentative and atypical. His period of greatest innovation was from 1945 to 1962, and these innovations—"anticultural" art, relating to the naïf, the primitive, the insane; nonpictorial, vestigial images; rough, sometimes organic materials—made him relevant to the youngest artists. His 1951 speech at Chicago's Arts Club, "Anticultural Positions," was the manifesto for a new era.

Dubuffet spoke of a revolution under way, a reversal of values in which primitive art, with its savagery, passion, violence, madness, supersedes the civilized, the "occidental." To Dubuffet, "culture" was the dead language of mandarins. What mattered to him was the "art of the streets," of daily life, of nature. He disavowed elaborate ideas and complicated analysis, the written word in favor of the voice. He discarded the myth of plastic beauty, the concept of beautiful objects and ugly ones; for Dubuffet, there were no ugly people, objects, or materials. Cinders, gravel, leaves, were as beautiful as marble or bronze. Art, for Dubuffet, addressed the mind, not the eye. It was, as for the primitives, for children, for the mad, a language. Painting was richer than words, capable of revealing inner voices and hidden values. It was more than "assemblages of shapes and colors." This was the revolution that Dubuffet had announced that winter morning at the Arts Club.

As the Neumann Citroën pulled up to Dubuffet's house that August afternoon in 1961, high over the Côte d'Azur in Vence, I had no idea what to expect. His perversity and irascibility were legendary. He was an aesthetic and social contrarian. When France blocked the departure of ships Israel had bought and paid for during the 1967 war, most of the artists donated work to Israel; Dubuffet's donations were to the Arabs. Years later, Dubuffet invited me to join him and his wife for lunch at the restaurant of the Gritti in Venice. A photographer came along and took our picture. I asked Dubuffet if I might have a copy, and when in explanation I said that I thought he was a great artist, his reproof was, "I am not an artist. I am a man of the streets."

Dubuffet was, I thought, remarkably hospitable and communicative the day we came. We sat for a while drinking coffee on the terrace outside his house. Then he did something none of us had anticipated. He suddenly asked if we would like to see his studio. I would never have dared ask, and this question may have been one of the few things that entered Mort's head which did not emerge from his mouth. The last series Dubuffet had exhibited, two years before, the *Beards,* had been in grisaille tones of brown and black. What he had been doing since, no one knew.

There had always been a certain rhythm in Dubuffet's palette. He would make a series, like the paintings of 1943 and the *Métros* of 1944, and the brilliant color would bleed out to monochrome in the next series, the *Hautes Pâtes* of 1945 and 1946 and the *Portraits* of 1947; then return to color again in the *Arabs* of 1948; bleed out in the *Corps de Dames* of 1949 and 1950, the *Landscapes,* India ink drawings, and *Tables* of 1951 to 1953; then rush into color again with the *Cows* of 1954 and the canvas and butterfly-wing assemblages of 1956; then bleed out with the later assemblages of 1957 and the sculptures, *Matériologies, Texturologies,* and *Beards* of 1959.

Through the open door of Dubuffet's studio that afternoon burst the most amazing blaze of color I had ever seen in his work—the little people, cars, streets, stores, and cafés of his new *Paris Circus* series. So buoyant was Dubuffet's mood that I dared ask if I might buy a picture I particularly liked, *The Fiat with Bumpers,* and Dubuffet later forced his dealer of the time, Daniel Cordier, to sell it to me. Cordier let it go grudgingly, for $8,000, because the *Paris Circus,* like the *Beards* before it, were very salable, and Cordier was using the Dubuffets to sell his other artists' work. In order to get one of the Dubuffets, a client would have to buy a menu of Cordier's other artists. It is said that this was the reason Dubuffet left Cordier's gallery two years later. The force that had brought Dubuffet to Cordier's gallery in the first place was apparently Dubuffet's major patron, Elie de Rothschild, who had served in the Résistance with Cordier.

When the Museum of Modern Art Dubuffet exhibition opened later that year, several of the important *Paris Circus* paintings were still listed as belonging to the "collection of the artist." When the exhibition reached the Los Angeles County Museum, a client of mine, Burt Kleiner, succeeded in snaring one of the huge paintings, *The Automobile, Flower of Industry,* but when it arrived at his house in Beverly Hills, it wouldn't go in the door. With the truckers at the door, Burt went inside and phoned to ask me if I would take it off his hands for the $16,000 he had paid. The Dubuffet hung in my Chicago apartment until I sold it at Christie's in 1990 for $3.5 million.

The Neumanns took me on another artist visit that summer of 1961, up to Vence again, to Chagall, and this time I knew exactly what to expect. Chagall's temperament was legendarily benign, and certainly his work held no surprises. He hadn't had a new idea since 1917, and had been doing much the same thing since the 1920s. We walked out onto the Chagalls' lawn on a splendid August day, the Côte d'Azur asparkle down below. We found Madame Chagall presiding over a birthday party for twin daughters of friends. The girls were mesmerized by the towering pyramid of a great fruitcake. Chagall was nowhere in sight. Suddenly he burst onto the lawn, wringing his hands. "I am in despair! When a woman is giving birth, she knows that sooner or later the baby will come! With this painting, I never know!"

Chauvinism is a problem with most places, but—except when football, basketball, or hockey is involved—not Chicago. Chicago has always been the last place to appreciate its own cultural accomplishment, and Rose and Mort Neumann were certainly no exceptions. When Tennessee Williams's *The Glass Menagerie* opened there in 1945, it took the critic Claudia Cassidy to berate the public into finally coming to the theater.

When the Second City Players started in 1960, the place was empty until improvisational political humor drew acclaim in the international press and people crowded in from everywhere.

During Chicago's golden age of collecting in the forties, fifties, and sixties, the collectors, courted by dealers all over the world, were ignored at home, even insulted. When the Art Institute opened exhibitions with black-tie dinners, the collectors were assembled in the galleries in street clothes and at ten o'clock the great doors swung open and black-tied Lake Foresters spilled out of the dinner.

Of all the collectors, none were more ignored, even ridiculed, by the establishment than Rose and Mort Neumann. The social climbers, like the Leigh Blocks, were embarrassed by the Neumanns' naïveté; they saw it as the gauche underside of their own ambitions when in fact Rosie and Mort had no ambitions at all. As their passion carried them through wave after wave of the avant-garde, the collection grew in fame, and their charming idiosyncrasies with it. Unlike the Blocks, whose oldest friends were afraid to solicit visits on behalf of the most august dignitaries—I once told Roland Penrose to get someone else to phone Mary; I didn't dare risk her fury—all were welcome at Rosie and Mort's. I cannot imagine anyone being turned away from 5555 South Everett or 53 East Division until Mort died in 1985 at the age of eighty-seven.

It was then that Rosie, whom no one could ever remember seeing without Mort, went into seclusion and the ivy started covering the windows. She became a recluse, and the yellow brick house a mausoleum housing one of the world's great art collections. Most of the art remained there with Rose until 1997, when her sons began to remove it to safer quarters. No one in the art world, which Rosie and Mort loved so much, or even in Chicago, whose only spirit their gatherings had provided for over thirty years, even noticed when Rosie died on May 13, 1998. She had simply disappeared when Mort died thirteen years before.

The art world continues to speculate on the collection's destiny. Auctioneers hover incongruously around Hubert at the cutting-edge openings he frequents. Before Mort died, the National Gallery staged a Neumann collection exhibition and gave a dinner in Rose and Mort's honor, but it was a halfhearted effort, a small affair in an upstairs room with a few of their friends, quite obvious in its objectives. No museum, certainly not the Art Institute, solicited their counsel or involvement, nor chose to honor their commitment and achievement during their heyday. I recently asked Hubert whether, had Rose and Mort been drawn more warmly into the Art Institute "family," the collection might have ended up with the museum. First he said "probably not," but then, after some reflection, he said he didn't know. I don't know either, but I knew Rose and Mort for almost half a century, and as inheritance taxes forced twenty-one works from the Neumann collection—only one of them a major painting, Picasso's 1909 *Seated Nude*—into Sotheby's in November 1998, I suspected that at least a substantial number of Rose and Mort's treasured paintings might have found a home at the Art Institute.

THE WAR OF THE MUSEUMS

On June 25, 1999, the press suddenly laid bare to the public the revolution that for years had been progressively striking fear in the hearts of museum professionals. The director of the Museum of Fine Arts, Boston, Malcolm Rogers, had summarily fired eighteen members of his staff, including Jonathan Fairbanks and Anne Poulet, veteran curators respectively of American decorative arts and European decorative arts, departments in whose collections the museum has long been preeminent. Five other curators quit or were fired in the autumn, capped by the resignation in December of Theodore Stebbins, the respected curator of American paintings. Fairbanks and Poulet had been escorted by security guards to the personnel office, where they were forced to hand over their keys and museum passes, and ordered to clean out their offices and be out of the building by 3 p.m. Rogers's "restructuring" plan was under way.

Rogers had fulfilled the mandate that had been handed him by the trustees; as one of them was quoted in the press as saying, "Malcolm has done a great job; he's livened the museum up and put it in the black. . . . [the] visitors eat, and buy in the shop." One of the world's great museums and one of America's oldest, Boston had been run into red ink by a Brahmin board that had finally embarked on a construction program it could not afford. New blood, even though it be businesslike and respectful of the museum's traditions and collections, was not welcomed onto the board, and when change came, it came suddenly and with the same kind of pent-up resentment that has beset others of the old institutions. The doors weren't opened; they were battered down. Alan Strassman, a trustee and former board president, opened an office at the museum during the tenure of Alan Shestack, a former director, where he took to reading Shestack's mail. Unsurprisingly, Boston could find no one to take the job until they hired Rogers, an unknown deputy director at the National Portrait Gallery in London.

What the museum world has come to call the "Boston Massacre," Rogers describes as "glorious decisions." The sympathetic press calls him a "Shake-up Artist." Some have described the Boston battle as one between the forces of art and commerce; others as between inertia and progress. But on one thing all agree. The Boston Massacre of 1999 sounded the cry of battle as surely as did the Boston Tea Party of 1773.

To those few who could spot them, the battle lines had been drawn a quarter century ago, in the very cradle of the modern American museum, Harvard University. The war, as it has evolved in those twenty-five years, is over the very concept of a museum's mission—the old model, a temple of connoisseurship and scholarship, called "elitist" by its antagonists; or the new, an entertainment palace and elementary art school, called "populist."

The old connoisseur museum director felt it his mission to show and teach people what they did not necessarily yet know about, to surprise and excite them with new images and ideas. He seemed to respect the public's intelligence. The new breed, groomed in management and fund-raising, lures the public with the familiar, with gold and jeweled objects, with fashion.

The public debate over the museum's very mission has also opened the political floodgates. There was a time when the museum's program was dictated by its trustees and their choice of director, by the nature of its collections and its chosen fields of activity. It was open to those who chose to enjoy and learn from its specific program. The William Rockhill-Nelson Gallery in Kansas City and the Cleveland Museum were particularly rich in Oriental art, the Art Institute of Chicago in impressionism, Toledo in Italian baroque painting, the Sterling Clark Institute in Winslow Homer and impressionism, and so on. But the museums' tax-sheltered status, with or without direct public subsidy, left them ultimately vulnerable to political pressure. The debate over mission, the demand by the "populists" that the entire community be addressed, leads all segments to demand equal representation, even if much of this activity flies in the face of the museum's historic strengths and program, and even if it means compromising the museum's aesthetic standards. Once the museum becomes an entertainment palace and elementary art school, the question can reasonably be asked, "Why not entertainment for everybody?" and "Why not education for everybody's children?"—on demand. Connoisseurship is for the "few," entertainment for the "many." Forget about the old dream of miraculously transforming some of the many into the few. The institution surrenders its own agenda and curriculum, even its choice of director. The political Pandora's box, once sprung open, can never be shut again.

In this new era of museology, a director's success has come to be measured by the crowds he attracts, the funds he raises, the buildings he builds, and how effectively he can dodge political cross fire. A prospective director who finds himself in the political crosshairs, who does not appear to fulfill the new criteria, has no chance of getting the job. Museum directorships go begging. Recently, both Detroit and St. Louis found themselves in this bind, directorless, on the political battlefield.

I drove past the Metropolitan Museum one February night in 1997. There, draped across the central bay of the facade was what seemed evidence that the tide was drowning the "elitists": a huge blue and gold banner proclaiming HAUTE COUTURE. That banner was joined not many days later by FABERGÉ IN AMERICA. The august institution was now pursuing crowds and big money with fashion and kitsch disguised as high art. This is not the Metropolitan's usual menu. Yet the 1997 program advertised by those flags was by no means unique. Exactly one year later, in February 1998, the main flag proclaimed GIANNI VERSACE. Versace, the subject of the wildly publicized exhibition, was a talented couturier, tragically shot in Miami, but the question remains as to whether couture is a serious subject for a great museum. In recent years, a certain part of the Metropolitan's public face—exhibitions or parties—has seemed to involve fashion.

Apart from the Metropolitan's staggeringly rich collections, which are constantly growing through benefactions, there have in recent months been such important exhibitions as *Winslow Homer, Tiepolo, Prud'hon, Dosso Dossi* and *Ingres*. But this random mixture of box-office frivolity with serious art reminds an "elitist" of a nice girl of good family who just once in a while goes out and turns tricks for some pocket change.

The brouhaha over the Brooklyn Museum's 1999 *Sensation* exhibition

Facade of the Metropolitan Museum of Art, New York, February 1996

focused public attention on the conflict of interest when a museum accepts funding from someone who wants to sell objects being exhibited. Mayor Giuliani used Christie's sponsorship and the funding of the objects' owner, Charles Saatchi, as his excuse for trying to censor the exhibition and penalize the museum, when in fact his motive was political. Certainly, as museums' costs escalate, and as their management becomes corporatized, they look more to corporations for funding, and the projects being funded relate more to the sponsors' products. The Metropolitan Museum showed Cartier jewelry and Versace dresses, the Guggenheim BMW motorcycles and Armani clothes. Clearly, the reason these companies spend all this money is to burnish their products in the museums' aura.

It is precisely this that concerns me more than the simple conflict of interest, the museum selling its prestige to market commercial products. The Brooklyn project at least involved art. Not so with dresses and motorcycles. This is the more troubling conflict. To the broad public, anything exhibited in these institutions is high art. So if dresses and motorcycles are exhibited in a museum of fine art, the message is that they are art. The public is being deliberately confused for commercial purposes.

In the old days, art museums were about real art—taking care of it, completing collections of it, exhibiting it. But these days American museums—with only a few exceptions—seem more concerned with crowds and money than art. In an article in the January 10, 1999, *New York Times,* Glenn Lowry, director of the Museum of Modern Art, relates museums to the entertainment industry. Box office is of course the entertainment industry's index of success. It is important to consider whether this sea change over the past quarter century—and with it, museums' preoccupation with endowments and construction programs—is for better or worse.

The end of the twentieth century is a watershed. These changes afoot are fundamental. Even as museum opening hours were being curtailed and staff layoffs announced, and amid claims of inadequate funds for acquisitions and scholarly exhibitions, plans proliferated for new buildings, galleries, courtyards, temples, and fountains. Massive fund drives were launched—$300 million by the Metropolitan Museum, $100 million by the Art Institute of Chicago—but only to build endowments or clear up deficits, rarely to acquire objects, or for scholarly pursuits. What expensive exhibitions took place were usually "blockbusters"—much like $100 million movie projects—directed at broad popular taste, guaranteed to make back their cost and turn a profit.

In this new climate, even a museum's scholarly projects can be distorted by box-office ambitions. The Metropolitan Museum's exhibition *Orazio and Artemisia Gentileschi, Father and Daughter,* scheduled for 2002, is a significant example. Orazio Gentileschi (1562–1639) was one of the great painters of art history. He initiated a tradition of objectivism, of formalism, in baroque painting that diverged from Caravaggio's emotionalism and drama. Caravaggio and Gentileschi were two towering figures whose personalities were at opposite ends of the emotional spectrum. Both were seminal influences on later seventeenth-century painters, Gentileschi most particularly on the Frenchmen working in Rome. Yet Gentileschi continues to be labeled, along with almost every other figure painter of the period, a "Caravaggist." Scholars sensitive to the essential difference between Caravaggism and Orazio's counter-Caravaggism have long awaited a monographic Orazio Gentileschi exhibition to clear up the misconceptions.

Gentileschi's talented daughter, Artemisia (1597–1651), was, like all aspirant women painters of the period, barred from the academy. Only because her father was a painter was she able to study the nude and become a well-known painter in her own right. Artemisia grew up under the powerful influence of her father's friend Caravaggio, who died in 1610 when Artemisia was thirteen. She shared Caravaggio's emotionalism, which may or may not have had to do with her gender. At the same time, as her father's assistant, she borrowed many of his themes, and even his compositions, in her own work. Because few of her works, or her father's, were signed, Artemisia's artistic personality remained shadowy for three centuries, her work often confused with Orazio's. The rise of feminism, the scarcity of important women painters, the drama of Artemisia's rape by Orazio's friend Agostino Tassi, and the ensuing trial have recently generated a wave of interest in her work. There have been books, exhibitions, symposia, and a feature film (*Artemisia,* 1998). She has become world-famous, pushing her father, of whose work there are fewer than sixty extant examples, even further back into the shadows. Despite all this exposure and fame, Artemisia remains a relatively minor figure, a competent painter, mired in the powerful tradition of Caravaggio.

Philippe de Montebello, director of the Metropolitan Museum, a respected art historian and member of the vanishing breed of museum men who actually care about objects, has long recognized Orazio Gentileschi's importance and regretted the absence from the museum's collection of an example of his work. Yet when Judith Mann, a young St. Louis Museum curator, hatched the idea, dear to feminists, of the father-daughter exhibition, to be mounted by St. Louis in conjunction with the Museo Capitolino in Rome and the Metropolitan, without whose powerful collaboration major loans would be unobtainable, the Metropolitan succumbed to the famous daughter's bait and signed on. Artemisia's box-office appeal was irresistible. The idea for the show, incidentally, started with an expensive mistake in St. Louis's collection—their purchase, some years ago, of a little painting on copper of *Danäe,* which they were almost alone in thinking was by Orazio Gentileschi, and is now supposed to be by Artemisia.

In the forthcoming *Father and Daughter* exhibition, it is certainly the daughter, not the father, who will grab the headlines; the public will be fooled into thinking it was she who was the great painter; Orazio's message will be obscured by Artemisia's dramatic Caravaggism; the artists Orazio influenced will be absent from the show; and finally, the loan of some 80 percent of Orazio's lifework will foreclose, for the foreseeable future, the possibility of a full-scale monographic treatment, which is urgently needed. Rape and political correctness are irresistible. Apparently the Metropolitan lacked enough confidence in its capacity to secure sponsorship for the exhibition it knew it should have done. The public, even the scholars, will remain more unenlightened than ever. Scholarship again takes a backseat to box office.

Trustee search committees now hire "head-hunting" firms to find "fund-raisers" and "administrators" to fill vacant directorships and run these new programs. At lunch some time ago, a leading museum headhunter told me that museum directors need not know about art; this can be left to the curators. The message was implicit: you can be either an administrator or an aesthete, not both. This comes not only from the headhunters but from the museum trustees from whom they get their directives. The thinking seems rooted in our Calvinist heritage: everything is black or white, never gray. In their lack of confidence in the aesthetes' ability to deal with fiscal and managerial problems, the trustees have increasingly taken over the basic conduct of museum affairs. But it is not only this doubt that triggered the devolution of power in the trustees and their refusal to relinquish it to the museum professionals. Economics played a crucial role.

Fueling the Art Market

In the 1960s and 1970s, the United States printed amounts of money far beyond what its productive capacity warranted, largely to conduct its manic counter-communist campaign in Southeast Asia. This inundation of world currency markets naturally caused massive inflation; museum budgets ballooned and the art market soared. At the same time, it incidentally created huge new fortunes, bigger even than those of the 1920s, transforming much of our society, particularly in New York, into a great plutocracy.

This newly minted money washing around the world—from Saigon black markets to Mideast oil kingdoms to American money-center banks to corrupt South American regimes and back to the money-center banks and off again to Japanese car manufacturers—not only eroded the purchasing power of the dollar but forced holders of the currency to search beyond traditional repositories for places to put it. Existing markets were either too small or too volatile. The currencies themselves fluctuated wildly and became prey to speculators. Bond and stock prices seemed bloated. The politically powerful Japanese farmers, in an effort to keep land around Tokyo agricultural, forced confiscatory taxes on real estate profits, and as the real estate market atrophied, Japanese banks and insurance companies effectively added to the money supply by making massive loans on the real estate, and prices took off, first in Japan, then throughout the world.

As these events unfolded, quantities of the money, although small by the standards of the financial markets, seeped into the art market. Art, however, proved unsuitable as a financial instrument, not only because of its illiquidity but because there is just not enough real art around. In the markets of the eighties, the "art" envelope got pushed far beyond the frontiers of genuine art—objects of aesthetic quality and art-historical significance—to include cookie jars, Mickey Mouse watches, duck decoys, comic books, and baseball cards. And as the art market soared, fueled by Japanese money, the press took off on a feeding frenzy. This attracted even more speculators and climbers, many of whom were members of the real estate and investment communities, where bankruptcies and layoffs were imminent, and who could not afford the losses they were about to incur.

The bloodiest fields of the art market were of course those where the speculators had been playing: the Japanese in impressionism, the School of Paris, and post-1960s American; Europeans in the twentieth-century Europeans and expensive contemporaries; and again the American speculators in the contemporary market. Which takes us back to the new plutocracy.

If the "free enterprise" system is the natural ordering of human society—and this seems borne out by the disintegration of various socialist systems—and some people are more enterprising than others, then the money flows to some and not to others. It is natural for people to want power, or at least to resent others who have power over them, and if in a plutocracy money is power, with more of it in circulation and more people making it, then the ante keeps rising—i.e., the amount of money it takes for this kind of society to devolve power on a newcomer. The pro-liferation of centimillionaires just between 1998 and 1999 was such that the entry level for the Forbes 400 ballooned from $500 million to $625 million, and the number of American billionaires from 189 to 278, of whom 19 were attributable to the Internet. Anyone—except for the occasional savage—who arrives in New York with this kind of money is courted frantically.

Contemporary Art: Ladder to the Stars

But there are also a number of people who, having garnered $50 million or so, think they are important, even if they can't get their pictures in *W.* In the 1960s, Ethel and Robert Scull pioneered another road into the limelight: art. They discovered that, with a relatively modest investment, they could become celebrities and also make a profit. Thus was launched the ill-fated contemporary art boom that climaxed in 1989 and tanked in 1990, leaving much carnage and many galleries out of business, and artists' lifestyles and psyches in ruins. The bubble burst when the specu-lators, who thought that the prices of the anointed artists could only rise, discovered that was not necessarily so and bailed out and ran for cover; and the social climbers found that once the bloom was off, owning a few trendy pictures no longer guaranteed membership on museum boards and councils or a picture in *W.*

This would be a gloomy picture indeed if it meant the end of the con-temporary art market. In the 1980s, anyone who predicted the bursting of the bubble was accused of trying to wreck the market. And if the rejoinder was that it was unhealthy for everybody, including the artists, to have the prices of thirty-year-olds pushed into the six and seven fig-ures—unhealthy and dangerous—and that all the anointed artists on the menu were not necessarily the best in the world—that there were some unheralded artists out there, whose work could be bought for $2,000 or $5,000 or $10,000, who were much better—you were pilloried for not liking contemporary art. "Contemporary art" was synonymous with that one little list of artists.

I suspect that a fair number of the "great" contemporary collectors in the eighties were not that interested in the art—just in the power and the profit. The unfortunate fact is that the whole contemporary art economy was built on quicksand—on six- and seven-figure sales. I sensed at the time a disturbing parallel to the junk-bond market. The ever-spiraling prices of that select group of contemporary artists implied that there was no downside. Just as Michael Milken could assure his junk-bond clients that he could always move the bonds on at a profit to another member of the circle, so the dealers could move the art at a profit to another client. Milken had a select buyer list that got first crack at the offerings of his select seller list. And the powerful dealers who represented the select artists had a select client list that got first crack at new work, with the implicit—or perhaps sometimes explicit—assurance that the next show's prices would be substantially higher. Guaranteed profit, along with the guaranteed power that owning these works conveyed.

Right now, new collectors are looking at the work of inexpensive emerging artists, many of them more exciting than their pricey 1980s and 1990s predecessors. These collectors are not demanding that the art get their photographs in magazines or guarantee them a profit. But at the same time, they are not being asked to make a serious financial commitment.

It was possible for a young dealer to make a living in contemporary art in the sixties and early seventies, when a SoHo loft rented for $100 a month and a whole cast-iron building cost $50,000. Now, at the present levels of gallery expenses, where even in an emerging art neighborhood like Chelsea, raw taxi garages are quickly rented at $15 a square foot, it is unlikely that many galleries can survive without six-figure sales, and only a handful will be able to achieve those levels again for contemporary artists. Now, at the outset of the twenty-first century, another bubble is inflating, and we can only await the moment when it bursts in the auction room.

The prosperity of the nineties was selective, but there were fortunes and incomes in this decade that far outstripped those of the eighties. Some of these were created in the entertainment industry, and lavish new gallery palaces opened in Beverly Hills to try to harness them to art. The device seemed to be to link art with power, and to reach, by means of massive publicity, an otherwise inaccessible market in a community which is not otherwise reached effectively by any commercial communication medium. The problem is that galleries this expensive, purveying contemporary art, cannot afford to show the work of emerging artists whose prices are not yet high enough to justify the wall space. So those whose work is expensive enough, but not necessarily good enough, will see their prices propelled even higher by the power-publicity machine. The question is, can these prices be sustained, or will another bubble burst? The entertainment industry is notably transient. What happens if a powerful person with a power art collection suddenly loses his power and consigns the art to auction, and the prices plummet? This happened to the social climbers and speculators of the eighties. Why not to the power climbers of the nineties? And what then will become of the artists and the galleries? Museums are still preoccupied with the box-office power of trendy artists. The position of galleries concerned with emerging artists remains economically precarious.

Old Masters: The Bargain Basement

As more of these vast amounts of money cascaded into the impressionist, School of Paris, and trendy contemporary markets, the gulf widened between them and the old masters. In the 1920s and 1930s, Lord Duveen had imbued old masters with social cachet as the newly minted megarich tried to create an aristocracy in the English mold. By the 1970s, the country had emerged from World War II and Vietnam-era inflation, and aristocracy was out and plutocracy was in. Power now derived from money, not lifestyle. Old masters became unfashionable after Duveen's death in 1939, their palettes too dark for the new interiors, the subjects generally too lugubrious, and their prices never recovered. Meanwhile, although prices stayed low, supply was imperceptibly diminishing.

Country after country closed its borders to the export of its artistic patrimony. The sources were drying up. Meanwhile, museums were being launched in more and more countries and cities all over the world, staked by new fortunes. Each of these museums would ultimately require a basic collection of western European art. Italy's and Spain's borders were closed, and, effectively, France's as well. Austria restricted exports of its major artists' work, as did Denmark. Even Germany had a shortlist of proscribed objects. The one remaining source was England, whose vast private holdings had been amassed in the days of the grand tours in the eighteenth century. And now England, staked by lottery money and its own team of 1990s megarich, was finally becoming protective, stopping, at least for a time, the export of most objects of any significance.

Export policy began changing radically in the early 1970s. In 1974 I had bought at Christie's in London Orazio Gentileschi's *The Penitent Magdalene* for £18,900 (at that time, $45,180). The painting had been consigned by the Earl of Elgin, whose forebear, the seventh earl (of Elgin marbles fame), had bought it through his Paris agent, Quentin Crawford, in 1803. The painting had hung since 1805 at Broomhall, the Elgins' seat near Edinburgh. Gentileschi, one of the greatest of the Italian baroque painters, had been brought to England by Charles I in 1626 and remained there until he died in 1639. The Broomhall *Magdalene* was commissioned by Charles I, apparently the first work painted by Gentileschi in England after he arrived there from France. The version owned by the Duke of Buckingham (in Vienna since the mid-seventeenth century, and now in the Kunsthistorisches Museum) was probably painted in France, acquired there from Gentileschi by Buckingham, and brought to London, where it must have inspired the king to commission the ex-Elgin version. Charles's *Magdalene* was seen and recorded in Gentileschi's London studio by Joachim von Sandrart (in his *L'Academia todescha . . .*) in 1628. The background of the Elgin Gentileschi therefore contains what must certainly be the first known landscape of England by any artist. This was a well-preserved work by one of the great foreign artists hired by Charles I, an artist so rare that fewer than sixty works survive: a painting from the king's collection, painted in England, containing the first English landscape, and coming from an old Scottish collection in a stately country house. There seemed to me at the time every reason for the Export Licensing Board to stop the painting and for a U.K. museum to buy it, under the law, at the bargain price it brought at Christie's. Yet the license was immediately granted and the Gentileschi went off to New York.

Orazio Gentileschi, *The Penitent Magdalene,* circa 1626–28

Collection Richard L. Feigen, New York

Twenty-one years later, on December 6, 1995, Orazio Gentileschi's *The Finding of Moses* came up for sale in London at Sotheby's. This painting, although larger and more important than the *Magdalene,* was not in quite as fine condition. Otherwise it had many of the same characteristics. It was commissioned by Charles I, painted in England around 1633, and was in the royal collection until 1651. It now came from another country house, Castle Howard, where it had been since it was acquired by the Howards in the Bridgewater-Carlisle-Gower sale of the Orléans pictures in London in 1798. Prior to the Sotheby auction, the National Gallery in London had for months, and until the very morning of the auction, been negotiating with the Howard family, but they could not agree on a price. Because it was assumed by everyone that the National Gallery would stop export of the painting and acquire it, regardless of price, I decided not to fly over for the sale. But I arranged to be on the telephone at six that morning just in case everyone else was discouraged by the National Gallery's determination. I was prepared to pay £3.2 million, based on the serious interest of curators of two American museums, but there was not one chance in ten of my getting it at that price. Just as the painting went on the block, the auctioneer repeated twice an announcement that I had never heard in my fifty years of attending auctions: that the National Gallery had been and was still negotiating for the picture, and that title would not pass on the fall of the hammer, as the catalogue terms spell out, but only after the buyer made payment, which no foreign buyer would make without an export license. No one had any idea whether that exception to the printed catalogue terms would have held up in court, but it seemed to impede the bidding. The painting sold for £5,061,500 ($7,744,000), less than the National Gallery had originally offered. It was bought by an anonymous collector, who turned out to be Sir Graham Kirkham, and apparently will remain in England, so the National Gallery lost its chance. The change in export policy over those twenty-two years was dramatic: same artist, same period, both Charles I pictures, both with similar provenances—one exported at £18,900, the other, certain to be stopped at over £5 million. Yet even with increased patrimonial protectionism and higher prices for the rarest and most important old-master paintings, Warhol, Basquiat, and Richter still cost more than almost any of them.

Orazio Gentileschi, *The Finding of Moses*, circa 1633

Private collection, England. Photograph courtesy Pyms Gallery, London

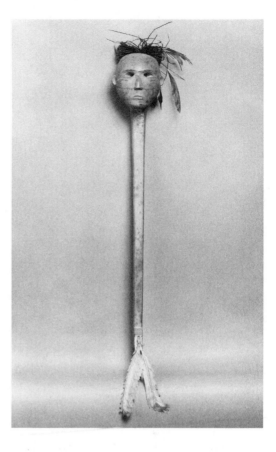

Iroquois war club, mid–nineteenth century

An extraordinary example of this export policy about-face also involved the Elgins. After my purchase of their Gentileschi at auction in 1974, I contacted Lord Elgin about the picture's early history. He sent me photocopies of the seventh earl's original correspondence and bookkeeping entries. We became friends, and over the years my family and I were frequent guests of Victoria and Andrew Elgin at Broomhall. On one of these occasions, I came in from jogging around the property and found Andrew and his son Charles opening some boxes in a small room off the main hall. The boxes, full of American Indian artifacts, had apparently not been opened since they were brought back from Canada in the mid-nineteenth century by the eighth earl, who had been governor-general. Fifteen years later, in 1989, my colleague Eugene Thaw phoned me from Santa Fe, New Mexico. He told me about his collection of American Indian objects, and wasn't I a friend of the Earl of Elgin? I said that I was, and he asked me if I thought Lord Elgin might sell his Iroquois ball-headed club. I had no idea what he was talking about, except that I remembered those boxes in the hall. I said that I did not have the impression that the Elgins were emotionally attached to the moccasins, beaded shirts, and ephemera I remembered, and that I would ask them. How did he know about the club? He'd seen it reproduced in an exhibition catalogue. How much would he pay? $225,000. I was astounded. Furthermore, said Thaw, it was not a genuine eighteenth-century war club anyway—only a nineteenth-century copy, made for presentation purposes, more or less for the tourist trade. Andrew Elgin was delighted with the price, and a deal was struck. Our shippers applied for an export license, and much to my surprise, export was stopped pending a hearing, and after that for another three months. Later that summer, while the war-club matter was still pending, I happened to be at a lunch in Florence with Tim Clifford, director of the National Gallery of Scotland and a member of the export committee on the Iroquois club. I told him how bizarre all this was. This Iroquois war club seemed to have, at best, a marginal connection with British culture, and certainly no aesthetic value. There were so many significant works of art leaving England because there was no money for the museums to buy them. Clifford assured me the club would get its license. But before the three months elapsed, the National Museums of Scotland bought the club for the full $200,000 invoice price. Quite a change from 1974, when the Elgins' great Gentileschi left at $45,000 without even a delay.

Another case was the Seurat *Channel of Gravelines,* which I sold in 1985 for the Butler family to Heinz Berggruen for $8,200,000. Export was stopped, for only six weeks, and the National Gallery could have bought it at that price. But the painting was granted a license. In 1995 Berggruen sold the painting to the National Gallery for £16 million ($24,600,000).

The gulf between old-master and modern picture prices, increasingly restrictive export policies, and dwindling old-master supply led me in the 1980s to the brink of a big financial deal. I had become convinced that the time was now or never to accumulate an inventory. But to do this took more capital than was available to the art business from traditional banking sources, which at the time did not even treat art as a fungible asset. These thoughts had been roiling around in my head for some twenty years when a friend of mine, one of Michael Milken's major clients, invited me to fly out to Los Angeles with him for Drexel Burnham Lam-

Georges-Pierre Seurat,
*Channel of Gravelines,
Grand Fort-Philippe,*
1890

National Gallery, London.
© National Gallery, London

bert's 1985 "junk bond" conference. These conferences had become legendary. During the week in Los Angeles, one of Milken's European colleagues put forth the idea of an art fund—a possible solution to my old problem.

Three meetings with Milken ensued, each for no more than ten minutes, the first two in his offices in Beverly Hills, the last in New York in October 1986. At the first meeting, I was put into a conference room with several of Milken's associates. After a time, Milken burst into the room, asked me a few questions, then came up with an answer. What amazed me was that, with no knowledge whatsoever of art or the art business, he had comprehended and solved all the problems I had been puzzling over for twenty-five years. Then he dashed out to another meeting, leaving his colleagues to sort out details. Milken's solution was to use my own company as a vehicle, rather than create a separate fund.

He was not interested in a capitalization of less than $200 million. At that point, no work of art had ever sold for more than $11 million, and sales even in the low seven figures were a rarity. I doubted that $200 million could be spent intelligently, particularly in the old-master field, where prices were, and still are, very low. So I balked, and Milken lowered the figure to $100 million, which still gave me pause. His formula called for me to invest $7.5 million. He would produce $42.5 million of additional equity. The balance of $50 million would be debt; as he described it, "high-yield securities."

The last of our meetings was at the Vista Hotel, near the World Trade Center. Milken was on a banquette across the huge lobby. An Oriental girl was at a small table near the hotel entrance taking the names of people with appointments and allocating time slots. Every few minutes, Milken adjourned a meeting on the banquette and someone else was ushered over for an audience with him. When my time came, I told Milken of my misgivings. I had started my company thirty years before. This was no new shoestring venture for me, where if it flopped I would simply go back to square one. The firm bore my name, and my reputation was at stake. I had serious doubts that, except over an extended period, we could acquire even $100 million worth of significant old masters. And could this $50 million debt be drawn down as needed, or did it all have to be borrowed at once? All at once, Milken said. In the form of "high-yield" securities—junk bonds—at an interest rate of over 15 percent. I asked him how, if I could not find enough paintings to buy, the debt would be serviced. He told me there was no problem—the money would be invested in other companies' "high-yield" securities that would provide enough income to service our own debt. So I went back to my office and discussed the whole project with my colleagues. We were too nervous to proceed, and I told Milken that, tempting as his proposal was, our decision was negative. Shortly after that, Milken was indicted and the junk-bond market collapsed. I have no regrets, but still sometimes wonder how quickly I could have gotten that money out of junk bonds and into old masters.

Art prices continued to escalate in the 1980s. The $1 million barrier had been broken on November 14, 1961, with the sale at Parke-Bernet to the Metropolitan of Rembrandt's *Aristotle Contemplating the Bust of Homer* for $2.3 million. Then, on November 27, 1970, the Metropolitan bought Velázquez's *Juan de Pareja* for $5.4 million. Armand Hammer bought the

Leicester Leonardo da Vinci Codex in 1980 for $5.6 million and modestly rechristened it the "Hammer Codex." When Wendell Cherry paid $5.8 million in 1981 for Picasso's *Yo Picasso,* I told him I thought he was crazy to reach into the stratosphere for what I considered an immature work, painted when Picasso was twenty. It was not that I ever doubted that art prices were going anywhere but up. In a *Time* magazine interview after the 1961 Rembrandt sale, despite the international tremors over the first seven-figure sale, I predicted that we would see a painting sell for over $5 million, and in 1970 we did. Curiously, I was interviewed by *Fortune* magazine after the Velázquez sale and I predicted that not only would the $10 million barrier be broken—which it was on December 10, 1984, with the sale of Rembrandt's *Portrait of a Girl* for $10 million, and again on April 18, 1985, with the sale to the Getty of Mantegna's *Adoration of the Magi* at Christies London for $10.4 million—but we would see paintings reach $50 million, and someday $100 million. We did, and, alas, we will.

By 1987 Japanese cash had inundated the market, and Allan Bond, staked by a Sotheby loan, grabbed van Gogh's *Irises* for $53.9 million. Then, in 1989, for the first time since the Velázquez, an old master, Pontormo's *Halberdier,* joined the Olympians and went to the Getty for $35.2 million. Again in 1989, Wendell Cherry proved me a fool by selling his *Yo Picasso* at Sotheby's for $47.8 million, a neat $42 million profit in eight years. Finally, just before the Japanese bubble burst, Werner Kramarsky sold the family's van Gogh, *Dr. Gachet,* at Christie's for $82.5 million, the same week as the Whitney Renoir, *Le Moulin de la Galette,* sold at Sotheby's to the same Japanese buyer, Ryoei Saito, for $78.1 million.

The message of all this was that, whatever the fluctuations, art had become irrevocably monetized, given status as a financial instrument. The amounts now being committed to individual objects were serious. Even financial institutions like Citibank no longer treated art as a luxury. Citibank now had a full-scale art advisory department and lent money to finance art purchases. Inevitable as all this may have been, with all that United States currency out there looking for places to park, it was bad news not only for collectors, priced out of many—but still not all—areas of the art market, but for museums, which may still one day want to augment their collections.

While old-master painting prices and those of antiquities have remained relatively low, strong, aesthetically oriented professionals are being diverted from the field by museums' preoccupation with money rather than objects. To find any light at the end of the dark tunnel, one has to go back to the origins of the American museums, to see what they are, how they got there, and what they ought to be.

Museums: Building the Bastions

Until the Civil War, the country was essentially dominated by a pre-Revolutionary aristocracy whose ties to Europe were still close enough that it felt little need to emulate European culture. And it was secure enough in its power to eschew snobbism. Things changed with the industrial revolution that followed the Civil War. New "robber baronies" were forged, new power amassed, and suddenly the country had a new plutocracy. One of the first things the plutocrats did was build museums, as well as libraries, operas, and symphony orchestras. The older American museums—the Metropolitan, Boston, Philadelphia, Chicago—all date from the 1870s.

There were two reasons for building museums. The first was a need to emulate European culture. The second was to form clubs to keep the new immigrants out. Massive waves of immigration to the United States had begun in 1848 with the political upheavals in Europe and the potato famine in Ireland. The Jewish immigration started from Germany in 1848 and continued from eastern Europe in the 1870s into the early twentieth century. Well before the turn of the nineteenth century, the immigrants had come to dominate important segments of the old power base—the Irish, politics; the Jews, the entertainment industry; and so on.

So the older plutocrats, the "robber barons," founded cultural institutions on whose boards the newer aspirants were cordially unwelcome. In those days, art seemed one of the trappings of the European aristocracy, to which their wives dedicated themselves to marrying off their daughters. Into their marble palazzi, and eventually onto the walls of their museums, went hundreds of paintings and objects brought back before Europe began stanching the flow of its patrimony to America. Family friends of the Philadelphia Cassatts—the Havemeyers of New York, the Potter Palmers of Chicago—began visiting Mary Cassatt in Paris and bringing back boatloads of impressionist pictures. Later, Duveen introduced them to old masters and Georgian portraits, as well as to prospective sons-in-law. And, starting with Isabella Stewart Gardner soon after his graduation from Harvard in 1887, Bernard Berenson had become their oracle for early Italian pictures.

All this was generally done under the aegis of museum directors cut from the same cloth as the trustees themselves. This tradition continued as the plutocrats' grandsons and great-grandsons graduated from Harvard and were trained by Paul Sachs, himself a snobbish German Jewish banker from Goldman Sachs. By the 1920s, in the American tradition of assimilation, the grandsons of the 1870s plutocrats had been transformed into an aristocracy. They and their Harvard-trained cousins ran the museums and built the collections without interference into the 1970s, until the museum economy began to spin out of control. And by and large, these Harvard-trained museum directors had gone into art because they loved objects, just as their brothers went into the Anglican Church because they loved God. They did not do it for the money, of which they had no need. They did it because they loved the scholarly life, they loved the objects, and they welcomed the chance to make their statements by building the collections and mounting exhibitions. When these men, who had entered the field because of their love of objects and whose taste had been honed in the Fogg Museum course, fanned out to museums across the country, the trustees could confidently attend to their business interests and merely come in for monthly board meetings because they trusted their director cousins' knowledge and motives. They did not have to watch the store because it was in good hands. They merely had to provide the funds.

Since the days of Charles Eliot Norton in the 1870s, Harvard had been the preeminent institution in the country, if not the world, for the study of cultural appreciation. The great British universities, Oxford and Cambridge, did not have departments of art history. Oxford even now has but one chair in the discipline, and there have thus far been only three occupants. I once asked the second of these, Francis Haskell, why this was so. He told me that the gentlemen students, who had come down to the university from the English country houses, had been surrounded by pictures all their lives and were expected to know about them. Art history was therefore not considered a legitimate academic discipline.

As for the collecting that filled these country houses, after the mid-nineteenth century this was no longer an active pursuit. The collections had generally been completed between the reign of Charles I, the grand tours of the first half of the eighteenth century, the foraging in France after the Revolution, and the resurrection of the early Italian painters in the first half of the nineteenth century. The British museums had been formed from these collections, and their work, too, was largely done.

Academic training in connoisseurship, the identification of a work of art by its qualities, was therefore really born in the United States, at Harvard. Boston was the first of the great American cities to produce, out of the mercantile prosperity of the post-Revolutionary period, a class of gentlemen scholars and aesthetes who either toured Europe, studied there, or became expatriates. This imported European culture began to permeate their native college, Harvard, and out of this atmosphere developed the study of works of art. These studies in connoisseurship reached their apogee in the eras of Paul Sachs and Sydney Freedberg. In their later years, in the 1950s, the Sachses would invite socially acceptable young people to Sunday lunches in their Cambridge apartment atop the Commander Hotel. The walls were covered with great drawings from the Fogg, drawings for which Sachs was responsible and to which he took free access. Lunch was served by a platoon of old German maids. I still remember my panic when Professor Sachs asked me, before one of those lunches, to identify a drawing on the wall. To these inquiries there was always a catch. In this case, as I recall, it was a Delacroix copy of a Holbein. I have never forgotten this moment in the dock, having for the first time to bore in on a work of art. This kind of atmosphere, this concentration on the qualities of an object—on connoisseurship—would now, even at Harvard, be deemed elitist, irrelevant, politically incorrect.

Changing of the Guard

Back recently for a dinner at the Fogg Museum, back on hallowed ground and basking in the old academic atmosphere, I happened to use the word "connoisseurship" in a conversation with one of the faculty. After all, there I was in its very cradle. My friend said, wryly, I thought, "We don't use that word around here anymore." Things had started to change at Harvard in the 1970s, as a new aesthetic doctrine took hold under Michael Fried, an associate professor who had arrived in 1969—the doctrine of theory over beauty, of contemporary "hard-edge" and "color-field" painting. This was the theology of Clement Greenberg, whose disciples had already captured the art history and studio art departments of Sarah Lawrence and Bennington colleges in the sixties. Greenberg had cleverly extended his battle with figurative art to the very frontier—the minds of the young—and now what more logical place to take hostage the incipient museum directors than Harvard? After effectively infiltrating the curriculum, Fried left Harvard in 1975.

Then, in 1980, Timothy Clark, a young British professor, arrived at Harvard. His fiery lectures were wildly popular. He preached a Marxist functionalism for art, not unlike the Stalinists' and Nazis'. Hundreds of Clark's acolytes fanned out into the art world, immersed in his theories. Although Clark left Harvard in 1988, his theology survives in a general insistence on "political correctness," "cultural diversity" and anti-"elitism," and this in turn now permeates many of our museums. Harvard had come a long way since the days of Paul Sachs and Sydney Freedberg, who had left for Washington in 1983. Reverence for the object seemed to have lasted at Harvard barely a century.

After the old robber barons had died and their great corporations' shares passed into the hands of hundreds of thousands of public shareholders, a new school, the Graduate School of Business Administration, was founded at Harvard, just across the river from the Fogg Museum, to

Paul Sachs, circa 1940

Courtesy of the Harvard
University Art Museums
Photographic Services.
© President and Fellows of
Harvard College, Harvard
University

Sydney J. Freedberg,
with bust of Bernard
Berenson, at the Villa I
Tatti, Florence, 1995

Photograph courtesy Mrs.
Catherine Blanton Freedberg

turn out managers for these companies. As the founders' second- and third-generation progeny changed roles from proprietors to trust beneficiaries, they also lost interest in art and their inherited museum trusteeships. And then the economic conditions of the post–Vietnam War period bore in on the museums in the 1970s.

As John Hess wrote in 1974, "The trustees know they are ignorant about art—they think their employees are expert in every aspect of it. This puts a strong-minded director in a position of power unknown to other executives in our society. . . . [M]useum trustees . . . jealously guard the secrecy of their actions and accept no limits on their powers, which they in fact delegate to their directors." This was the situation on the eve of the revolution.

A new era was ushered in by Thomas Hoving at the Metropolitan Museum. The trustees, led by Douglas Dillon, thought they were getting an art-loving, trustworthy connoisseur director in the old mold. What they found themselves with instead was a power-hungry politician, an aspirant to a cultural commissariat in the Kennedy "Camelot." Ostensibly to cope with ballooning costs, Hoving launched what would become a national nightmare: giant mail-order businesses retailing reproductions of museum artifacts and neckties; rental of museum premises for social and business functions; retail shops in shopping malls. Hoving still went after important objects—in retrospect, it seems, largely for the sport and the publicity—funding the purchases by selling off paintings, some of them irreplaceable and of great importance, in some cases against the specific wishes of the donors.

The most heinous example involved the collection of Adelaide Milton de Groot, who had, in a precatory clause in her will, specifically stated that should the Metropolitan Museum wish to dispose of any of her pictures, she did not want them sold but conveyed to the Wadsworth Atheneum in Hartford, Connecticut. Cavalierly ignoring her wishes, Hoving presided over the sale of a number of her pictures in 1971 and 1972, including Henri Rousseau's great *Monkeys in the Virgin Forest,* one of the masterpieces of twentieth-century painting, as well as three paintings by Max Beckmann. The disposition of the Rousseau was conducted by the curator of paintings, Theodore Rousseau, who sponsored its sale to his friend Frank Lloyd of the Marlborough Gallery, ostensibly for Giovanni Agnelli, but in fact resold under mysterious circumstances

Thomas Hoving, 1972
New York Times Pictures

through the Nichido Gallery in Tokyo to Mitsui & Company. The mystery was intensified by the fact that the museum reportedly received only $600,000, after Rousseau had been offered a price in excess of $775,000 by a California collector, Jack Levin. Levin had flown in at my urging from Los Angeles on October 21, 1971, to bid at Parke-Bernet on Mrs. Robert R. McCormick's Rousseau, *Exotic Landscape*. Despite my pleas, he had stopped me from bidding beyond $500,000, and Norton Simon bought the picture for $775,000. After the sale, I took Levin and another old friend, Janice Levin, to dinner. Theodore Rousseau was sitting with a group of people at the next table. I introduced him to Jack Levin as an important new collector who could become a valuable friend of the Metropolitan. I also mentioned that only an hour after the auction, Levin was already regretting, as I warned him he would, not pushing beyond the $775,000 and buying the Rousseau. Although John Walsh, at the time the Metropolitan's chief curator, had assured me they were not selling the de Groot Rousseau, I told Theodore Rousseau that should they change their mind, Jack Levin would pay the Metropolitan more than

Henri Rousseau,
Monkeys in the Virgin Forest, circa 1907

Private collection

the auction price. The de Groot Rousseau was an even finer picture and in better condition. Eighteen years later, by which time the Metropolitan Rousseau had long since disappeared into the chairman's office at Mitsui, Mitsui brushed aside an overture in the $75 million range.

As for three of the four de Groot Beckmanns,* including the powerful 1947 *Self-portrait with Cigarette,* the sale to his friend Serge Sabarsky in 1971 was engineered by the curator of twentieth-century art, Henry Geldzahler. Sabarsky paid $95,000 for all three pictures, but payment was arranged to be delayed for a year, until Sabarsky had had a chance to resell the Beckmanns. None of the three major dealers in Beckmann's work, neither Catherine Viviano, Allan Frumkin, nor I, was even consulted about the values. The *Self-portrait* alone is now worth over $3 million.

In 1972 Hoving and Rousseau sold to their friend Lloyd—who years later, as a convicted felon in the Rothko scandal, went into hiding in the

---

Sacrificial Meal, 1947, G.750, coll. Stephan Lackner; *Self-portrait with Cigarette,* 1947, G.752, coll. Museum am Ostwall, Dortmund; *Sleeping Woman with Fishbowl,* 1948, G.779, coll. Serge Sabarsky.

Max Beckmann, *Self-portrait with Cigarette,* 1947

Museum am Ostwall, Dortmund. Photograph: Claus Körber

Bahamas to escape prison—van Gogh's *The Olive Pickers,* which had been bought for the Metropolitan by Mr. and Mrs. Richard J. Bernhard, generous patrons and collectors. The painting was passed to Lloyd for $850,000. It is now conservatively worth $50 million. Dorothy Bernhard was dead by 1972, and in offhandedly mentioning the impending sale to her son Robert, and in stressing the redundancy of *The Olive Pickers,* Hoving and Rousseau, for reasons that are still shadowy, deliberately misrepresented the museum's van Gogh holdings. The family was told that the Metropolitan owned three versions of *The Olive Pickers,* including the Bernhard picture, when in fact this, the first and prime version, was the only one the Metropolitan had, the others being in the National Gallery and the Enid Haupt collection.

Geldzahler had borrowed a group of Joseph Cornell boxes from my personal collection for his 1969–70 exhibition, *New York Painting and*

Vincent van Gogh,
The Olive Pickers, 1889
Private collection

Sculpture: 1940–1970. At the time, he asked if I could get my friends Eleanore and Milton Gordon to change their minds about lending their great 1947 Gorky, *The Plough and the Song.* The Gordons refused. They didn't want a bare wall, and they liked their picture. I said, "What if I can get the museum to lend another great picture in its place?" I was thinking of the de Groot Beckmann triptych, *The Beginning.* The Metropolitan apparently thought so little of it that it wasn't even hanging. I told the Gordons that it was a masterpiece, greater even than their Gorky. They finally agreed, and Geldzahler jumped at the idea. So the switch was made, and the Beckmann hung on the Gordons' wall for four months. I was there for dinner one night, and they said they were in love with the Beckmann. I said, "I don't blame you. So am I. Would you consider an outright swap of your Gorky for the triptych?" They asked me what I thought. "If I can work it out, do it." They said, "Go ahead." So the next morning I phoned

Geldzahler, for whom postwar American painting outranked everything else in the history of art. He was delighted with the idea. But somewhere up the line at the Metropolitan, perhaps with Rousseau or Hoving, the idea snagged, the swap never happened, and the Gorky and Beckmann were switched back after the exhibition.

Joseph Cornell died on December 29, 1972. I suggested to Geldzahler that the museum hold a small memorial exhibition of the twenty-one Cornells in my collection. While the boxes were at the Metropolitan, I had an idea. My family was about to vacate our house on Seventy-ninth Street, where I had built a special double-sided glass wall to encase the Cornells, and there was nowhere in the new apartment to safely place them. I asked Geldzahler if the museum would consider a swap of the whole collection for the Beckmann triptych, which still wasn't being exhibited. He jumped at the idea. This time it was apparently approved all up the line. But just before the deal was to have been consummated, John Hess's story about the de Groot scandal broke in the *New York Times*. Until then I had had no idea that de Groot had specifically ordained in her will that nothing be sold. I phoned Geldzahler and told him I could not be a party to this. The deal was broken off. The triptych stayed at the Metropolitan. All nine Beckmann triptychs are now safely in museums, seven in this country, two in Germany. But the Hoving regime roared on, setting an unfortunate example for the country's museums and hastening the end of the era when trustees trusted their directors, and directors their curators, to handle museum affairs.

The Corporate Takeover

With the museums' new activities came new administrative problems. This administrative deluge was beyond the capacity of the old trustees. So into their ranks, into the ranks of the handful of trustees whose board memberships constituted a badge of social status they were unwilling to see smudged by those whose company they deemed less flattering, but who, because of their commitment to art collecting, might have prevented the scandals of the previous period, they inducted a new breed of museum trustee, the Harvard Business School–type corporate CEO, just as, a generation earlier, professional administrators had replaced their fathers on their own corporate boards. The very last thing the socially driven trustee nucleus wanted was "boat-rockers," trustees who knew something about art and had the time and inclination to ask questions about museum acquisitions and deaccessioning of objects, and about exhibition policy, let alone about the overall direction the museum was taking. It was all right for a prospective trustee to be an art collector, even a brilliant businessman, as long as he was willing to give millions, be satisfied with the honor of naming a new gallery, go about his own business, and not poke his nose too closely into museum affairs—in effect, not "rock the boat." In general, notwithstanding the country's supposed commitment to "rugged individualism," just as eccentricity is suffered impatiently, so boat-rockers—people who aspire to effect change—rarely make it into clubs or onto boards.

As museums began to commercialize, to adapt to 1970s inflation, exhibitions also veered away from an emphasis on scholarship toward a preoccupation with box office. Hoving launched the trend by pretending to be a politically correct Kennedy populist when in fact he was an ambitious cynic who had no trust in the public's intelligence. He merely served up what he thought they wanted, what would sell, or what would sell himself—like the patronizing and ill-fated *Harlem on My Mind* in 1969, during which a Rembrandt was defaced by a vandal—not what would enlighten. And the virus spread throughout the country. Commercialization seemed the answer to the ballooning fiscal problems, many of them caused by the very commercialization intended to cure them, and by the crowds generated by all this intensive marketing.

The new CEO trustees provided an added dividend. Although they themselves, unlike their patrician predecessors, had no personal fortunes to fund the museums' expanding activities, their companies welcomed the publicity from subsidizing the tidal wave of "blockbuster" exhibitions. There was a great deal of corporate money available for endlessly recycled impressionist and postimpressionist exhibitions—exhibitions whose box-office success could be guaranteed more surely than anything confected in Hollywood.

The new trustees were accustomed to hands-on administration. Just as they would not expect directors of their own companies to delegate complete control to a CEO and merely appear at monthly meetings to rubber-stamp decisions, they did not expect to appear at monthly museum board meetings to rubber-stamp museum directors' decisions, particularly art-oriented directors who presumably could not balance the budget or raise money. The problem was that few of these trustees collected art, knew anything about it, or even cared. For some, membership on a museum board represented membership in an exclusive club; for others, a responsibility to their community or their company.

There were a few exceptions on large museum boards. Some trustees are knowledgeable specialists in certain esoteric fields that do not command much public attention—antiquities, prints and drawings, the decorative arts. These departments often have their own consultive committees, benefactors, and sometimes their own endowments, and function as museums within museums. Trustees dedicated to these rarified disciplines are usually involved only with their specific department, not with the museum as a whole. They do not "rock the boat," and are left alone. Not having these sophisticated trustees involved with core museum affairs is in one sense a loss, in another a gain. Because, unlike painting departments, these departments are not high-profile, their curators' acquisitions, exhibitions, and fund-raising are not interfered with by the director, development department, or other trustees.

It is for this reason that a curator of Greek and Roman antiquities like Carlos Picón has been able to form his committee at the Metropolitan Museum, create new collectors of Greek and Roman antiquities and inspire seasoned ones, and build impressively on the museum's collection. Meanwhile, the European paintings department has been conspicuously inactive, probably because this area of the museum commands more public attention, and thus the attention of powerful trustees and the development department.

It is for the same reason that the Art Institute of Chicago was able to build a great prints and drawings department under two curators, Carl Schniewind and Harold Joachim, even while the museum at large was suffering serious damage in the era of a weak director, John Maxon, and an autocratic and meddlesome president, Leigh Block. Because of the relative autonomy of prints and drawings curators, the positions have been attractive to acquisitive connoisseurs like George Goldner, who built a formidable collection at the Getty and is now doing so at the Metropolitan Museum. It followed that their efforts to develop new collectors were not interfered with, that there are perhaps five times as many collectors of old-master drawings as paintings, and that the market prices for drawings are relatively higher than for paintings. Meanwhile, the European paintings departments are moldering all across the country, there are few museum acquisitions and almost no collectors, the market is almost dead, and historic old-master firms are downsizing or closing.

The problems now besetting American museums are to a certain extent rooted in the confusion between membership on a board of a corporation—a profit-making entity where everything focuses on the "bottom line"—and participation in a nonprofit institution whose primary objectives are not about making money. In cases where the new museum trustees have had expertise in the former, they usually have no qualifications whatsoever for the latter. But since American museums are private foundations and the boards self-perpetuating, and with no shareholders to vote on board membership, the power is not likely to shift to more qualified hands. The incumbent trustees are rarely willing to relinquish power.

One of the more unfortunate imports to the museum field from the corporate world is the use of head-hunting, or, more properly, executive search firms, to fill directors' jobs. Head-hunting works for corporations because they are basically similar to each other, their problems are similar, the job descriptions within their corporate structures are more or less synonymous, and there are too many candidates for anyone, even someone in the field, to know about. A marketing executive can market soap or cigarettes. A turnaround specialist can turn around a sick drug chain or a sick fast-food chain. At the end of the day, every company is after the same thing—a profit. You do what you have to do to make it, hopefully without abusing your employees, your franchise, or the government.

Museums of course don't work like that. They bear the same generic name, but their missions differ. The Des Moines Art Museum addresses Iowa. It concentrates on twentieth-century art and Iowa artists, like Grant Wood. It does not get into earlier centuries, and it does not try to do things of international or historic importance that will draw the world to Des Moines. The Kimbell Art Museum, on the other hand, has built a great collection of old masters and stages exhibitions and symposia of such significance that scholars come from all over the world each time they have an opening. Fort Worth is not markedly more accessible than Des Moines, nor is it that much more important a city. The New Orleans Museum, in a city much more attractive to visitors than Des Moines or Fort Worth, focuses its exhibitions and acquisitions on French art, catering to the city's Cajun history.

In their last two searches for a director, the trustees of the Dallas Museum—numbering an unwieldy ninety-eight—were presented with some options. Were they going to treat Dallas and Fort Worth as a single metropolitan complex, and therefore not duplicate the old masters of the Kimbell or the Western art at the Amon Carter Museum, or were they going to treat Dallas as a separate city and do it all on their own? Were they going to try to carve out a niche, perhaps around their significant holdings in Mondrian and Brancusi, or their pre-Columbian collection, and try to draw the world to Dallas, or were they going to serve their own community, with its substantial Western orientation and Hispanic population? They finally hired Jay Gates away from the Seattle Museum. Gates decided to leave the old masters to Fort Worth and build on Dallas's impressionist and twentieth-century holdings and the city's private collections, and work from the early nineteenth century forward. By late 1998 Gates had moved on to the Phillips Collection in Washington, and Dallas had hired Jack Lane, a specialist in contemporary art, who had been replaced as director of the San Francisco Museum of Modern Art by David Ross, fresh from his controversial directorship of the Whitney Museum, who had in turn been replaced by Maxwell Anderson, formerly director of the Art Gallery of Ontario, a scholar in Roman antiquities. Throughout these games of musical chairs, the trustees seem to have no clue about where the museum is going. It is hardly surprising that no director satisfies them.

The trustees of the Wadsworth Atheneum in Hartford, Connecticut, more recently had a similar decision to make. The museum had been blessed with a brilliant director in the thirties and forties, A. Everett ("Chick") Austin, Jr., who had built an internationally important collection ranging from Caravaggio and Gentileschi to contemporary surrealists like Cornell and Max Ernst. Austin staged the first performance of

Gertrude Stein's *Four Saints in Three Acts.* He made the museum a vortex of vanguard activity in the thirties. Because of the wealth of its collection and contribution to art history, as well as its proximity to New York, several of the world's great museum directors made themselves available during the search. Although through several interviews the trustees seemed largely unaware of the various directions in which they could take the museum, they selected Peter Sutton, a former curator at the Boston Museum, more recently at Christie's in New York. Sutton, a respected specialist in seventeenth-century Dutch painting. He apparently had to impress the trustees with his ability to address their primary concerns— fund-raising in a distressed economy, and a perceived responsibility to the local constituency and the substantial minority population. But in late 1999, Sutton departed—no one outside the museum board knows why—and the search is on again.

In general, as far as trustees' overall responsibilities are concerned, whether the money is their own or the corporations' they represent, they have come to believe that whoever does the funding should make the key decisions, whether or not they know anything about what they are deciding. The museums begin to be deprived of professional guidance.

Museum professionals, after all, deliberately choose to go into a field that does not earn big money. They have expertise, but no money and no power. The business people have the money and the power, but no expertise, although the power often stimulates the illusion of expertise.

Some secret insecurity apparently plunges men into a power struggle, whether in government or in culture. The danger is that once achieved, power can metastasize into megalomania. In the cultural arena, the rich and powerful, having taken control of institutions, think of themselves not as patrons of artists but as their collaborators.

One day in the 1960s, I was sitting in Ethel and Robert Scull's apartment waiting for Scull to get off the telephone. I overheard the conversation. He was negotiating for, or rather demanding, a huge tract of land in Colorado for a Walter De Maria earthwork. It took a few minutes for me to realize that Scull was talking to the secretary of the interior. It was also apparent that Bob Scull had come to think of himself, not De Maria, as the artist.

This was an early symptom of the corporate culture that would in three decades engulf our museums. As it evolved, there was no better example of this confusion of roles than Thomas Krens, director of the

A. Everett Austin, Jr., 1936

Wadsworth Atheneum Archives.
Photograph courtesy Estate of
George Platt Lynes

Guggenheim Museum. Krens arrived at the Guggenheim in 1988 from the directorship of the Williams College Museum. While at Williams, he had developed, for nearby North Adams, the visionary concept of the Massachusetts Museum of Contemporary Art. It was to occupy, with cutting-edge contemporary art, the twenty-eight-building complex of a derelict nineteenth-century cotton mill. In propelling this concept—which was conceived not only to provide a milieu for experimental art projects but to restore a historic site and alleviate the old mill town's poverty and unemployment—through the Massachusetts political bureaucracy, Krens developed the skills and boardroom fluency that would later enable him to recruit megarich benefactors for his visionary Guggenheim projects.

Packing the formidable power of new Guggenheim board members' purses, Krens was able, by 1997, to consummate what must stand as his monument, Frank Gehry's brilliant Guggenheim Bilbao, certainly one of the great structures of the twentieth century. Krens refers to it as his "collaboration" with Gehry. It must be said that, however extravagant his

Thomas Krens, circa 1992
Photograph: Hugh Hales-Tooke

creative claims, Bilbao never could have happened without Krens's extraordinary deal-making skill.

Krens met with James Rosenquist in November 1996 to discuss a projected retrospective of his work. He further mentioned in that meeting his intention to buy for the Guggenheim all of Rosenquist's large-scale paintings, and his frustration at having been outmaneuvered by the Museum of Modern Art for Rosenquist's legendary *F-111*, which it had recently bought from the Cleveland collector Richard Jacobs. Krens claimed that he had been willing to pay $500,000 more than the Modern for *F-111*, which, although the exact price was never revealed, would have made the cost to the Guggenheim some $5.5 million. Krens then alluded to a new, ninety-foot-long painting for the projected Berlin Guggenheim that would outdo the eighty-six-foot *F-111*.

Jim Rosenquist asked me to attend a meeting at Krens's office to negotiate this commission for him, and the sale to the Guggenheim Bilbao of an earlier painting, *Flamingo Capsule.* I went into that meeting at two o'clock on February 4, 1997, with Rosenquist, Krens, his deputy director,

Lisa Dennison, and Krens's assistant, Max Hollein, thinking that a 1996 Beckmann project I had undertaken for the Guggenheim had put me in good stead to act for Rosenquist.

I had organized for my own gallery for February 1995 an exhibition that had been on my mind for almost forty years, *Max Beckmann in Exile.* When the German government was unable to provide an insurance indemnity and the costs escalated out of control, I handed the exhibition to Krens, who scheduled it for 1996 at the SoHo Guggenheim. There was no advertising, but the reviews—particularly by Robert Hughes and John Updike—were overwhelming, and the exhibition drew big crowds. Some of the loans had been difficult to secure. In one case, the American ambassador to the Netherlands had to intercede with the Stedelijk Museum in Amsterdam. In several instances of museum "hardball," I had to promise loans from my own collection to secure Beckmann loans. In the end, the exhibition even included seven of Beckmann's nine monumental triptychs.

For the February 4 meeting, Krens spread out on his vast desk the plans for the Deutsche Bank's Berlin Guggenheim. The bank was to commission a painting ninety feet long for the largest wall. Rosenquist did a quick calculation and figured the height at eleven and a half feet. There was one point on which Krens was specific: the commission was Rosenquist's, but only if the painting could be completed in time for the building's opening on September 5 (a date that was later superseded), and if an acceptable price could be arrived at. I turned to Jim. "Can you do it, James?" "I can do it." Jim knew, and I knew, that he was probably

James Rosenquist, *The Swimmer in the Economist,* 1997

Deutsche Guggenheim Berlin.
Photograph: Peter Foe

the only major painter who could commit to a work of this scale on such a schedule and come up with a worthy result.

When the negotiations turned to money, Krens said, "We buy at the dealer's price. . . ." We weren't talking about the artistic value of the painting, and certainly not about the depth of Deutsche Bank's pockets. Krens was clearly on the corporate side of the table. Krens then said, offhandedly, "Of course there will be curatorial 'oversight.' This is a collaboration." He mentioned Michelangelo and Pope Julius II and the Sistine Chapel. A vision flashed through my head of Julius's ferocious fights with Michelangelo, the Pope on one occasion supposedly mounting the scaffold, bashing Michelangelo with his cane, and threatening to throw him off. The thought of Krens, six feet four, up on the Aripeka scaffold was frightening. During the seven ensuing months of skirmishing on terms, contracts, and payments, the commission grew from one ninety-foot painting to two more, a forty-eight-footer and a twenty-footer, and the studies for all three. Meanwhile, at each stage the price decreased.

The most exciting aspect of the whole commission, as far as I was concerned, was the prospect of the forty-eight-foot painting hanging in Bilbao for the opening of the Frank Gehry building, which Jim had seen at an early stage on a visit with Krens in the spring of 1996, and which I was to see at the Pritzker Prize dinner in June 1997.

On July 31 a fax arrived from Lisa Dennison apologizing for not getting back to me sooner because everything was "extremely hectic." She said that they would "like to proceed with this acquisition," but that "the agreed-upon price must reflect a substantial discount from the market values." Further, that since a painting commission is "analogous to an architectural commission" and Krens's "work with Frank Gehry is tantamount to a collaboration and had gone through many stages of review and commentary . . . we expect that Jim, Robert [Rosenblum] and I will be able to communicate on a similar level, and that our 'critique' will be part of the creative process. . . ." Shades of Julius II. So much for the artist's solitary struggle. No contract arrived until December 15, and the first payment installment followed on the thirtieth, over ten months after Rosenquist started working on the project, and two months after he finished it.

Under the old order, museum trustees placed confidence in the director because of his commitment to art. Krens, archetype of the new breed, commands confidence with his fluency in corporate-speak and salesmanship. Supersalesman to the megarich, Krens sees museums as part of the entertainment industry, and himself as an industry "investment banker." For Krens, even more than for the Modern's Glenn Lowry, art is a form of entertainment, a leisure-time activity. The new museum is an entertainment palace, and crowds its measure of success. In Krens's words, he is "reinventing the museum for the twenty-first century." In "globalizing the Guggenheim," he is "rocking the boat." This is the way of the future. Krens is the master builder, the visionary. In this he calls to mind Bob Scull and the De Maria earthwork. The builder, the deal-maker, becomes the artist. Artists themselves are interchangeable, even expendable. If it's not a Rosenquist painting or an Oldenburg *Soft Shuttlecock,* then it's a scarlet Dine neo-*Venus* or even a motorcycle. If it's not a Rauschenberg retrospective, then it's *Giorgio Armani,* scheduled for 2000 at the Guggenheim, or *Norman Rockwell,* featuring the work of an illustrator famous for his sentimental magazine covers and infamous in the serious art community—into whose face Krens seems to love to throw his box-office numbers—scheduled for 2001. Never mind if there isn't enough real art to fill the burgeoning palaces. If you can't get one artist or one object, you get another, like booking films for a cineplex. Krens's vision is the art.

The corporatization of the American museum has not been all bad. The Bilbao Guggenheim project is an example of at least one positive result. Corporations build buildings. In this sense, they are the present-day incarnations of Renaissance patrons. When architecture becomes art—large sculptures, with a function—the patron, whether corporation or corporatized museum, becomes an art patron. To bring to fruition an architectural project advanced enough to qualify as a work of art requires a facilitator with taste, sophistication, energy, vision, and the capacity to communicate all this to the corporate sponsor. Tom Krens is just such a facilitator, and it is in this sense that he is the architect's collaborator.

This is as good a point as any to digress to make some comments on art and architecture. In a talk on November 21, 1997, at the University of Virginia Graduate School of Architecture, fresh on the heels of a visit to the opening of Frank Gehry's great Bilbao Guggenheim, I addressed the subject of "Art and Architecture," how architecture is an art form that, unlike art—at least art since the dawn of humanism—must also serve a function.

There is of course architecture that serves its function but is not art, just as there is painting and sculpture that serve no function and are still not art. There are two ways in which the disciplines intersect. Architecture can be a house for art, or can itself be a work of art. With Frank Gehry's Bilbao Guggenheim, there came into existence an eloquent example that is both. It was on this hazy area, where art and architecture overlap, where they serve each other, that I focused that evening in Virginia. Gehry's masterpiece seemed to usher out an old millennium, with its old debates, and usher in a new one, with new clarity, new possibilities.

Museum architecture must, of course, house the art. In designing museums or art collectors' residences, the architect must be more or less sensitive to the art, must create an environment that is more or less hospitable to it, and must more or less subordinate his own statement to the art it is supposed to contain. He was not, in the past, supposed to make a muscular statement, to create a cacophony, to fight with the art. Form was supposed to follow function. Louis Kahn's Kimbell Art Museum in Fort Worth was regarded as the most successful house ever built for art. Others were Renzo Piano's Menil in Houston and Beyeler in Basel, and Marcel Breuer's Whitney.

The other way the two disciplines interact is when the architecture becomes art, when the architect is in effect a sculptor. In these cases, function was supposed to follow form, but when the most gifted archi-

Guggenheim Museum Bilbao, 1997

Photograph by David Heald. © The Solomon R. Guggenheim Foundation, New York

tects thought of themselves as *sculpteurs en grand,* it rarely did. Frank Lloyd Wright made the New York Guggenheim a big sculpture—in my opinion of arguable quality—but it does not function as a house for art, or for that matter for people working with art. Like Wright's other structures, in terms of wall space and light, it is inhospitable to art, and even to people. Mies van der Rohe's structures, mostly steel and glass, accommodate art reluctantly. There is little wall space. Mies himself owned mostly little Paul Klees that would not fight with his spaces. He squabbled with Kandinsky, whose paintings did. The sculptures that are intermittently placed in front of Mies's Seagram Building are in obvious conflict with the architect's artistic statement. In 1967 I commissioned Hans Hollein to remodel a New York town house for my gallery. After the building was completed in 1968, the architectural statement was so strong—the chrome, the fabric, the colors—that some purist artists, like Bridget Riley, quit my gallery. Hollein, competing for museum commissions, has since mellowed and learned how to modulate his work to accommodate art.

Some structures, like those in the Désert de Retz, strayed so far from the functional into the realm of fantasy that they were truly sculptures. But sometimes, rarely, a structure achieved a functional purpose and at the same time took its place as significant sculpture. The architects were in effect artists. The disciplines intersected—the Pyramids, the toll-houses of Ledoux, the Brooklyn Bridge, the Getty tomb, the Simmering gas containers, even the Seagram Building. Sullivan turned us to the sculptural at the turn of the last century, and the cause was powerfully embraced by the Wiener Werkstätte, Charles Rennie Mackintosh, and Frank Lloyd Wright. No one denies that Sullivan's ornaments are sculpture, any more than they do Gaudí's.

In the past, when the call went out for a building to house art, the architect was expected to stick to function, to avoid a strong statement of his own, and I suspect that in general this should continue. Few architects are artists, just as few artists are architects. But now something new is upon us, a fusion, a genuine dialogue between art and architecture, in which the artist respects the architect and the architect the artist—artists all. In Bilbao, Frank Gehry said to James Rosenquist—two of whose works hung in the new building—"Jimmy, I hope this isn't intimidating for the artists." Rosenquist said, "Intimidating? Frank, it's inspiring!" I was standing next to Claes Oldenburg and Coosje van Bruggen waiting for the King and Queen of Spain to arrive at the Bilbao opening dinner; we looked up at their ghostly *Soft Shuttlecock,* lent from the New York Guggenheim, drooped high above us over a balcony, and I said, "Claes, I wish it could stay here," and Claes, who couldn't take his eyes off it, said, "So do I."

Bilbao is a ringing call for dialogue, for insemination of each discipline by the other. In the avalanche of press, Bilbao has been called the last great building of the twentieth century, and, by the *Chicago Tribune,* the first of the twenty-first. Gehry's building is a shout of optimism, a call for this fusion of art and architecture, of form and function, with neither following the other. The architect values the artist's imagination, and the artist the architect's. Artists see architectural parameters, a framework on which to pull together their ideas, like a stretched canvas contains a painter, a block of stone a sculptor. This dialogue is particularly important at a time when artists are pushing the envelope—into photography, video, and beyond.

It is the gray area where art and architecture overlap—where it is difficult to tell which is which—in which the visionary flourishes. Some
projects of the past, like Etienne-Louis Boullée's and Hollein's, were
barely achievable in architectural terms. Could they or could they not be
built? Some, like Buckminster Fuller's geodesic domes, were hard to tell
apart from sculpture. Some sculptures, like Tony Smith's models and
Claes Oldenburg's drawings, could have been projected into buildings.
It is perhaps Frank Gehry's love of art and his intimacy with artists that
have helped push him out onto the edge, to launch the third millennium
with its first masterpiece. Many ideas will spring from it, and many old
ones will be discarded.

But Bilbao's message goes beyond architecture. It goes to man's spirit,
and to art as the expression of its aspirations, as salve for its wounds, as
relief from its misery, as its source of pride, as an agent for unification
among men in an age of separatism. It is also, incidentally, a demonstra-
tion that great art is great business. Before Frank Gehry's building was
completed in October 1997, 450,000 visitors were predicted for the first
year; 1,360,000 made the pilgrimage. $160 million was added to Bilbao's
decayed, hopeless rust-belt economy. Basque separatist terrorism in the
1980s had destroyed the steel and shipbuilding industries and left thousands unemployed, desperate, and angry. Frank Gehry's great building,
constructed by the Basques themselves, gave them pride in their skills.
The world acclaimed their work and came in droves to see it. The sepa-
ratists declared a cease-fire, and it still holds. Frank Gehry's genius gave
the people a vision of a fuller life, just as the forces of separatism not so
far away in Yugoslavia have produced only hopelessness and death.
Gehry gave us a Chartres Cathedral for the twenty-first century, a declaration of man's determination not merely to survive but to aspire and
prevail. This, as Anthony Lewis pointed out in the April 17, 1999, *New
York Times,* is a historic declaration of the power of art.

Unfortunately, not every architectural project of the new breed of
trustees has been as successful as the Guggenheim's. The board of
Chicago's Museum of Contemporary Art set about choosing an architect
for its new building, to be placed on one of the finest museum sites in
the world, acquired with the intervention of the governor of Illinois.
Every major architect in the world wanted the commission. Although
there were some nominal professional "advisors" who presumably had

some input with regard to the "shortlist," the committee assigned to make the final choice consisted of those who had donated $1 million or more for the building. Their credential was their money. For reasons that remain obscure—perhaps, despite a nominal commitment to contemporary art, a pervasive conservatism of taste—they chose Josef Kleihues, an urban planner little regarded in his native Berlin. Most critics and architects have found the building to be an architectural disaster. Some Chicagoans are prepared to live with it because it exists and nothing can be done about it. I was told that the early politics were intense, and that, so much did some major donors fear a radical design, if Kleihues had not been selected, funds would have been withdrawn and there would have been no building at all. As it turned out, perhaps that would have been for the best. In a city internationally known for its architecture, the contrast between what might have been and what is has had a depressing effect on the community.

Interestingly, on June 1, 1997, on a flight to Madrid the day after the Pritzker Architecture Prize dinner at the almost-completed Bilbao Guggenheim, I found myself seated next to Rafael del Pino, CEO of Grupo Ferrovial, the contractors for the job. He told me the construction cost was $89 million, below the $100 million budget, for a building of 256,000 square feet, or $347 per square foot. The Chicago Museum of Contemporary Art cost $46 million for 150,000 square feet, or $307 per square foot. Jay Pritzker himself, whom I had implored to intervene when Kleihues's model was unveiled, turned to me at the Bilbao dinner and said, "We could have had something like this!"

New Trustees, New Directors, New Problems

The cover story in the November 20, 1996, issue of *Business Week* was "The Best and Worst Boards." It was a "report card" on "corporate governance." The Campbell Soup Company won the contest overwhelmingly. CEO David W. Johnson was quoted in the article as saying, "The board is my boss. . . . [T]hey need to feel this guy knows his cookies and his soup." The article had stated that "every director was as familiar" with the details of the company's "ambitious new strategy" as was "Campbell's flamboyant CEO, David W. Johnson." The article interested me because it makes obvious the reasons why the new crop of museum trustees has got it so wrong. They consider a museum board's role, like that of a corporation's, to be one of governance, not oversight. They speak the same language and have the same educational and professional backgrounds. They are in fact often the same people. Serving on a museum board is effectively like serving on another corporate board, but less demanding. The corporate director, knowledgeable in business and aware of what is expected of a director, schools himself in the intricacies of the company's business, and for this he is compensated. He assumes that a museum should be run in a businesslike way, and brings only his business skills to the table. And for this rudimentary contribution he receives no compensation. There is no way that he can do his homework in fields whose expert practitioners on the staff have Ph.D.'s and decades of scholarship behind them. Yet art is a field in which almost everyone thinks he knows enough. And beyond this, the museum's objectives are entirely different from those the corporate CEO is accustomed to. It is not supposed to make money. It is sufficient to merely break even, aided by endowment income and admission fees. Its objectives are, or should be, to enlighten the public and conserve the collection.

But when a museum search committee interviews a candidate for a vacant directorship, it expects the candidate to come with hat in hand and address the committee chairman as a prospective boss, just as a candidate for corporate CEO would address his prospective board chairman. Notwithstanding the fact that in the latter case the chairman, as a fellow businessman, has the qualifications to make a judgment, whereas in the former, he has none whatsoever. The strong museum director, of whom, alas, few remain, is therefore at a disadvantage when he is interviewed for a new post. Like most competent professionals, he may suffer fools—particularly those who pretend to knowledge in his field—with little patience, and he expects, if he gets the job, considerable autonomy. He rarely then approaches the museum search committee with the appropriate measure of humility. If, after all, the job were CEO of an aeronautics company, the board would scarcely pretend to aeronautics

Timothy Clifford, 1998

expertise; it would trust the applicant's scientific qualifications. But somehow everyone seems to think he is an art expert, and presumably if a museum director is an art expert, he cannot also have expertise in administration and fund-raising. Both assumptions are not of course necessarily correct. But since neither the new trustees nor the new museum directors belong to the old boys' club that controlled the field until a quarter century ago, the trust is no longer automatic. And since the problems that concern the trustees are now primarily financial rather than aesthetic, they are certainly not in a mood to grant autonomy to someone trained in the humanities rather than economics. For these reasons, two of the most respected museum directors in the world were recently turned down for important jobs: Dr. Edmund P. Pillsbury, former director of the Kimbell Art Museum in Fort Worth, for the National Gallery of Art in Washington, and for the Cleveland Museum; and Timothy Clifford, director of the National Gallery of Scotland in Edinburgh, for the Victoria and Albert Museum in London. Both of them are known to be somewhat authoritarian, as befits their distinguished records, and neither would expect to be much interfered with by his board unless he failed, over a period of time, in the mission he had undertaken. Had they been named to the directorships for which they had been interviewed, the director's power would have grown in proportion to the diminishment of the board's. The search committee chairmen must have sensed this, and the applicants were turned away.

Incidentally—and probably unknown to the search committee chairmen and the headhunters they had hired—both Pillsbury and Clifford had also proved to be fine administrators and fund-raisers in their previous posts. Finally, having failed to find an appropriate job in 1999, Pillsbury left the museum world to open an art gallery in Dallas.

The administrative problems of the National Gallery derive from a different, though curiously related, source. The gallery is unique in several respects. It is some sixty years younger than the older museums. It is the product of the benefactions of a single family, the Mellons. The board of trustees has only nine members, of whom four—the chief justice, the secretary of state, the secretary of the treasury, and the secretary of the Smithsonian—are ex officio. Two of the remaining five trustees have been members of the Mellon family, and two, until recently, were husband and wife. The director was always appointed by Paul Mellon, or with his accord, and the relationship was always directly between the two of them. There was no outside fund-raising. The Mellons were the only benefactors. The board was window dressing. The Mellons' act of generosity to the nation was unprecedented, and could never happen again in an age of special interests, meddling by Congress, and ideological warfare.

Paul Mellon was himself an anachronism, the Brahmin progeny of the robber-baron era, yet, unlike most others of his class and generation, he remained passionately committed to art. He was the best kind of Maecenas an institution could possibly have—rich, generous, unobtrusive, gentlemanly in every way. Much like the Founding Fathers, Mellon was unable to conceive of ulterior motives or conflicting interests. Since he never thought of the National Gallery as a monument to himself, when he stepped aside in 1985, he stepped back like a gentleman. This was his code. Like few other cultural benefactors, he did not retain control, either from his retirement or from his grave. Curiously, it was this very diffidence that contained the seeds of the gallery's problems.

Paul Mellon's Brahmin colleagues on the boards of the Metropolitan, Boston, Philadelphia, and Chicago, whose founding families' interest in art had waned before the National Gallery was even founded, had already ceded control to corporate CEOs. But when Mellon stepped back, he ceded control to no one, trusting that its affairs would be conducted as they had always been. When J. Carter Brown, who had always

Edmund P. Pillsbury, 1997

worked closely with Paul Mellon, resigned as director in 1992, Edmund Pillsbury expressed interest in the position directly in a letter to Paul Mellon. Pillsbury had previously received and refused an offer unprecedented for an American: the directorship of the National Gallery in London. Pillsbury knew Mellon well, and in fact had been director of the Yale Center for British Art, donated by Paul Mellon, before going to Fort Worth. Yet Mellon refused to intervene in the selection of Brown's successor, leaving it entirely up to the incumbent and undersized board.

As for the National Gallery's fund-raising in the post-Mellon era, the gallery's unique prestige and national importance should give it priority over any museum in the country. This would, however, require a substantially larger board of trustees, people of wealth and importance dispersed around the country. To expand the National Gallery board requires, by its charter, an act of Congress. In an age when the arts have become an ideological battlefield, any such effort would be frustrated by political pressures, from Jesse Helms on the right to Jesse Jackson on the left. The only person who might have circumvented the politics, perhaps in a plea directly to the president, was the original benefactor, Paul Mellon himself. Again, Mellon failed to usher his institution into the new era, to provide a transition to the day when it could no longer depend only on the Mellons. Mellon represented the ultimate example of the old-style, noncorporate chairman, trusting in his director, understanding and caring but not interfering. Yet he left the gallery with an undersized board, unable to properly compete for funding, floundering in a new era when museums are springing up everywhere. The National Gallery represents, in a way, the ultimate breakdown of the old system. With Carter Brown's departure, there were no collegial hands in which to entrust the gallery's destiny, and no board of corporate CEOs to take over.

The effect of all these developments in the museum field is to discourage aspiring young people from entering the field. If one of them has a dream of groundbreaking exhibitions and visionary acquisitions but is told that a museum director's job is really about administration and fund-raising, he is likely to aim for teaching, writing, or even art dealing. And at the curatorial level, if the message is that the director is unlikely to support the curators in any exhibition projects except box-office bonanzas, and ignores acquisition recommendations in favor of building the museum's endowment, prospective curators will divert to other callings. One of the country's leading curators of European paintings was told by the director of one of the great museums, in a recent interview for the chief curatorship, that his responsibilities would be purely administrative, that he would not be concerned with the collections. When he responded that it was the collections in which he was interested, he heard no more about the job. Another talented young curator presented two exhibition projects to his director, was never given an audience to discuss them, and heard nothing for months.

Some museums, perhaps self-conscious about blatantly subordinating art to business, have tried dual directorships, held by a coequal administrator and director. The system was instituted at the Minneapolis Institute of Arts in 1960. Their director at the time, Richard Davis, was cut of the old Brahmin cloth. He deeply loved objects and had superb taste. Furthermore, his wife, Phyllis, was a Minneapolis Pillsbury. All this put him in a position of trust, allowing him to cultivate collectors like the Donald Winstons and Sam Maslons. Davis's acquisitions for the museum ranged from Poussin's great *Death of Germanicus* to Beckmann's triptych *Blind Man's Bluff*. But, as is not uncommon with those of his generation and class, Davis was no businessman. Not only was he a poor administrator, but he deaccessioned some redundant but potentially valuable paintings, including an 1896 Monet, *Matinée sur la Seine*. He sold a number of these, not at public auction, but to a colorful and controversial dealer, Julius Weitzner. He then failed to record and communicate to his board which proceeds had been used to pay for which acquisitions. In later years, the trustees supposed of course that the acquisitions could have been made without selling anything, which was not the case because the money was not available. Donald Winston, although a passionate collector and one of the museum's most generous benefactors, was not a man of great wealth. Although he stepped in and put up the money so Davis would not lose the Poussin and the Beckmann, he had to be paid back. Davis was also a passionate collector of drawings himself. Although he avoided conflicts of interest between his own collection and that of the museum, his personal collecting gave sufficient appearance of a conflict of interest to justify what ultimately amounted to his demotion. Davis's problem was not so much what he did as how naïvely he did it. Minneapolis later, in 1995, paid millions of dollars for another 1890s Monet. But Davis's acquisitions are what helped make Minneapolis a great museum. After a messy battle between factions of the board, Davis was demoted, and an administrative co-director was appointed in 1960. The arrangement failed, and Davis left and retired from the museum world. In 1972 Minneapolis reverted to a single directorship.

Another museum that had tried a dual directorship was the Art Institute of Chicago. The museum had gone through a stormy period in the 1950s, the kind of turmoil the Lake Forest trustees were unaccustomed to. Saddled with a weak director, Daniel Catton Rich, and his mistress, Katherine Kuh, the domineering and ambitious twentieth-century curator, the trustees accepted Rich's resignation in 1958, and Kuh's in 1959, after she failed to be named director. The board then decided to split power evenly between a director of fine arts, John Maxon, and a director of administration, Alan MacNab. But the tension continued during a protracted power struggle, as MacNab increasingly intervened in curatorial affairs. MacNab resigned in 1966, Maxon was demoted, and Charles Cunningham was appointed full director. When Cunningham retired in 1972, the trustees again fell into the trap of appointing an administrator, Lawrence Chalmers, as president rather than director, in an effort to placate Maxon, who reported to Chalmers, and his protector, Leigh Block. The Art Institute's turmoil continued for another six years, with Chalmers fighting to retain power and refusing to resign until he was forced out in 1978. It took the trustees two more years to find and appoint James Wood as full director in 1980.

As far back as my relationship with the Art Institute had extended, over half a century, there had never been a senior curator of European paintings. This contrasted sharply with the Department of Prints and Drawings, where Harold Joachim succeeded Carl Schniewind, and Douglas Druick succeeded Joachim, and which is consequently one of the world's great cabinets of prints and drawings. The European old-master paintings collection, on the other hand, seems to have chronologically stopped with the Ryerson bequests in the 1930s.

In 1988 a signal opportunity presented itself to Chicago. Sydney Freedberg, eminent scholar and teacher, author of the standard *Painting in Italy, 1500–1600* and the authoritative monograph on Parmigianino, might suddenly be available to Chicago. The National Gallery had hired Freedberg as chief curator on his retirement from Harvard in 1983. In retrospect, everyone, including Freedberg, wondered why they had engaged him, since the field in which he was preeminent was exactly the one to which the then director, Carter Brown, and his predecessor, John Walker, had some sort of Calvinist aversion. It was, precisely for this reason, the area in which the National Gallery's collection needed the most help. Freedberg had no conception of the set of jaws into which he was sailing. His suggestions, which should have been invaluable, were invariably disregarded, and he resigned in 1988.

The older generation of museum directors, trained in connoisseurship at the Fogg, had died off, along with their curators. They were succeeded by a new breed of director, taught that administrative skills were the order of the day. There remained in training, however, younger men and women, lovers of art, many destined for teaching and writing, but some still aspiring to museum careers. They never dreamed, in the early years of this new order—the late 1970s and 1980s—how difficult it would prove to be to get a hearing for their exhibition and acquisition ideas, and how they would be saddled with the burden of staging redundant "blockbusters," all in the name of "keeping the doors open."

It seemed to me that connoisseurship might be dragged back into Chicago's foreground, that potential museum patrons might be educated,

John Maxon, circa 1965

Photograph courtesy of the Art
Institute of Chicago

form collections, and bequeath them to the Art Institute, as they used to do. But to accomplish this would require a senior scholar with sufficient credentials to operate at the pinnacle of the city's power structure. It would also require, as it turned out, colleague staff members who would not feel threatened by so august a figure, and who would not fear diversion of the community's virtually unlimited resources from development projects to acquisitions.

As to any threat to the titles or areas of authority of the incumbent staff, the Metropolitan Museum seemed to have provided a formula. It had imaginatively invented a title for Sir John Pope-Hennessy when he arrived there in 1977: "consultive chairman of the Department of European Paintings." The rationale was that it would be difficult to insert so eminent a figure into the existing staff structure. To whom, after all, could he report? Not even the director, Philippe de Montebello, who was many years his junior. And certainly "the Pope," as he soon became known, could not be saddled with departmental administrative responsibilities. "Consultive chairman" was the perfect title. And in this role, Sir John, reporting to no one, with no obstruction between him and the nucleus of key trustees, almost immediately became the most powerful figure at the museum.

But Sydney Freedberg, a contemporary, colleague, and friend of Sir John's, although an equally distinguished figure, was of a very different temperament. Freedberg had no interest in power, in influencing a museum's overall policies. Nor was he interested in the kind of clubby, Berensonian society that Pope-Hennessy enjoyed presiding over, though he, like Pope-Hennessy, had been a member of Berenson's circle at I Tatti, in Florence, and had served as chairman of the I Tatti Council. If Freedberg had been engaged in this consultive role in Chicago, his only interest would have been to offer his counsel.

This is exactly what Chicago needed: a scholar in the field in which the museum was notably weak, who could offer advice on acquisitions and exhibitions; who had the standing with other institutions to obtain otherwise inaccessible loans; and who carried the authority to reach out to the community and encourage it to collect and help the museum. I discussed this with Freedberg, and he seemed enthusiastic. Commuting on an intermittent basis from his home in Washington posed no problem. But my suggestion to various officials of the Art Institute appealed to no one except Katherine Lee, a former employee of my Chicago gallery, daughter of the former director of the Cleveland Museum, at that time assistant director of the Art Institute, then director in her own right at the Virginia Museum of Fine Arts, and appointed in 2000 to her father's old job as director of the Cleveland Museum.

In another attempt to put curatorial and administrative affairs at parity, the Metropolitan Museum adopted the failed formula in 1978. The director, Philippe de Montebello, and the president, William Luers, were nominally coequal. But since the museum's basic thrust was fund-raising, the curatorial side, under Montebello, was subordinated to development. The failure of the system was acknowledged and a promising step taken in 1998 upon Luers's retirement. Montebello acceded to the full directorship. An administrator was appointed, reporting to Montebello. This augurs well for the Metropolitan, and perhaps for the whole museum system.

Sir John Pope-Hennessy,
1971

Photograph: Anthony Crickmay

The Los Angeles County Museum searched for a director for months, appointed Michael Shapiro, fired him after a year, searched for months again, was refused by a number of candidates, then appointed an administrator, Andrea Rich, and in 1996 finally found a director, Graham Beal, willing to report to her. Again, aesthetics took a backseat to administration. Beal resigned in 1999 to become director of the Detroit Institute of Arts. A Los Angeles trustee told me that, with Andrea Rich in control, the museum didn't need a director. Prior to her appointment in Los Angeles, Rich had had no art or museum experience. The headhunter's words seemed to be coming true: museum directors are administrators. Art can be left to the curators.

One of the most egregious cases of trustee interference occurred in early 1996. The Toledo Museum of Art has an international reputation for the quality of its old-master painting collection. A former director, Otto Witmann, built an outstanding collection of Italian baroque paintings. A successor, Roger Mandle, also loved objects and continued to build the collection, and this continued, for a time, under Mandle's successor, David Steadman. The people of Toledo, Ohio, had reason to be proud. Suddenly, in 1993, members of the Toledo board, the new corporate CEO breed of trustees, forced a reassessment of the entire museum organization and its objectives. Corporate management consultants McKinsey and Company were hired to analyze the structure along business lines. The result was a "senior management team" consisting of an "audience development team leader," the director, and an "asset development team leader." This "senior management team" makes all of the museum's decisions. Reporting to these "team leaders" are three other team leaders to "Development"; none to the director; and four to "Assets." One of those reporting to "Assets" is "Collection Management." "Collection Development," meaning the traditional curatorial heart of the museum, is now only one of the eight areas under the heading of "Collection Development," and in fact is listed fourth, under "Registrarial," "Librarian," and "Security." So much for connoisseurship, which might be required for the acquisition, conservation, and exhibition of objects of art, the traditional concerns of museums. The new corporate trustees' concerns were with "development"—of "audiences" and "assets."

McKinsey's key blunder is of course its failure to understand that systems designed for profit-making enterprises do not work with nonprofit institutions because their objectives are, or should be, different. A museum's international, or even local, stature is not measured by how much money it makes, or how big its audiences are. If a museum is no longer held in esteem by other museums, and by scholars, domestic and foreign, it will ultimately lose even its local support. If the curatorial departments are downgraded and the curators become demoralized, distinguished scholars with Ph.D.'s reduced to parity with registrars, librarians, security guards, researchers, and even conservators, the museum will be unable to hire any curators at all. The naïveté of the McKinsey plan would be absurd if it did not have such tragic implications for American museums.

The effect of all this is apparent in the recent rush for the directorship of the Frick Collection, a splendid collection with an august reputation, but with limited funds for acquisitions and limited space for exhibitions. Yet it is a tantalizing job for the surviving dinosaurs of the old order, connoisseurs who love objects. I had been asked for advice about the Frick museum directorship by two of the ablest museum people in the world.

One of the two, someone whose capture by the Frick would have been a coup not only for the Frick but for the city, had been expunged from the shortlist by the headhunter, Nancy Nichols, without even an introduction to the trustees. In the end, the Frick was lucky to get Sam Sachs, the highly regarded director of the Detroit Institute of Arts. No headhunter should have been needed, though, to discover Sachs's availability; his monumental problems with Detroit's City Council's racial politics, and its control of the museum, were known throughout the field. The battle he had waged for so long to free the museum from Detroit's politics was finally won only weeks after his departure.

If the trustees wanted to keep the Frick exactly as it always was, it could only be a cemetery of dreams for any ambitious museum man wanting to pursue a career, rather than end one with grace and elegance. Yet here was a traffic jam for the directorship of this little gem of a museum, and the reason is clear: the Frick is still about objects, connoisseurship counts, the museum is not dedicated to the turnstile. The place remains uncontaminated. The question, I suggested to one of the trustees, was: What do the Frick trustees want the museum to be? A mausoleum for Henry Clay Frick, his home just as he left it, buying almost nothing, lending nothing, borrowing little? Or do they want to widen the vision, add exhibition space, raise money for acquisitions, and expand the constituency? It seemed to me that the answer was the latter, and, with Sam Sachs at the helm, the Frick could be an example for other institutions.

However, the effect on American museums of this diversion from connoisseurship to money is already visible. The great museums aspired, from their inception, to cover the various fields of the visual arts in a comprehensive way. In paintings, for instance, certainly the Metropolitan, Boston, Chicago, and Cleveland originally intended to cover all the significant areas—Italian, French, Netherlandish, German, Spanish, English, and American from the thirteenth at least through the nineteenth centuries.

This mission differed sharply from the great European museums, with the exception of the National Gallery in London and the National Gallery of Scotland. The European museums generally began as princely collections—the Louvre, the Prado, the Uffizi, Dresden, Munich, Vienna, the Hermitage, Stockholm. These museums are extraordinarily rich in specific areas: the Prado in the Spanish court painters, the Louvre in Louis XIV's collections and Napoleon's predations from Italy. Being offshoots of their national governments and with limited funds, they usually do not try to cover every field. The National Galleries of London and Edinburgh, on the other hand, were founded as museums, not royal collections, as late as 1824 and 1850, respectively. Since England retained its monarchy, the monarch retained the art—with the exception of Charles I's great collection, which was dispersed when England beheaded its monarch. These two British museums, like their American counterparts, try to cover all the fields of painting. Recently, using lottery and government money and private benefactions, they have competed effectively with the Americans, much to the Getty's frustration.

As administrators and fund-raisers started running the American museums, the collections seemed to stop growing in fields these people simply did not understand or like. The National Gallery, rich in early Italian and Netherlandish paintings, has few Italian paintings of the seventeenth century, and almost no mannerism, simply because John Walker and Carter Brown, former directors, did not like them. One wonders why such enlightened men would not have filled these gaps, even if these periods were not to their personal taste. Were they predecessors of today's administrators because they were responsible to only one man, Paul Mellon—as benign a benefactor as he was? Or was it some streak of the Calvinism with which our culture is riddled that made these directors abhor the distortions of mannerism and the drama of the baroque? Not perhaps coincidentally, the Metropolitan, Boston, and Chicago Italian collections also virtually stop in the mid-sixteenth century and are also almost devoid of mannerism. If, as the Toledo trustees believe, their McKinsey plan is the blueprint for the future, one wonders whether these distortions will ever be set right.

From the standpoint of museum trustees, the most important issue is to put the institution on a sound financial footing. The way to do this is to solicit contributions to the endowment and turn a profit with blockbuster exhibitions. The most effective way to get major endowment contributions seems to be to sell trusteeships. The price at the Metropolitan is apparently $10 million, but the customers have to be people who will not rock the boat.

The problem is that old money is usually tied up in trusts and not available in big chunks. Also, old money is not much concerned with prestige or more trusteeships. As for the new money, of which there is a vast amount, it took brains to make it, and brainy people are usually unwilling to release their money to less brainy people to spend as they see fit. They want some input. This input is usually considered "boat rocking" by the incumbent board. Since the boards are clubs designed to keep out those whose membership would not enhance the social status of the incumbents, some rich new prospects are denied trusteeships. Guarding their turf like territorial lions, the incumbents ignore the fact that these are public institutions, supported by taxpayers' money, and that to deny an institution access to funding or talent for one's personal social gain is a violation of fiduciary responsibility and a blatant conflict of interest. Quite apart from financial support, some of these talented new businessmen can provide invaluable counsel, help prevent blunders like the Metropolitan de Groot scandal, and solicit their peers for even more funding. But just as strong museum directors are kept at bay by trustees unwilling to relinquish power, so potentially strong trustees are unwelcome for the same reason.

I recently encountered the director of one of the two museums I had approached on the Gentileschi *The Finding of Moses,* and asked him why he hadn't let me bid. There was nothing to lose. He said, "We didn't have the money." "No museum," I replied, "has the money, except the Getty, and they weren't bidding." The Getty would have wanted the Gentileschi, but they were threatening to the British because of their expensive predations and did not want to waste one of the few arrows left in their quiver on a lost cause, needlessly infuriating their already "spooked" British colleagues. "Why not sell an unrestricted Monet of your stock of thirty-odd, some of which you can't even hang?" "We would never sell a work of art to buy something!" The American Association of Museums rules, by the way, specifically permit this.

To exacerbate the problem, almost every museum seems to have "Chinese walls" between centuries in their paintings departments; if they deaccession a nineteenth-century French picture, for some reason they will only use the money for another nineteenth-century French picture. This policy ignores redundancies and market opportunities. The Art Institute of Chicago, the Metropolitan Museum, and the Museum of Fine Arts in Boston, for instance, are rich in impressionists because of the histories of their collections, and poor in Italian baroque paintings. Even with the Japanese largely gone from that market, impressionist prices are bloated and prices for seventeenth-century Italian pictures depressed. Why not then deaccession a single redundant impressionist and plug multiple holes in the collection while there is still time, before the British finally slam the door on exports? A strong museum director might suggest this, and imaginative trustees might support him. But strength and imagination are not, alas, in current fashion. I asked the director, "Why don't you develop relationships with some of the new young tycoons who live in your museum's own neighborhood so you can approach them on projects like the Gentileschi?" "Who, for example?" I suggested the name of a young collector who in the last few years has built not only a great fortune but one of the most sophisticated art collections in the world. This man has a genuine passion for beautiful objects. "He would have understood the Gentileschi and why you need it. He probably would have helped." "Nonsense," said the director, "all he does is buy things for himself. He has never given us a penny." I said, "Of course he hasn't. His passion is for objects. I can't imagine him giving money to a general fund." Why would anyone who has no interest in power or prestige, who is smart enough to have become so rich so quickly, who so loves art, give money to buy more temples, fountains, courtyards and galleries?

Museums must look to the objects to generate money, not to money to generate objects. To build an endowment in order to generate income to balance the budget and maybe, one day, buy some art, is wrongheaded. The theory seems to be: if you ask a donor to fund an acquisition, it will drain money from the endowment. The theory is wrong. Those individuals who can be tapped for an acquisition are not the same ones who will contribute to a general fund. Further, if a museum mounts important, enlightening exhibitions, if it sponsors scholarly symposia attended by eminent authorities in the field—as the Kimbell Museum has consistently done—the scholarly world and the press will applaud, and the museum's community will hear the applause and respond with pride—and money. The same holds true for acquisitions. The Kimbell is again the example. Crowds come to Fort Worth for no other reason than because the Kimbell is so acclaimed for its exhibitions and acquisitions. It is not because the Kimbell has such a huge endowment and so much money for acquisitions. It has the money because a few donors are so proud of what the former director, Edmund Pillsbury, did, and had such confidence in his taste, that they funded his projects. The objects generated the money, not the money the objects. The program, and the Kimbell's reputation, promise to continue under the new director, Timothy Potts.

Museum trustees could take the long-range view, relinquish some of their power, and decide that a new generation of directors can love objects and also be effective administrators and fund-raisers; that if help is needed in administration, the administrator should report to the director, not the other way around, because these are, after all, cultural institutions whose course can only be charted by professionals in the field who have knowledge of the alternative directions a particular museum can take. If the tides of war turn us back closer to the old order, legions of young connoisseurs should emerge to direct our museums into the new millennium.

JULIEN LEVY

There was a breed of man, born around the turn of the century to families made affluent in the aftermath of the Civil War, Yankee or German Jewish, educated at Harvard in the humanities and connoisseurship. They were neither brought up nor educated to make money, which their families had in greater or lesser abundance. They became educators, publishers, museum directors, art collectors and dealers, but also scholars and, above all, gentlemen. The glorious and lamented brigade included the likes of Wright Ludington, Joseph Pulitzer, Edward Warburg, Lincoln Kirstein, Henry McIlhenny, Henry Clifford—and Julien Levy.

Julien Levy was around my father's age, and in a sense he was a surrogate father, that is to say a friend, of the previous generation, with whom I could have a dialogue over shared interests. I had come back to Chicago in 1957 to open a gallery. I found the city a hotbed of collecting, either with an affinity for the imagism native to Chicago—German expressionism and, most particularly, surrealism—or New York abstract expressionism. Julien had closed his own gallery nine years earlier, after Arshile Gorky's suicide, and was living with his wife, Jean, in the Berkshire foothills of Bridgewater, Connecticut. Looking back forty years, it seems incredible that all the seminal figures, of whom Julien was certainly central, were then still in their fifties. Many of the former expatriates, like the Levys, and many of the European artists in flight from the Nazis had fled from Paris to Litchfield County: Joan Miró, Alexander Calder, Yves Tanguy and Kay Sage, Robert Penn Warren, and Malcolm Cowley.

Julien was an eloquent link to those romantic Paris years of the twenties, and as my commitment to surrealism intensified, it took me little

Julien Levy with Max Ernst on Long Island, 1944

Collection Jean Farley Levy

time to locate him. The more time I spent up there with Jean and Julien, the more I mourned the failure in 1946 and 1947 of my boarding school, the Gunnery, in nearby Washington, to introduce us to this local excitement, when all the artists and writers were in their forties and in full feather. What lectures they could have given us, Julien in particular, and what studio visits we could have made. . . .

A generation separated us, but Julien was my spiritual contemporary. Julien lived and died a naughty kid. The downstairs toilet in Bridgewater was plastered with erotica. There was never anything new, no young artist, too far-out for Julien.

There were evenings in Paris in the late fifties and early sixties that would progress from Jean's and Julien's tiny Left Bank entresol, in which I could barely stand up straight, to a Chinese restaurant behind Saint-Germain-des-Prés, and thence to Julie and Man Ray's studio-bedroom behind Saint-Sulpice, and whereas Man Ray bemoaned his yesterdays, Julien always talked about tomorrow.

His own gallery having closed in 1949, and with no source of income, from time to time Julien had to sell one of the objects salvaged from his inventory, hanging in Bridgewater, a trove of surrealist treasure, and he made me his agent. My commission was 10 percent. My New York branch opened in 1963 and I began to split my time between Chicago and New York. When I married and moved to New York in 1966 I needed a Chicago gallery director, and Julien suggested his own gallery secretary until 1941, Lotte Drew-Bear. From that point on, our representation of Julien intensified to the point where Lotte and our Chicago gallery became a veritable reincarnation of the old Julien Levy gallery. Lotte regarded its artists and program as the gospel, believing not only in Joseph Cornell, whom I had shown since 1958, and Gorky but in artists like Leonid, Berman, Tchelitchew, and Leon Kelly, none of whom had ever caught on, and whom she continued to support.

As the values of some of Julien's paintings began to climb in the sixties, he became concerned about the flammability of the frame Bridgewater house, and he shipped much of the collection for safekeeping to the Yale University Art Gallery. Although they were not for sale, in 1971 I suggested that several of the major works—including Max Ernst's *Vox Angelica* and Gorky's *Love of a New Gun*—be shipped to us for loan to museums that specifically needed them. I suggested the Ernst be lent to the Art Institute of Chicago and the Gorky to the Cleveland Museum, to which Julien enthusiastically agreed.

I had, incidentally, sold Julien's Gorky *Days, Etc.* in 1965 to a Chicago collector (for $35,000), who consigned it back to us in 1971, at which point, hoping for Julien's sake and mine to place it in a public collection, I sent it to the National Gallery for purchase consideration at the owner's price of $55,000; it was turned down and returned to us. Chicago had been the international vortex of surrealist patronage in the 1950s and

Arshile Gorky, *Love of a New Gun*, 1944
Private collection

1960s, but the Art Institute had little surrealism to show for it. Not only was surrealism considered "contemporary art," but its Chicago patrons were Jewish, and the museum didn't harbor much affection for either one. The loan of Ernst's *Vox Angelica* plugged a major surrealist hole in the museum's collection.

It was this contact with Chicago, reinforced by my sale to the Art Institute in 1963 of Julien's great 1943 colored Gorky drawing (for $9,000), that led to the museum's first purchase from Julien in 1975 of works from his seminal photographic collection and his subsequent donation of the balance. A valuable alliance had, in effect, been forged between Julien and the Art Institute. It could have been even more valuable.

In December 1972 Julien finally decided to sell *Vox Angelica*. The price he set was a not unreasonable $275,000, which included our $25,000 commission. Both Julien and I wanted it to go to the Art Institute, where it had been hanging on loan, and where it would do much to permanently plug that hole that had been gaping even throughout Chicago's banquet surrealist years. Even Leigh Block, self-promoted dictator of museum policy and, despite a powder room full of little Mirós, no fan of surrealism, had acknowledged the need for an Ernst. No greater Ernst existed than *Vox Angelica*. I felt certain the painting would stay in Chicago. But I didn't count on Jim Speyer, the part-time amateur curator of contemporary art. He countered with an offer of $250,000. I told him Julien wouldn't sell it for less, that I had already given a lot to the museum, including a Nolde painting, and wasn't going to relinquish my commission. I said, "Jim, you're going to let *Vox Angelica* go for $25,000?" Well, he did, and off it went into a private European collection.

I considered my relationship with Jean and Julien rock solid. I had been Julien's acolyte, doing what I could to see that he was accorded the respect due him during the years

Max Ernst, *Vox Angelica*, 1943

Private collection

when surrealism, although acknowledged in Chicago, was internationally in the shadows. In 1965 I had arranged an exhibition in my Chicago gallery in homage to Julien and borrowed back many works he had sold in the old days. I flew Jean and Julien out to Chicago for the opening and put them up at the Ambassador East Hotel near the gallery on Division Street. Among the paintings I borrowed was a masterpiece from my old friend and client Wright Ludington, Dalí's *The Accommodations of Desire.* Julien had sold it to Wright in 1941. I had, over the years, handled many important pictures for Ludington, and I certainly intended, during the exhibition, to see if he would let me sell the Dalí. Jean and Julien walked over to see the exhibition in the afternoon before the opening, and when they came back that evening, Jean rather defensively announced that Julien now owned the Dalí, that he had phoned Ludington from the hotel, obviously at her urging, and had bought it, and that "Julien was entitled to it." Julien was, after all, much more the artist than the businessman, and Jean the artist's wife, a breed with which I had long experience.

Julien died in 1981. After years of commitment to the man and to his achievement, I expected to be at least consulted on the liquidation of his collection. Perhaps he had left it to a museum. I had no idea. But I was not even among the first to learn that Jean was consigning it for sale to Sotheby's. I wanted to make a case for a large-scale memorial exhibition, possibly in my gallery and perhaps continuing on a museum tour. When I phoned, I was diverted to a lawyer, who told me brusquely that "dealers" should submit their proposals in writing, and that in any event it was all going to Sotheby's. Being treated like a *commerçant* by my old friend's widow, artist's wife though I considered her, was painful. But when I reread Julien's *Memoir of an Art Gallery*, finally published in 1977 after the manuscript was lost for years under a flowerpot in the Paris entresol, I always stop where Julien says, "[Lotte] was until recently an important executive in the Chicago and New York galleries of my friend Richard Feigen—the man who did much for the Surrealists, giving them shows and stimulating the interest of Chicago collectors in the late fifties," and all is well.

ARTISTS' VESTALS

Artists' women—wives, girlfriends—are supposed to be impossible. No other group fits this description. Why are all these women "impossible"?

It seems to derive more from their status as artists' companions than from their gender. The fact is that until the present generation, male artists far outnumbered females, so the consorts were usually women. This will not necessarily always be so.

Since Linda Nochlin's explosive article, "Why Have There Been No Great Women Artists?" in the January 1971 *Artnews,* there have been reams of books, papers, articles, and symposia on the subject. Feminist ideologues have intermittently declared Artemisia Gentileschi as great as her father, Orazio, and ranked Raquel Ruysch, Vigée-Lebrun, Marguerite Gérard, Mary Cassatt, and Georgia O'Keeffe with Chardin, Fragonard, David, van Gogh, and Winslow Homer. They simply are not as great and do not have equal rank. It has nothing to do with their sex. It has to do with history.

Until art started to be made for its own sake at the end of the fifteenth century, it was made for the Church, and women had no place in the Church. From the sixteenth century on, painting—at least anything but still lifes—was considered an unsuitable profession for women, they were banned from the academies and guilds, and unless their father was a painter, they had no way of learning how to draw the human figure from the nude.

Except in the case of the performing arts, making art is not a collaborative effort. It requires an independence and confidence that most women were denied. Women were conditioned to take care of others and be taken care of, not to take care of themselves—not to be confident of their own abilities, not to seek to achieve mastery—not to be great artists. "Greatness" is almost defined by independence. Nothing is "great" that is not on the cutting edge, the cutting edge involves risk, to take risks takes courage, to have courage takes confidence and independence.

Artists' women, denied independence, bore an added burden. Since making art is a solitary pursuit, while the artist was alive the wife sulked in his shadow, doing wifely things like keeping his house in order and his friends at bay while he communed only with his muse.

As James Rosenquist once put it in reply to an audience question in Seattle, sometimes he goes to sleep and when he wakes up the picture is painted. Then, when he starts putting it on canvas, it's like he's chasing a star, and then when he gets near that star, he sees another one in the distance and off he chases after that one. Not even an artist communicates in his sleep. And once he's on his way, it's not like driving a car. He doesn't discuss the geography with his companion. Once he gets there, there's nothing to talk about. It's there on the canvas, or whatever it's done on or in, for anyone, including his companion, to see. For the companion this is usually a lonely and frustrating life.

This, by the way, seems true for all the disciplines except the performing arts, where sometimes the companions practice their art together and communicate through chamber music or on the stage. At least they are on the same timetable. When both are visual artists, one of them is invariably more famous—it has usually been the male—and the woman, usually outliving the man, fumes in the shadows until he dies, like Sonia Delaunay, Sophie Täuber-Arp, Lee Krasner, and Dorothea Tanning.

During the artist's lifetime, the woman, relegated to manager, typically became financially and socially ferocious, like an insecure man married to a rich woman, proving every day how financially acute he is by being "impossible" in all his dealings. Under French law, the widow becomes keeper of the flame, signator of unsigned works, arbiter of authenticity, and sometimes, as with Madame Wolfgang Wols, fabricator of fakes, whether or not she was the wife of record when the work was executed, and even if she doesn't understand the work very well.

In late 1957 and early 1958 I began to make frequent buying trips to Paris, and I befriended a number of the surrealists, most of whom were still in their fifties. Matta was thirty-eight. He ignited my imagination and galvanized my interest in contemporary art. It was obvious how he had come to have such a powerful effect on the New York artists in the early 1940s, and why, according to Harold Rosenberg, Gorky wanted to keep Matta to himself. Matta, born in Chile of an affluent Basque family and trained as an architect, was accustomed to the good life. He was never the starving artist. A man of great taste, he bought beautiful properties—an apartment facing the church of Saint-Germain-des-Prés, a seventeenth-century house at Montfort-l'Amaury outside Paris, a property on the island of Panarea in the Mediterranean, a house in London—and restored them splendidly. He collected African art, and once bought a wonderful little Max Ernst painting from me, *Henry IV, la lionne de Belfort, un ancien combattant,* 1935, which was later stolen from his Paris apartment and has never resurfaced. He had a cellar at Montfort-l'Amaury with the best wines. He collected erotica—I remember him showing me a wild Japanese scroll painting he had just bought. And whenever he spotted in some shop an erotic necklace he wanted for his wife at the time, Malitte, he would buy it or swap a painting for it.

Matta made light of his early paintings and never wanted to talk about them. He knew how good they were and how much time they had taken him to paint. Matta's talent was prodigious. He could whip up a painting in a couple of hours. And it was these paintings that he used as currency for whatever he wanted to buy. So when he complained to me once that his prices were lower than those of his colleagues, like Ernst and Tanguy, I told him that with his paintings all over Paris, everybody was competing to sell them. Matta's work from 1937 to 1945 was enormously influential, particularly for the New York painters. But then in 1945 he seemed to collapse into worldliness and complacency. How tough it must be for an artist to stay out there on the cutting edge, risking everything, when he isn't hungry. I always felt that if Matta had been hungrier he might have been one of the great painters. He certainly had the ideas, and the technical ability to execute them.

I saw a lot of Matta in those days. In 1960 I rented William Rubin's wonderful duplex apartment on the Quai de Bourbon on the Ile Saint-Louis, complete with his art collection, including such classics as Matta's *The Earth Is a Man,* 1942 (at the Art Institute of Chicago), which I later sold to Joe Shapiro; and André Masson's *Antilles,* 1943 (Musée Cantini,

Matta, *The Earth Is a Man*, 1942

The Art Institute of Chicago. Gift of Mr. and Mrs. Joseph Randall Shapiro (after her death, dedicated to the memory of Jory Shapiro by her husband), (1992.168). © 1999 Artists Rights Society (ARS), New York/ADAGP, Paris

Marseilles). Both of these, the respective artists' masterpieces, were painted in the United States during their exile during the Nazi occupation of France.

Matta frequently phoned to ask what I was doing that evening. He liked to go to fancy parties. One evening Nathan Cummings, the Chicago collector and founder of Consolidated Foods, was giving a big black-tie party on the Seine. He had hired two *bateaux-mouches,* one for the guests and one for the Paris Ballet to perform on, sailing side by side, blocking the Seine for normal traffic; there was chaos on the way back in the early morning hours when boatmen were trying to make their daily market deliveries. When I told Matta what I was doing that evening, he insisted that I get him invited. I got hold of Nate Cummings at the Plaza Athénée. Word about the party had leaked, or been leaked, and he was deluged with requests for invitations. I said, "Nate, this is Matta, the famous artist." I was amazed that he had never heard of Matta. In the

Victor Brauner,
photographed by
Man Ray, 1934

© Man Ray Trust. Artists
Rights Society (ARS),
New York/Telimage, Paris
1999

end, I managed to get Matta invited and he charmed everyone, particularly the ladies. Another day Matta phoned and said I had to come with
him that evening to a concert at the Théâtre de l'Odéon. It was Karl-
heinz Stockhausen's debut in Paris. The whole avant-garde was there.
And so it went. But by that time Matta's serious work was fifteen years
behind him. One day he sent a *pneumatique* to Brauner and made a date
for us to visit. On the way, he explained that Brauner had no money at
all and was close to starving. He and his wife, Jacqueline, lived in a
squalid metal shed, partly open to the weather, that had once belonged
to the Douanier Rousseau, at 2 bis, rue Perrel. We had been invited to
lunch, which as I recall consisted largely of mashed potatoes, which I ate
sparingly because it was apparently all they had.

Brauner was shy and said little during lunch. Matta asked him to show me some paintings. While Jacqueline cleared things away, Brauner took us to the section of the shed he used as a studio. Although I responded to the formal aspects of Brauner's work and sensed the authenticity of the imagery, his mysticism baffled me. I understood little of what he was talking or painting about. He was the second of the three artists I have encountered who were on an entirely different planet than the rest of us. The first had been Joseph Cornell, and the third, Ray Johnson.

Practically everything Brauner ever painted was still in the studio. He had sold almost nothing since he arrived from Romania in 1930. One of the earliest and finest works, *La Porte* (now in the Los Angeles County Museum), was painted on a small door because Brauner had no money to buy materials. Matta had told me that Brauner was a visionary. He pointed out the self-portrait in the painting, noting that Brauner's left eye was blinded, and that the panel was dated 1932. Then he told me how Brauner had actually been blinded. On the night of December 27, 1938, the surrealist group had been assembled in a Paris bistro. Oscar Domínguez, a Spanish painter of little talent, became enraged at Max Ernst and threw a bottle at him. The gentle Brauner stepped between them and caught the bottle in the same eye he had shown blinded six years earlier.

I was embarrassed to ask this shy artist for prices. Matta, on the other hand, was so anxious that Brauner get some money that he took the list of paintings I was interested in to Jacqueline, who was busy at the other end of the shed. She obviously handled the family's business matters. The prices Matta came back with were so high I told him to tell the Brauners I would think about it.

Matta put intense pressure on me for the next few days. I finally went back to the Brauners', looked over the paintings, and struck a deal. I would organize an exhibition in my Chicago gallery, the first retrospective ever held of Brauner's work. I would buy fifteen paintings outright at the prices Jacqueline had set, less the dealer's 50 percent discount. The other fifteen paintings would be sent on consignment, also at a 50 percent discount. Brauner would write a poem for each painting for the catalogue. Matta offered to translate each one into English from the Braunerese French. This would certainly make the catalogue a document—as indeed it did, for now, whenever copies from the 1,200-copy printing turn up in a bookseller's catalogue, they are expensive. The date for the show was set, I gave Jacqueline a check for the total of about $12,000—in those days, and at the Brauners' standard of living, enough to support them for three years—and shipment was arranged with Maurice Lefebvre-Foinet, the color merchant and shipper of choice of all the artists. Jacqueline also appointed me Victor's exclusive world representative.

Soon after our studio visit, I heard that Matta had been touting me among the artists as Brauner's savior. One of the occasions was a dinner I gave for André Masson at the Méditerranée, across from the Théâtre de l'Odéon. Another was a dinner I gave the Brauners at Chez Albert, on the Avenue du Maine, near where they lived. At the time, I was seeing a beautiful, tall, and very blond woman called Colette Escarra, who came from an affluent family in the sixteenth arrondissement, and whose only connection with the art world was an aunt, the renowned concert pianist Nicole Henriot. The artists were dazzled by this warmhearted, elegant, Nordic-looking girl—particularly Hans Bellmer, whose erotic imagery and strange behavior quite frightened Colette.

The dinner party took place during the autumn game season, and Chez Albert specialized in game. The menu was tall and pages long, a veritable encyclopedia of fauna. My own French was quite fluent, but I didn't know what half the things were. Nor even did Colette. The problem was ornithological, not linguistic. Brauner reached for Colette's menu and proceeded to draw a picture of each of the birds, and the beasts, to show her what they looked like. When he finished, we had what amounted to a surrealist Audubon. When we were leaving, I handed the menu to Colette and told her to keep it, that someday it would be valuable. Colette later married the publisher Jacques Firmin-Didot. She had several children, and then Jacques was tragically killed piloting his own plane, leaving behind a young and beautiful widow. Years later, while visiting New York with her second husband, she rang me and we all had a drink. She had matured into one of the most elegant women I have ever seen. I asked her whatever happened to the Brauner menu. She still had it.

Two weeks before the 1959 Brauner exhibition in Chicago, the paintings had not arrived. It turned out that of all the airlines, Lefebvre-

Foinet had chosen TWA, which was on strike. The paintings turned up in a hangar at Orly. I was furious and told Lefebvre-Foinet to hand them over immediately to another shipper. Brauner cabled that unless we used Lefebvre-Foinet, as much as he needed the show, he would have to cancel it. I couldn't understand this at all. I phoned Matta, and he explained. Maurice Lefebvre-Foinet was a hero. Not only had he given materials to all the artists when they had no money, but at the risk of his own life, he had hidden Brauner, who was Jewish, in a cave during the war. Once when Brauner came to my hotel to see one of the paintings he had executed in wax in the early forties, he told me the reason these paintings were done in wax was that during the war, when he was in hiding, he wasn't able to get any pigments.

The exhibition was a succès d'estime, but nothing was sold. Meanwhile, Jacqueline and Victor, in their intermittent phone calls, had taken to calling me "cher papa." In one of these calls, Jacqueline frantically asked me to rush more money to them. I asked her what the problem was. The money I had paid them was supposed to last at least another two and a half years. She said that Victor needed a proper studio to work in. Their shed had been condemned for some building project. The artists' community was up in arms that the shed that had housed both Rousseau and Brauner was to be torn down. I, for one, had written a protest letter to the *Herald Tribune.* But Jacqueline had spent the whole $12,000 as a deposit on a $100,000 studio in a fancy new building in Montparnasse. Now the $88,000 balance was due, and, "cher papa, if it isn't paid within two months, the $12,000 deposit will be forfeit."

I phoned every client who had ever heard of Brauner. I told them how great he was and explained the urgency of the situation. I said that the consigned paintings could be bought for the retail price, less our 50 percent commission, and I would absorb the shipping expense. A number of the paintings went out to the clients on approval, and I had some hope that if I couldn't sell $88,000 worth—which as I recall was more than the cost of the whole exhibition—we could at least make a dent in the debt and perhaps get some forbearance on the balance. On New Year's Eve, a cable arrived from Jacqueline. She had doubled the prices on the consigned paintings for the New Year, 1959. I panicked. The Brauners had no telephone; Jacqueline used the public phone in the neighborhood bistro. I cabled her, and she finally phoned back. I told her that I had sold nothing, that I was desperately trying to raise money for them, and that I had eight paintings out on approval with no profit margin for me. She said that was too bad, that the new prices stood and that was that. Now all I could do was hope that none of the clients kept the pictures that were out, because for each one that was sold I would lose 50 percent. In the end, without further salesmanship on my part, only one was sold, and on this I took my loss. The rest went back to Lefebvre-Foinet, along with my one-year representation of Victor Brauner.

Then somehow, for no apparent reason, and just as would later happen with Man Ray, Brauners started to sell, and the "impossible" Jacqueline was bailed out and the fancy apartment was paid for and finished and Victor lived out his days in the luxury to which he was certainly entitled.

In 1969 I bought a fine little painting by Kandinsky, painted in the Parc de Saint-Cloud around 1904. It was a typical Kandinsky of the period. But oddly, perhaps uniquely, it bore in the lower right corner the apocryphal signature "Münter 06." The only reason I could think of for this was some kind of 1906 joke with his painter mistress of the time, Gabriele Münter. That it was a Kandinsky, I was absolutely sure. To get it baptized as a Kandinsky, though, I had to go to Nina Kandinsky. I made an appointment, took the painting to Paris, and my wife and I went out to see Madame Kandinsky in Neuilly. As I walked over to her with the painting in my hand, from a slight distance she said, "That's a Kandinsky of 1904." But when I handed it to her and she read the inscription, she said, "This is not a Kandinsky." According to Nina, no Kandinsky ever owned by Münter was a Kandinsky. Nina of course didn't even know Kandinsky when Münter was his mistress around the turn of the century, but she could never forget that Münter was bequeathed all the works Kandinsky had kept from this most valuable pre–World War II period. Notwithstanding the fact that Münter had given her vast collection of 132 paintings and many drawings and watercolors to the Städtische Galerie in Munich in 1957, five years before she died. After a time, I was forced to sell the painting as a Münter.

Then there was Eugénie Kupka. She also lived in Neuilly, in a depressing, cluttered, dirty house, in an enclave, she told me, where Jacques Villon had also lived. Madame Kupka was a very fat, slovenly woman, and I recall a housekeeper or companion, also slovenly but not quite as fat. I also have an unpleasant memory of the smell of the place. At that time, in 1958, nobody was paying any attention to Kupka, nor had they ever, and Madame Kupka had in that house almost all of his major works. One might ask why I made so many trips out to that disagreeable place to visit a woman who was herself so disagreeable. I had, after all, become an art dealer in 1957, and although I wasn't entirely convinced, as not only Eugénie but a few critics had claimed, that Kupka was the first "abstract" painter—or even if he was, that this fact was so important—I was convinced that he was a painter of substance whose work deserved attention. And that I could make some money from it. So off I went on my trips to Neuilly, stopping from time to time at places like the Dior boutique to pick up chic scarves, which pleased Madame Kupka.

It seemed that no one else had indicated any interest in buying Kupkas, and Madame Kupka was certainly interested in selling. I went through all the paintings, which she had stored in an attic. She made a list of the paintings I wanted. It included such key works as the huge *Grand Nu, plans par couleurs* of 1909, which I sold in 1959 with all its preparatory drawings to Geraldine and Andrew Fuller, who gave it to the Guggenheim Museum, and the even larger *Localisation de mobiles graphiques* of 1911 (now in Madrid, Fundación Thyssen-Bornemisza).

After several of these tedious layings-on of scarves, there came a visit when we got down to business, which it turned out was where Madame Kupka wanted to be all along. I took out a notebook and pen and asked the prices of all the major pre-1918 paintings, which she gave me in businesslike fashion, in "old" French francs, and I noted them on my list. Then we made a deal for the whole list. Madame Kupka grudgingly included all the preparatory drawings and pastels for the *Grand Nu.*

I told her I would have the money wired within the week, and that as soon as it arrived in her account my shippers, Lefebvre-Foinet, would pick up the paintings. Madame Kupka bared her teeth: "Mais non, monsieur, je n'accepte que des devises, en francs français." I told her that of course I did not have with me what then amounted to around 30 million francs (in today's francs, 300,000, or, at the time, around $60,000). Nor, because of currency controls, could I wire the money to myself in France without making an official purchase that the vendor would have to record and pay taxes on, which Madame Kupka was clearly not dis-

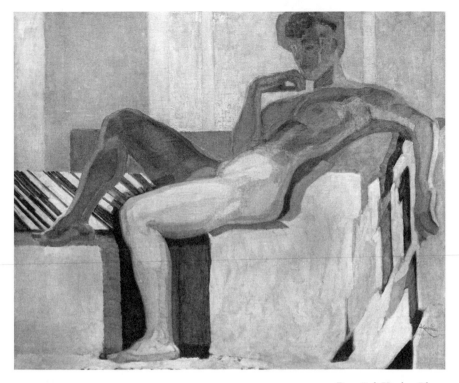

František Kupka, *Planes by Colors, Large Nude,* 1909–10

Gift, Mrs. Andrew P. Fuller, 1968. The Solomon R. Guggenheim Museum, New York (68.1860). © The Solomon R. Guggenheim Foundation, New York

posed to do. Nor could I leave the country and smuggle the bills in without risking a stop at customs and a visit to a French jail, about which of course Madame K. could not have cared less. It was obvious that František Kupka had never had to concern himself with business matters. No matter how strenuously I protested that I had no way to produce the French currency, she was prepared to forgo the deal. Finally we agreed to meet a week later, when I would return with the money.

I went back to the Hotel Pont-Royal, phoned my office with instructions to buy the francs and wire them to me in Zurich, and off I went to Switzerland. In those days the biggest bill was 1,000 francs (about $2), so this involved some 30,000 bills, and I left the Hotel Baur au Lac to find a large but inconspicuous suitcase. When the francs arrived some four days later, they barely fit, camouflaged by a bunch of dirty shirts, into the suitcase. When the plane landed in Paris, I went through the green line, "nothing to declare," and no one stopped me.

Back at the Pont-Royal, it suddenly occurred to me that I could not go out and leave my suitcase in the room, and the hotel safe was too small. So I ordered some food and stayed in the room that night. Allowing for Madame Kupka's sybaritic hours, I waited until eleven the next morning to phone her. There was no answer. Nor was there all that day or evening, nor the next or the next. Panic set in. All through Christmas I stayed in my room, until finally, on New Year's Day, my morning paper announced that the night before, the franc had been devalued and 100 old francs had become 1 new franc.

On January 2, the fat housekeeper finally answered the phone and Madame Kupka agreed to see me that afternoon. I had been trapped in that room for over two weeks. I rushed out to Neuilly to get rid of the suitcase. When I opened it, she started counting the money like a croupier, and when she finished she asked me where was the rest. I said, "What rest, Madame? They're all here, 30 million francs, just like on our list." "Oh no," said she, "the franc has been devalued. You owe me 12 million more." "But Madame, we had a date to meet on December 14, before the devaluation, and I've been trapped in my room with these francs for two weeks, all through Christmas." If I wanted the paintings, I would have to go back to Switzerland and get the remaining francs, which I did. Lefebvre-Foinet came to take the pictures, hoisting the *Grand Nu* and *Localisation de mobiles graphiques* out of the second-floor window. When I was finally sprung to have a meal with friends, I told them the story and everybody laughed. They asked how I could have been the only person in France not to know the franc was going to be devalued.

In 1958, during the Arp retrospective at the Museum of Modern Art, Jean Arp was staying with his lady, Marguerite Hagenbach—later, after many years together, to become Marguerite Hagenbach Arp—in an apartment on West End Avenue. I had at the time two fine India ink "dada" Arp drawings of 1917. As a sort of introduction to Arp, I brought them to New York from Chicago and met with Arp and Hagenbach on West End Avenue. The moment he saw the drawings, I knew he wanted them back. I said, "If you would like them, we could make an exchange for something more recent, perhaps a small sculpture." Arp was pleased, we agreed to consummate the swap on a future trip to Switzerland, he gave me their address and phone number in Basel and Hagenbach's in Paris, and I left the drawings with them.

The next time I was in Europe, I phoned Basel. No one answered, nor did they in Paris. The next trip the same, and the next. I wrote Arp a letter confirming, subtly, I thought, our arrangement. There was no answer. This went on for over two years. One day my friends Marilyn and Jim Alsdorf dropped into my gallery and I told them the story. Jim laughed and said, "You gave Arp the drawings." "I did not! I can't afford to give away $1,800 presents." "You don't know Hagenbach." A nagging feeling—that I had been had—set in.

Some months later, I found myself again at the Baur au Lac in Zurich and gave the operator a list of phone numbers to try. Rather hopelessly, I put Arp's Basel number on the list. Suddenly the operator rang and said, "Mr. Arp is on the line." I told him I was coming to Basel the next day, and could we meet. I really had no other reason to go to Basel. We made a date to meet the next afternoon at their apartment.

As soon as I entered the apartment, filled with Arps and Mirós and Ernsts, Hagenbach's disapproving presence filled the room. We chatted for a while, and it was just as if I hadn't been trying to make contact for a couple of years. It was as if Arp had been expecting me all the time. As I glanced around the room, I spotted two tiny bronzes, of recent vintage but quite salable, sitting on a shelf. I ventured, "Monsieur Arp, about our arrangement for the two 1917 drawings. Would those two little sculptures work?" Hagenbach sprang into action. "We have prepared the exchange." She went into another room, brought back a package, unwrapped it, and handed me two collages of recent date, of miserable quality, unsalable even for $400. I gently explained that it would be difficult in the current market for me to recoup my $1,800 from the collages, and might I have the two bronzes instead? Arp thought that was fair, but Hagenbach said, "Absolutely not!" Arp, a kindly man, prevailed. The flame still flickered; the keeper would have to wait a bit longer.

There is a story about Olga Tamayo which I include here not because I ever considered Tamayo an artist of great consequence, or because I know much about their relationship, but because he was, after all, an artist, famous at least in Mexico, and Olga, as far as I knew, was not.

The Pont-Royal was, as I mentioned, the Paris art-world hotel in the late fifties and sixties. Most of the collectors and museum people stayed there, and so did visiting artists, writers, and composers. They had at the desk what they called the *livre d'or,* which they would ask each distinguished guest to inscribe. The manager once showed it to me, and most of the inscriptions, drawings and a few bars of music, were cursory and must have been done while the artists were handing over their passports. There was a more elaborate Chagall drawing, but he must have been able to whip up a standard Chagall while he stood there registering. There was a quite beautiful Tanguy watercolor in the book, and I asked the manager about it. He said that Tanguy, whom I never knew but who was certainly the sincerest of the surrealists, was the one person who insisted on taking the book with him to his room.

I was at the hotel one June, I think it was around 1960, at the same time as my friends Rose and Mort Neumann, the eccentric art-collecting couple from Chicago. Mort said, "Richard, there's a party tonight for Tamayo. Come with us." I asked Rose what kind of party it was. She said it was a dinner at an apartment on the Quai des Grands-Augustins. We walked over from the hotel to a beautiful apartment with windows on the Seine, full of men in blue suits and elegant women. Very subdued and formal. I walked into the library and started chatting with the hostess, whom I didn't know. It was not very long before we heard some horrendous screaming coming from the salon. Everybody rushed to the room. There, while the guests stood gaping, was an older woman beating the hell out of a younger one, most of whose clothes had been torn off. The older woman was screaming over and over again, like some kind of maenad, "You fawk my hosban! I keel you! You fawk my hosban! I keel you!"

No one was doing anything to stop them. It seemed entirely possible that the older woman might carry out her threat. I usually avoid confrontations, but I went over and tried to calm them down and threw my coat around the naked lady. The battle ended, and then finally the evening, and the Neumanns and I walked back to the hotel around one-thirty in the morning. The lobby was like a tomb. The antique elevator, with its open fin-de-siècle cage, creaked up to my floor.

Just as I was finally getting into bed, the whole place was jarred by the ringing of my telephone. I thought it must be some kind of emergency. I couldn't imagine anyone back in the United States being unaware of the six-hour time difference. I picked up the phone to hear, "Feigen. I luff you. Here is Olga Tamayo. I come to you." Until the phone rang, I had almost succeeded in quieting my nerves, but now my heart started pounding again. "Mrs. Tamayo," I said, "I am very honored. But it is very late, and I am very weary. Why don't we have a coffee in the morning?" "I am Olga. I luff you. I come to you." "Mrs. Tamayo, it is very late. You must not come to me." "Feigen. I luff you. I come to you." "Mrs. Tamayo, you must not come to me. And now I am so tired I must hang up." And so I did. Again the shattering ring of the telephone. "I am Olga. I come to you." Again I hung up. Again the phone rang. This time I did not pick it up. I cringed. Then I heard the creaking elevator. I remembered how she had mauled that lady at the party. I hid behind the armchair in the corner of the room. I prayed that the door was locked. Then the pounding on the door. "I am Olga. I come to you." More pounding. "I come to you." I was sure the whole hotel was awake by now. Then, after what seemed like an eternity, the pounding stopped. "Oh. I onnerstan! You are weeth a fren!" Then the creaking elevator again. After some minutes, I ventured out from behind my chair and to the door. Could she have slyly sent the elevator down and be there waiting for me? Another five minutes and I took a gamble. She wasn't there. Then, as I glanced down, I saw what had happened. In some moment of prescience, before going out to dinner, I had put my brown shoes outside the door, and then, when I got back from the dinner, my black ones as well.

There were the consorts of other artists whom I knew little, like Lee Krasner Pollock and Dorothea Tanning Ernst, both of whom quite terrified me, and Elaine de Kooning, or knew not at all, like Mesdames Léger and Braque. I have no firsthand stories to tell about any of them, but each has that legendary monster reputation. Tanning, a very beautiful woman, is a surrealist of substantial talent, and developing under the influence of Max Ernst's more powerful artistic personality must have driven her to the fury with which she explodes when referred to as a woman artist, or as Mrs. Max Ernst. Kay Sage, from an august American family, also influenced by Yves Tanguy, but less talented as a painter than Tanning, was finally driven to shoot herself. Julien Levy, the pioneer dealer—really more a surrealist himself in terms of his temperament and contribution to art history than a dealer—told me the story of how Sage, a Connecticut neighbor, invited him to accompany her when she went to buy the pearl-handled pistol to shoot herself. Julien recounted in his 1977 memoir how Sage had tried, as early as 1939, to convert Tanguy into a Connecticut country gentleman. Was this an effort to derail him onto her track, to communicate with him by homogenizing their backgrounds? As for Krasner, the hell of living with Jackson Pollock has been recounted many times. I suppose she had to consider herself—and be considered—an artist to make it in the circles and times in which she moved. But I never thought she was much of an artist, and I don't believe many people thought otherwise until Pollock died and she grabbed the flame and people had to treat her like an important artist to get to Pollock's work.

Thus, among these were consorts of the first category, the housewife-managers; and those of the second, who were true companions. In the latter group, usually neither artist nor consort had a genuine artistic temperament, famous though the man may have been, and thus the two of them could work together as partners in fraud. So it was with Gala and Salvador Dalí and Julie and Man Ray, and others who are still alive and happy and shall go nameless.

I remember evenings in the late 1950s and 1960s when Jean and Julien Levy and I, and sometimes Roland Penrose, took Julie and Man Ray to dinner at a Chinese restaurant just behind Saint-Germain-des-Prés, with Man wailing all the while about the unjust neglect he had been suffering all those years. After dinner we would repair to the Rays' one-room apartment-studio behind Saint-Sulpice, where Julie would proceed to try to sell me Man's work, which, except for the old photographs, I found execrable. It was sad and, for me, embarrassing. These two Americans had been together all those years in that studio, apparently never officially married but devoted to each other, and now quite destitute. Finally, late one night, when it was obvious I wasn't going to buy any of Man's paintings or objects, Julien said, "Why don't you show him the Rousseau?"

So Man went over and pulled out a large painting, quite strange, of cliffs on the Brittany coast, with, as I recall, girls in wooden shoes looking out to a stormy sea. It was signed "H. Rousseau," but the subject matter was unlike that of any known Rousseau. Julien said, "Maybe Dick can sell this for you." I asked Man on what basis he was so sure this was a Rousseau. He said that he had found it while strolling through the Marché aux Puces with André Breton, and that Breton had agreed that it was a Rousseau. And furthermore, there was a pencil inscription on the stretcher, "salon d'automne 1906," and he and Breton had found a 1906 salon checklist in the Bibliothèque Nationale in which there was listed among the Douanier Rousseau's entries a *"paysage breton."* There was of course no size or other identification. I asked Man, "Who accepts this as a Rousseau?" "I do. Man Ray does." "That unfortunately is not enough, not if you want a Rousseau price. Who else?" "Braque, Léger, Brancusi . . ."—he rolled out the whole pantheon. Except the only one who counted, the expert on Rousseau, Picasso. I said, "What about Picasso?" who by the way had, in the early days of the century, even before Max Weber introduced him to Rousseau in 1908, discovered several Rousseaus lying around unidentified in Left Bank junk shops. By then Picasso owned a formidable collection of Rousseaus.

"Oh, Picasso doesn't matter," said Man. "Oh yes he does," I said, "he's the only one who does matter." Man wanted $50,000 for the picture, worth, if an undisputed Rousseau, $100,000 at the time, perhaps $5,000 if only a good primitive carrying a purported Rousseau signature. "Well, I had a fight with Picasso, and he won't accept the painting." That left me with nothing, except my own hunch that this was indeed an offbeat Rousseau. It had that attitude of naïf wonderment before nature, the childlike strength and assurance of composition—no sophisticated uncertainties—the palette of the early work of the late 1890s, and the plastic power.

So there was my job: proving it was a Rousseau. Lefebvre-Foinet picked it up and shipped it to me in New York. I showed it to everyone who knew anything about Rousseau. Alfred Barr could not say it was a Rousseau, nor could he say it wasn't. James Johnson Sweeney wasn't sure either. I had X-ray photographs taken in quadrants. They showed no pentimenti and revealed nothing. It was like a paternity test. Nothing indicated it was not a Rousseau, but there seemed to be no way to prove it was. It occurred to me that the only proof would be to find someone still alive who might have seen the painting in the 1906 Salon d'Automne, more than half a century earlier. The only survivor I could think of was Daniel-Henri Kahnweiler, the legendary dealer of Picasso, Braque, Léger, and Juan Gris, born in 1884 and now in his eighties.

Soon after, I gave a dinner in Paris in Kahnweiler's honor at the Grand Vefour in the Palais Royal. At the time, it was still one of Paris's great restaurants, and certainly the most beautiful. I was not as adept at seating dinner parties as I have become since my divorce, and this particular table bore the seeds of potential disaster unless the *placement* was executed with great delicacy. Working against my natural grain, which is to come bounding downstairs tying my tie as my first guests are picking up their drinks, I arrived at the Grand Vefour a full half hour early. Although my own seat was to be in the center of the banquette facing half the guests, I took a temporary seat on the outside so I could greet everyone. I went to work on my *placement.* It was imperative to keep two of the people as far away from each other as possible: Mary Block and Alain de Gunzbourg. Mary and her husband, Leigh, were known everywhere as being among the world's great art collectors. Mary had everyone in the art and Chicago social worlds terrified of her volatile personality, particularly after she had consumed some alcohol. And this night I had not stinted on the wine.

Before her marriage, Mary had been an accomplished advertising executive in her own right. So, for these several reasons, the very last thing to do was treat Mary Block as some sort of housewife. Her personality was uncannily captured in her portrait by Ivan Albright, the painting she so hated that she had given it to the Art Institute of Chicago as soon as it was finished. Now that I think of it, Josephine Albright was one of the few artists' wives who cannot be included with the "impossibles." I can only think that the reasons might be that, first, Albright did not act or live like an artist, nor Josephine Albright like an artist's wife. The Albrights were social-registered Brahmins living in a Gold Coast town house. Jo was the self-assured daughter of Joseph Medill Patterson, heiress to one of America's great newspaper fortunes. Provincial Chicago society, oblivious to Ivan's world-class status as an artist, gave Jo more rank than Ivan.

The Baron Alain de Gunzbourg was a very baronial but impecunious baron, married to the intelligent Seagram heiress Minda Bronfman, she of prodigious fortune. Alain was given to such baronial pursuits as shooting, and to the conviction that women belong in the kitchen or the bedroom. He was not shy about forcefully presenting these convictions. It was obvious that the briefest contact between Mary—the rich, powerful, spoiled professional woman—and Alain—the impecunious, insecure, macho husband of a prodigiously rich woman—would be as explosive as nitrogen and glycerin.

Suddenly, at eight-fifteen, just as I thought I had it figured out, Kahnweiler appeared over my shoulder, fifteen minutes early. I jumped up, offered him the chair next to me, and ordered some wine. It was at that point that I asked him if indeed he had visited the 1906 Salon des Indépendents. Notwithstanding the sixty-year hiatus, Kahnweiler remembered that indeed he had. I asked him if he remembered the Douanier Rousseaus. In specific, a strange painting with Breton girls looking out to sea. Alas, Kahnweiler had no recollection of the Rousseau. He had apparently been transfixed by the fauves at that salon.

All during our predinner conversation, I had been sneaking glances at my seating plan. Then, before I could complete it, the guests started to arrive. In my panic, I kept my seat facing the banquette, opposite from where I should have been, and the sides of the table, though not the head and foot, were reversed. There, to my horror, were Mary Block and Alain de Gunzbourg sitting next to each other at the end of the table. It was only a matter of time before the explosion. The first words I heard from that end of the table were "How dare you!" The rest of the evening erased itself from memory.

In any event, judging from the sophisticated artists Kahnweiler had associated himself with after his famed exposure to the *Demoiselles d'Avignon* in Picasso's studio in 1907—Picasso, Braque, Léger, Gris—it was not surprising that a naïf had gone unnoticed at the salon. There went my one surviving eyewitness, and any chance I had of proving Julie and Man Ray's Rousseau and alleviating their poverty. After spending much time and money on it, and still harboring the nagging suspicion that it was indeed a Rousseau, I shipped the painting back to Paris. I have never seen it since, and I have no idea what happened to it after Julie's and Man's deaths. But by some miracle, it was not long after the Rousseau was returned that the Rays' fortunes dramatically improved. Suddenly Man Ray's paintings became fashionable and started to sell. The stimulus, as I recall, was the staggering $750,000 that his *A l'heure de l'observatoire: Les Amoureux* brought at the Copley sale at Sotheby's on November 5, 1979. This was the huge painting of red lips floating over the horizon which I had tried to get Estée Lauder to bid on for her cosmetics company. It supposedly found a wall on some Greek yacht.

The point of the anecdote is, of course, that the relationship of Julie and Man Ray was atypical of artists and their wives. Despite his eccentric trappings as a charter dadaist, Man Ray did not seem to me to have a genuine artist's temperament. Julie and Man Ray were a nice bourgeois Jewish couple working happily as partners to pull the wool over everybody's eyes and sell Man's work. Julie never faced real solitude and never became such an "impossible" individual. They were "impossible" together.

The same was true of Gala and Salvador Dalí. Gala, always taking her best shot, went off with Max Ernst while she was married to Paul Eluard, and when Dalí arrived in Paris from Spain, she said that since he was going to be the richest of them all, she was leaving with him, and leave she did, for the rest of their lives, partners in fraud at the St. Regis Hotel. Dalí acted strange—he waxed his mustaches and spoke every language with an incomprehensible accent, pretending to have no mother tongue. But Dalí really wasn't strange at all. I remember him well, sitting there every day at lunch at his table in the doorway of the St. Regis dining room, watching to see who would walk by. One day I was walking by with Tony Curtis. Tony spotted him and asked to be introduced. From that very afternoon on, Curtis was deluged with phone calls, invitations, inscribed books and catalogues. Finally, after a week of this, Tony pleaded to be cut loose. Later, I also arranged a meeting for Dalí and Matta in the King Cole Bar. They hadn't seen each other for twenty years. But that's another story. And it was also in Tony Curtis's suite in the St. Regis that I arranged to screen the wonderful films that Joseph Cornell gave me to show him while Tony was down with a fever. That too is another story.

There were others whose relationships with their artist husbands was only related to me secondhand. For instance, Quappi Beckmann, whom I knew only after Max Beckmann's death. She was an aristocrat, quite reserved, so I never got to know her very well. I do remember that Quappi, I thought quite extraordinarily, was the only one to refuse to lend her triptych *The Argonauts* (now at the National Gallery of Art in Washington) to the Whitechapel Gallery exhibition in London in 1980–81. One would have thought that the widow would have had the greatest stake in making the project complete and historic.

It is in our generation that fundamental changes are taking place in the relationships between men and women, and women have achieved equality with men as artists, both in their numbers and in their level of achievement. The question is whether the husbands—artists and nonartists—will be able to cope with artist wives, independent women often more famous than the men, and come to terms with the same creative isolation to which women traditionally had to become accustomed.

Was the case of Ana Mendieta and Carl Andre a portent of things to come?

On September 8, 1985, Ana Mendieta, a gifted thirty-six-year-old Cuban artist, wife of the sculptor Carl Andre, fell or was pushed from a thirty-fourth-floor Greenwich Village window. Andre was arrested, then exonerated in a widely publicized murder trial that had the art world passionately divided. Ana and Carl were two powerful creative personalities, equals in talent. Was Andre's anger triggered by an inability to deal with this equality? Will men be able to handle the solitude—the women taking care of themselves and not of them? Will their reactions to women's artistic autonomy be more violent, generating mutations more horrendous, more "impossible" than we have known?

THE BUTE "TRUMBULL"

At the end of the day, an art dealer is usually left with two assets: a collection of objects he could not or would not sell, and a collection of stories he could not tell. Some never get told because one of the protected players outlives the dealer. Sadly, one of my stories can now be told because John, seventh Marquess of Bute, died in July 1993. I was unaware that John Bute had never revealed any of this story to his family until his son, Lord Anthony Crichton-Stuart, head of the Old Masters painting department at Christie's in New York, telephoned me in the spring of 1996 asking for information about the version of John Trumbull's *General George Washington at the Battle of Trenton* formerly hanging at the Bute dower house, Dumfries House in Ayrshire, now removed for sale with other Bute furniture and pictures at Christie's in London in July 1996. Anthony had noticed that my name appeared in connection with the painting in the family records. I said, "Anthony, do you know the story about this picture?" "No." "Well, I promised your father I would never tell anyone, but now that you're going to sell the painting, I'll tell you the story."

During a drive through Scotland in September 1975, my wife and I were invited by the Dowager Marchioness of Bute, the seventh marquess's mother, to spend the weekend with her at Dumfries House at Cumnock in Ayrshire. Dumfries is a glory of English architecture and decoration, the best-preserved Robert Adam house in the United Kingdom. The third Earl of Bute ordered all the furniture from Thomas Chippendale when the house was built in 1759, and even had Chippendale design the picture frames. There is, for instance, in the drawing room a dashing portrait by Sir Thomas Lawrence of the fourth earl, later first marquess, as a young Spanish grandee (to which rank he had been elevated as British ambassador to Spain), whose Chippendale frame is but a feathery carving of gilded leaves pinned to the wall, certainly one of the most extraordinary picture frames in the world. The house, the furniture, the pictures—mostly seventeenth-century Dutch, for which the Bute collection is renowned, and the bulk of which is at the family's principal seat, Mountstuart, on the Isle of Bute—are of exceptional beauty and, because the family has long had money, are splendidly preserved.

We had been at a state dinner at the White House the previous January. During drinks in the East Room before dinner, Marvin Sadek, then director of the National Portrait Gallery, announced quite audibly to a cluster of fellow guests that the full-length portrait of George Washington which had hung as a Gilbert Stuart in that spot since it was purchased by the government in 1800, and which the White House still maintains is authentic, was not in fact by Stuart. The romantic legend that Dolley Madison had cut it out of its frame to save it when the British burned the White House in 1813, though without foundation, had supported the painting's attribution to Gilbert Stuart and its cherished place throughout its subsequent history, though Stuart himself had denied painting it from the time it was first hung in the White House in 1802. The painting still hangs in the East Room as a Stuart, but subsequent scholarship has tended to agree with Sadek, finding no stylistic evidence to support the ascription to Stuart.

Sadek's comment had turned my mind to two other full-length Washington portraits, the two versions of the Lansdowne portrait. One belonged to the Pennsylvania Academy of the Fine Arts. The other, the prime version and the only one universally considered to be completely by Stuart, I knew to be owned by the Earl and Countess of Rosebery, who also lived in Scotland, at Dalmeny House in South Queensferry. Both versions had been commissioned from Stuart by William Bingham of Philadelphia in 1796. The first he gave, in his wife's name, to the Marquess of Lansdowne, like the third Earl of Bute a supporter of the American cause during the Revolution; the other he kept and later bequeathed to the Pennsylvania Academy. In January 1975 they both happened to be on loan to the National Portrait Gallery in Washington, where the Rosebery version remains to this day.

Robert Muller, after John
Trumbull, *General George
Washington at the Battle of
Trenton*

© Christie's Images, Ltd., 1999

The White House dinner was a festive affair, honoring the ill-starred
Ali Bhutto of Pakistan, full of Democrats who had been in purdah all
during the Nixon years and were now being welcomed back by President
Ford in a charming gesture of reconciliation. But during dinner and
dancing I fantasized, like a committed art dealer—particularly since
Candice Bergen had taken off with the House photographer after
dinner—about replacing the disputed Washington with the Roseberys'
picture.

Back in New York, I wrote the Roseberys outlining my idea. With the
exception of Gilbert Stuart's portraits of America's founding heroes, his
paintings were virtually unsalable and were likely to remain so. The
"Lansdowne" Washington had enormous historical—and monetary—
value in the United States, little in England. I had a client who I thought

would pay some $3 million for the painting and donate it to the White House, on the occasion of the impending bicentennial, to replace the disputed portrait. Further, the Rosebery picture was already outside England, and I doubted there would be any difficulty procuring an export license, but I sensed that this might change if the Roseberys held on to it much longer. As far as I could see, the Stuart had no particular relevance to the Rosebery family. Lord Rosebery's forebear had merely bought it after it was exhibited at the Philadelphia Centennial in 1876. Finally, there could be the satisfaction of sending back to its rightful home a real American icon. My efforts at persuasion extended through a dinner I gave for the Roseberys in my New York apartment in 1978. In the end, it turned out that the portrait was in a family trust and could not be sold.

We had arrived at Dumfries House that September in 1975 on an overcast Friday afternoon. I was amazed at the splendid Adam facade rising at the Dumfries House turnoff out of the flat, dull Ayrshire countryside south of Glasgow. The gracious Lady Bute had us shown to a wonderful bedroom. The furniture, including a great canopied bed, was part of one of the most famous suites of furniture in the world, still intact at Dumfries after 216 years, thanks to the Butes' continuing affluence. The bedroom walls were covered with works by the Italianate Dutch painters, a school in which I was deeply interested. But we rushed down to dinner, and there, dimly lit in the dining room, was a full-length Washington portrait. I went down to look at the painting again on Saturday morning, but it was impenetrably dirty and there was little light even during the day. It was clearly a version of a Trumbull painting at Yale. And it was this image to which I turned after the Rosebery project collapsed. Trumbull's *General Washington at the Battle of Trenton,* the prime version, at Yale since 1806, was an image used on a number of American postage stamps, almost as celebrated as the "Lansdowne" Stuart.

On Sunday Lady Bute took us a short distance down the road to see Dumfries' sister house, Auchinleck, the home of James Boswell and his descendants. Auchinleck was built around 1760. Although the literature does not ascribe it to Adam, it is architecturally as beautiful as Dumfries, and Lady Bute said that Adam definitely was the architect. By 1975, however, dry rot had set in. The Boswells, unable to afford to restore it, had

John Trumbull, *General George Washington at the Battle of Trenton*, 1792

Yale University Art Gallery, New Haven. Gift of the Society of the Cincinnati in Connecticut

moved out shortly before, and the first eighteenth-century windowpanes had already been smashed by vandals. This was the one sad note in a lovely Scottish weekend. When I got home, I made a vain attempt to interest Yale, home and publisher of the Boswell papers, in acquiring and restoring Auchinleck as a Yale study center.

But the first priority following my failure with the Roseberys was to research the Bute portrait. John Bute knew nothing of the painting's background. He was under the impression that his father, the sixth marquess, had bought it in the 1930s. That, at least, was when Bute thought it had found its way into the Dumfries dining room. But a reference to the Bute version in the standard book by Theodore Sizer, *The Works of Colonel John Trumbull,* seemed to imply otherwise. Sizer treated the Bute painting as an autograph replica of the Yale version, dating from Philadelphia, 1792–93, or London, 1794, and placed it at Dumfries House as the property of the sixth marquess. More homework revealed that John Bute's forebear, the third earl, First Lord of the Treasury in 1762–63, broke with King George III and his prime minister, William Pitt, over Great Britain's draconian taxation of the American colonies. When the Revolutionary War broke out, Bute became an ardent partisan of the American cause. So it did not seem strange that his son, the fourth earl, who succeeded him in 1792, would have commissioned a portrait of the father of the new country.

Trumbull, whose ambition as a painter was to document the American Revolution and its heroes, was commissioned in 1790 by the city of Charleston, South Carolina, to paint a portrait of Washington at the battle of Trenton. The portrait was completed in 1792, but the Charleston officials found it too emotional and rejected it. Trumbull painted a second portrait, which they accepted. The first version was purchased in 1806 by Yale University with funds supplied by the Society of the Cincinnati, an organization of officers of the American Revolutionary army and their descendants.

Trumbull had, until the French Revolution, been an avid Federalist, pro-French and anti-British. But the bloody events of the Revolution, the incessant crash of the guillotine, turned him into an anti-French, antimaterialist, pro-British Republican. He had even become estranged from his old friend Thomas Jefferson when he got into a violent argument with Virginia Representative William Giles at a dinner at Jefferson's home in 1793.

Trumbull left for England in 1794 as secretary to John Jay on his mission to negotiate a treaty with England and settle the peace. Trumbull apparently took with him a small replica, whereabouts now unknown, of the first version of the Washington portrait. He left the replica in Benjamin West's London studio for delivery to an engraver, Poggi, who engraved it in 1796 and published it in 1797.

Resident in London as Jay's secretary since 1794, Trumbull was flattered to be appointed in 1796 the fifth commissioner of the Jay Treaty Commission, established to resolve the remaining disputes on commercial matters and on the American frontiers. Two commissioners were appointed by the British and two by the Americans. Lots were drawn to appoint the fifth, and the Americans won. The United States selected Trumbull as the potential tiebreaker. Trumbull was to remain in England in that capacity for a full ten years, not returning home until June 27, 1804.

So another piece of the puzzle seemed to fall into place. There was every likelihood that Trumbull, friend of the Founding Fathers, recently converted to a pro-British, anti-French Republicanism, would, during those first years of his stay in England, become acquainted with a Scottish peer whose father had been so active a protagonist of the American cause. I mentioned all this to John Bute, who had been unaware of the pro-American activities leading to his forebear's daring rupture with his own monarch.

Once the distinguished provenance of the Bute portrait seemed to have been established, the next step was to contact my client to see if he would be interested in buying the nation a Trumbull instead of a Stuart. It made no difference to him as long as the White House saw fit to hang it in the East Room in place of the questionable Stuart. His motives were not entirely altruistic. I had sketched a tantalizing picture of presidential gratitude and White House invitations.

Using the same arguments as with Lord Rosebery, I explained to Lord Bute what a service he would be doing the country by selling his Washington portrait. This time it worked. He agreed to a sale at $1,537,000, payable before delivery to our transporter. I phoned my client, he agreed, I cabled confirmation to Bute, we added our commission and invoiced the client, and the deal was done. It seemed to be one of those nice transactions that work to everyone's advantage and actually accomplish something. I had a good feeling when it was concluded. The only piece of the plan I hadn't put in place was to offer the Trumbull to Clement Conger, the White House curator. But since I assumed at the time that the word of Marvin Sadek—as director of the National Portrait Gallery and an authority on Stuart—would be accepted, even by the White House, I also assumed that Conger would be ecstatic to replace the "Stuart" with the Trumbull. In retrospect, I am not so certain they would have taken the "Stuart" down, since they still, years later, consider it authentic. But in any case, a place of honor would certainly have been found for the historic Trumbull, and its donor duly honored.

The client promptly paid our invoice by wire transfer, I bought the pounds sterling, and they were transferred to Bute's account. Our London shipping agents trucked the painting down from Scotland, and in due course it arrived in New York. Anxious to remove 180 years of grime and show the Trumbull to Clem Conger and the reigning Trumbull scholar, Irma Jaffe, I had it delivered directly from Kennedy Airport to the conservator, Marco Grassi, to be cleaned.

A few days later, I took a phone call from Grassi in my bathtub. For years I have been told that I will be electrocuted using the phone in my bathtub, but like a cigarette smoker, I have always done it and probably always will. Grassi said, "Richard, I have bad news." "What?" "The painting isn't a Trumbull." It felt like the electrocution. Grassi is a good friend, and not given to wild statements, particularly about artists on whose work he claims no expertise. "There is an inscription at the bottom right, 'J. Trumbull/1792./Philadelphia/by R. Muller/1797.' " Panic in the bathtub. So the painting was a copy by Muller in 1797 of the little replica, left with Benjamin West in 1796 for engraving, of the portrait commissioned by the city of Charleston in 1792 and sold by Trumbull to Yale ten years later.

Almost physically sickened, I started to compute my finances minus the $1.6 million. The next thing I did was phone John Bute. I did not want to discuss my problem on the telephone. It would be too easy to say at long distance, "I'm terribly sorry, Richard, but the funds have been committed. You're the professional. You're supposed to know what you're doing. You made an offer. It was accepted by our trustees. I'm afraid nothing can be done." So I merely said, "John, there is an important matter I would like to discuss. Can you see me tomorrow?" We made an appointment for late the next afternoon in Bute's London office. I got no sleep at all on the overnight flight. When I stepped into Bute's office, I blurted out, "John, I have a terrible problem. The portrait is not by Trumbull. It was miscatalogued by Sizer. It was so dirty only the restorer could see the copyist's inscription under laboratory light. It's a copy of the original at Yale. I will have to return my client's money right away." I was afraid of what would come next. But John Bute was a gentleman. He agreed to rescind the transaction and refund the money. But he was leaving for a month in the Caribbean and would make the arrangements when he returned. The painting should be shipped back to Dumfries House. And it was important that nothing whatever be said, ever, about the sale, or the rescission. The great load off my shoulders, I flew back to New York. A month later, Bute deposited the £674,000 in my London account. Before it was transferred back to my client, the sterling had to be changed into dollars. In that intervening month, the dollar had fallen against the pound, and I took a $56,000 loss. I considered myself lucky.

In the weeks and months that followed, Irma Jaffe came to see the rediscovered Trumbull that her predecessor Sizer had so definitively catalogued. Agnew's wrote on behalf of a museum, asking for an exhibition loan. To these requests, and others over the next few months until they subsided, I simply replied that because of disagreement in the Bute family over the sale, the painting had been returned. And nothing more was said about the matter until Anthony Crichton-Stuart telephoned asking for information twenty years later. The "Trumbull" was estimated by Christie's in the Bute sale at £20,000 to £30,000. It sold for £210,500, a price no Muller had ever approached. And as I looked at it hanging at Christie's before the auction, the one last thing I would have liked to have done was see the Muller copy side by side with the original at Yale. I had a feeling that the Muller was just as good, maybe better. Trumbull was, after all, more of a patriot than a painter.

BAKSHEESH

On Saturday, April 27, 1996, an article by Souren Melikian appeared in the *International Herald Tribune:* "Destroying a Treasure: the Sad Story of a Manuscript." As soon as I read the headline, I knew what Melikian was writing about, and I knew that this blood was on my hands. A story twenty years old came rushing back to memory, the story of the biggest deal I ever blew.

The 1970s were awash in corporate payoff scandals, Kashoggi arms deals, Saudi princes' distributorships. But none of the newspaper stories of all this "baksheesh" provided a manual on how to do it, just that it was common to some cultures, mainly Middle Eastern, but not to ours, and that our government frowned on it, even when it bolstered our exports. As for art, we knew vaguely of payoffs in Japan, but we weren't involved because we never dealt directly with the clients, private or institutional, only Japanese dealers. We never had any idea how many intermediaries there were, or how many times they marked up the prices. We were uneasy about the inflation we suspected at the end of the chain, but in the last analysis were glad to be doing the business we did.

In 1994 we heard about a Roy Lichtenstein, *Girl with a Hair Ribbon,* worth perhaps $3 million, sold to the new Tokyo Museum of Contemporary Art for $6 million. This was only a small part of the $63 million they had already spent. I was interviewed by the Japanese press in 1996 about the value of a Magritte sold to the city of Utsunomiya for a new museum for $5.9 million, worth about a quarter of that. But no one knew who got paid off in these deals, only that the sellers at the beginning of the chain got nothing like the prices at the end.

We knew about a "Rembrandt" that started its peregrinations in Indianapolis on the eve of its exclusion, as a damaged studio work, from the forthcoming Rembrandt catalogue raisonné, and ended up being peddled to a private Japanese museum as an autograph Rembrandt for tens of millions of dollars. When I spotted it in the museum's fancy catalogue and alerted the director, hoping to spare the Japanese from ultimate disenchantment with art in general, an irate letter arrived from the museum's dealer castigating me for blowing the whistle, and claiming they were getting the Rembrandt Research Project to reverse itself—effectively, telling me to mind my own business.

We had no idea who in between got paid off on these deals, just that someday it would all hit the fan. All this baksheesh was as foreign to our culture as Arab women crashing the immigration line at Fiumicino Airport. Would we pay bribes if we knew how and to whom to pay them? Some would, some wouldn't; for some it would depend on the circumstances and who, if anyone, was getting hurt. But the bottom line is that we didn't know how. At least I didn't. Therein lies the tale of the biggest deal I ever blew. And the dismantling of a masterpiece, the full weight of which I feel upon my shoulders.

The international art market had collapsed in the spring of 1970. Nixon, in office for two years, and in a misguided effort to dampen the Vietnam War inflation that his two predecessors and he had created, simply and suddenly cut off the money supply. Many of the art collectors of the day, high-flying Americans using money borrowed on illiquid collateral, went broke and had to stop buying art and start selling it. For the only period that I can recall in more than forty years, there was simply no art market at all, until the autumn of 1971. It was then that the Japanese came along.

About three years later, rumors began to circulate of serious buying for the Empress of Iran—Picasso, Pollock, de Kooning—either for herself personally or for a new museum of modern art in Tehran. Hard information was difficult to come by. The dealers involved were understandably tight-lipped.

Not knowing whom to contact in Iran about modern European paintings, I figured that the key to the Iranian door might be a spectacular Persian object. The problem was that I knew nothing at all of this very specialized field. I learned that one of the leading authorities, Toby Falk, had recently left Sotheby's in London and struck off on his own. I phoned him in the autumn of 1974 and asked him to let me know of the next available Persian masterpiece, whatever the price. It was not long before Falk phoned to offer me an important manuscript.

In 1954 Baron Maurice de Rothschild had consigned for sale to Rosenberg & Stiebel in New York three Persian manuscripts. The manuscripts remained unsold for several years, and upon Maurice's death his son, Baron Edmond, became the consignor. The two smaller of them, one of which was the *Gulistan of Sa'di*, finally sold to John Goelet, who by 1974 had the *Gulistan* on loan to the Houghton Library at Harvard University. Although the *Gulistan* contained only three miniatures, they were of great beauty and importance. One of them dated from 1486 and was attributed to Behzad, the greatest of the Persian painters.

The other manuscript, perhaps the supreme treasure in Persian art, the *Shahnameh,* or *Book of Kings,* containing 258 miniatures, was sold in 1959 to Arthur A. Houghton, chairman of the Metropolitan Museum board. It became known as the Houghton *Shahnameh.*

The great manuscript had been commissioned for the royal library by the Persian ruler Shah Tahmasp early in his reign, which began in 1524. It was conceived in the 1520s, was actively worked on during the 1530s, and was added to in the 1540s. The book tells the story of the Persian empire from its birth in legend until its collapse in the middle of the seventh century. Edmond de Rothschild's asking price was $450,000. The Metropolitan Museum found the price too high, and Rosenberg & Stiebel persuaded Rothschild to reduce it to $360,000 for the museum, but they still did not act. Finally, Rosenberg & Stiebel succeeded in selling it to Houghton for the $360,000 figure, but payable in installments, one half by October 26, 1959, and the balance by the end of that year. Edmond de Rothschild cabled approval of the terms. Stuart Cary Welch, a professor at Harvard and curator of Islamic art at the Fogg Museum, acted as advisor to both Goelet and Houghton in their purchases.

In a rush to find something for the Iranians, when I initially phoned Falk I also contacted Welch, knowing at the time only that he was an authority in the field, not that he had been involved in the sale of the Rothschild manuscripts. Welch subsequently tried to take advantage of my ignorance by bringing to my office for sale a Persian miniature that even I recognized as inferior.

The Iranian ambassador to the United Nations in the mid-1970s was Fereydoun Hoveyda. He was a painter much committed to artists and

Sultan Muhammad
(assisted by Mir
Sayyid'Ali), *The
Death of Zah-Hak,*
circa 1522–40
A folio 37 verso,
from the Houghton
Shahnameh

© Christie's Images, Ltd.,
1999

the arts. He and his German wife were known for their jolly soirées at the Iranian ambassador's residence on Fifth Avenue and Eighty-fourth Street, with extravagant wine and food, and a glittering if somewhat *retardataire* guest list. I still remember with some horror spilling red wine on Paulette Goddard's white gown at a Hoveyda dinner party. I don't think Andy Warhol missed a single one of those events.

When Falk phoned me later in the autumn of 1974, it was the Goelet *Gulistan* that he was authorizing me to sell. The manuscript was at that time in safekeeping at Harvard. The price was $400,000 net to Goelet, and Falk had conveyed to me the authority to offer it to my prospective client, the government of Iran. My agreement with Falk was that we would split the commission between us. I had no idea what the manuscript was worth and I decided to play it safe and offer it to Iran for $450,000. If successful, Toby Falk and I would each earn $25,000. It was not, after all, the commission on this object I was after, but entrée to the Iranians' European paintings program.

The *Gulistan* seemed exactly what I needed, and I phoned Ambassador Hoveyda, arranged a meeting at his office on Third Avenue, and gave him the details. He was excited. He called back soon after to arrange a viewing of the manuscript for the empress's representative. Goelet, however, did not want it viewed at Harvard because he did not want Harvard to know the manuscript was being sold. Since it would take some time to arrange with Harvard its withdrawal and transport to New York, a meeting was arranged several weeks later at the Goelet family offices in the Seagram Building. I left with my wife on a trip to California and planned to return in early December for the viewing of the *Gulistan* with the empress's representatives and the ambassador. I've learned that you can never count on anything in the art business—there is as much intrigue and backstabbing as in any business in the world, and to worsen matters, the objects are unique and irreplaceable—but about this particular deal I was as confident as I've ever been. The manuscript was of singular importance, the Iranians' pockets were as deep as the oceans, and as far as I could tell, the price was reasonable. The Iranians were excited enough to bring a number of dignitaries together in New York for the meeting.

While in San Diego, I got a phone call from my office. Goelet's secretary had phoned to say the meeting was canceled and the manuscript was not for sale. Mr. Goelet had left for Europe and could not be reached. No explanation, no excuse for the Iranians. I was far worse off than if I had never offered them anything. I phoned Toby Falk, who knew Goelet, but he could provide no explanation. I had too many battle scars from seventeen years in the business not to know when a deal had been glitched by somebody, but by whom or why, I could not guess.

I later learned from Toby Falk, who at first had been reluctant to tell me, that it was Stuart Cary Welch himself, the Harvard professor, who, having learned of the impending meeting and sale, contacted Goelet, convinced him that I had no experience with Persian art, and persuaded him to consign the manuscript instead to a protégé of Welch's, Terrence McInerney, whose employment Welch had arranged with Robert Light, a Boston drawings dealer. Welch then sold the *Gulistan* and Goelet's other Rothschild manuscript to a London friend, Aboulala Sudavar, who still owns them and now has the *Gulistan* on loan to the Freer Gallery in Washington. When Falk told me who was responsible, I could not understand Welch's motive. Perhaps it was his long-standing involvement with these particular manuscripts and his desire to officiate over any change in their ownership. As it turned out, Welch's derailment of my *Gulistan* deal was to have more devastating results than any of us could have imagined, particularly someone who cared as much about the Houghton *Shahnameh* as Welch supposedly did.

I phoned Hoveyda and made what apologies I could. He was genuinely upset: "What will I tell my queen?" I cannot stand dealing with "runners" who abound in the art business and do not control what they offer, and who at the end of the day usually can't produce. I refused to allow myself to be thought of in this category by the Iranians, or anyone else for that matter. I somehow had to figure out an alternative, if for no other reason than for the sake of my pride and reputation.

Desperate for a substitute for the Goelet *Gulistan,* I thought of the other ex-Rothschild manuscript, the Houghton *Shahnameh.* Arthur Houghton had unstitched the ancient binding in 1970 and donated 76 leaves, containing 78 miniatures, to the Metropolitan Museum in honor of the 2,500th anniversary of the Persian empire. He intended to give or bequeath the balance, 180 leaves of miniatures, the original binding, which had been rebacked in the nineteenth century, and the entire 1,006 pages of text on 503 leaves, intending that the manuscript be ultimately reunified. He did not donate the whole manuscript in 1970 because he had no need for the entire tax deduction that year, and because he was so attached to the greatest of the miniatures that he wanted to retain them for his lifetime, framed, on the wall of a "Persian Room" he had created at his home, Wye Plantation, on the eastern shore of Maryland, near Chesapeake Bay. In 1998 Wye was to emerge from its former obscurity as the repository of one of the world's great rare book and art collections when it served as the site of the historic Israel-Palestine Peace Accord. Houghton later confessed to me that the seventy-eight miniatures he had donated to the Metropolitan were the least important, leaving the best to be reunited later. It was the Metropolitan's exhibition of these miniatures in 1972 and John Canaday's August 27 *New York Times* review, "A King's Book of Kings, or, The Sleeping Beauty"—in which he called the exhibition "perfect," a "triumph"—as well as the museum's publication of a sumptuous coffee-table book, *A King's Book of Kings,* that had first brought the manuscript to my attention.

Everyone, most particularly the Metropolitan, knew the balance of the manuscript was destined for the museum. Securing it for the Iranians was an impossible project. Arthur Houghton was a former chairman of the museum, and I didn't even know him. But another thing I have learned about the art business is that if you think something is impossible, one day someone else will think of it and do it. What had I to lose?

It was clear that the Houghton *Shahnameh* ought to be reunified in its original binding. Among the many miniatures, created by a number of artists over a span of many years, some were clearly masterpieces, but in a museum as rich as the Metropolitan, the complete manuscript would merely add a large group of Persian miniatures to the Metropolitan's already substantial holdings. In Iran, however, this would be the greatest national treasure. If a sale could be arranged, and couched in the proper terms, it could serve as a gesture from our country to theirs. In 1974 the American government was making a great effort, for military reasons and because of a potential oil shortage, to cement relations with Iran. If Iran was interested, Arthur Houghton could get a high price, and I could earn a big commission.

When I phoned Houghton, I frankly expected, if I was put through to him at all, to be cut off by a crusty old WASP. Instead, he turned out to be about the friendliest stranger I had ever encountered. We set a date for Monday, March 31, 1975. He confirmed the invitation in a letter dated March 24, enclosing a map and inviting me for lunch and to spend the night.

I flew to Dulles from La Guardia the morning of the thirty-first, rented a car, and arrived at Wye Plantation at ten in the morning. The Houghtons were charming, and it very quickly became "Richard" and "Arthur and Nina." Nina Houghton was much younger than Arthur and very intelligent and attractive. Arthur showed me through the library, which, in addition to his famous rare book collection, included the large series of Fragonard drawings for *Orlando Furioso* and a spirited little Rembrandt, *Head of an Old Man,* the smallest oil painting by the artist. Then Arthur showed me, with considerable pleasure and pride, his "Per-

Rembrandt van Rijn,
Head of an Old Man,
1633

Private collection

sian Room." These finest of the *Shahnameh* paintings were magnificent. The walls were alive with action and ablaze with color.

I digress here with the story of what happened to the little Rembrandt I saw that morning at Wye Plantation. In 1984, nine years after my visit to the Houghtons in Maryland, the Rembrandt, *Portrait of a Girl,* came up for sale at Sotheby's in London. It was consigned by the Paine family of Boston, a member of which was my friend Diana Paine. I discussed the painting with Saul Steinberg, and he authorized me to bid up to $8 million. I flew to London and found the Rembrandt in fine condition. At the sale, I was pitted against a Citibank representative, and when the bidding reached $10 million, I stopped, having exceeded Saul's limit by $2 million. Citibank's bidding technique was not sophisticated enough to fool anyone, and I was certain they were prepared to go on, and that if

I continued, I would not only not get the Rembrandt but would wreck the Rembrandt market in the process. At that point, the highest price ever achieved for a work of art was £2.2 million for the Leicester Codex on December 12, 1980. I knew Steinberg well enough to know that he would have wanted me to go on, but my job is to read my clients' minds, and at the same time save them from mistakes. My policy is that if they don't want my initiative, they should hire a robot. The final price of the Paine Rembrandt, which I had underbid, was $10,523,000.

I went back to Claridge's and telephoned Arthur Houghton. I wanted to reach him before the London Rembrandt news hit the press and started to confuse the market. After all, had it not been for my underbidding, the Paine Rembrandt would have sold for about $4 million. I succeeded in making a deal with Arthur for the little Rembrandt I had seen on my visit nine years before, and arranged to send someone from my office down there with a certified check to pick it up, though Arthur hadn't asked for one. Then I phoned Saul. He said, "Did we get it?" and when I told him what had happened at the auction, he was desperate: "I should have gone to the sale myself! I wouldn't have stopped!" I said, "Saul, that's why you shouldn't have been there. We would just have spun our wheels, spoiled the Rembrandt market, and roiled the whole art market. But I may have a surprise for you when I get back to New York next week." "What is it?" Saul demanded. "I'm not telling you. You'll see when I get back." He kept insisting I tell him, and I kept refusing.

My assistant phoned me in London to tell me that the Rembrandt had been fetched from Wye Plantation and was safely delivered to my office. I returned from London the next Wednesday, December 17, in a heavy rainstorm, went directly from Kennedy Airport to my office, and picked up the Rembrandt, which was still in the leather case Andrew Mellon had had made for it, and in which he had passed it on to his son, Paul, and Paul in turn to Arthur Houghton.

When I arrived, Gayfryd and Saul were still upstairs dressing for a dinner, so I took the little Rembrandt into the library and set it up in its case on a table. Saul came down, buttoning his shirt, spotted the Rembrandt from across the room, grabbed me and kissed me on the cheek, then rang Gayfryd upstairs. "Honey, come downstairs! We just bought a Rembrandt!" I hadn't even quoted a price. "I don't care if you're not

Michiel Sweerts, *Plague in an Ancient City,* circa 1650

The Los Angeles County Museum of Art. Gift of The Ahmanson Foundation

dressed! Come downstairs!" I've met few collectors in over forty years in the business with Saul's eye and his passion.

In 1995 Saul suffered a stroke at the premature age of fifty-four, and he decided to sell eight paintings, among them the great Michiel Sweerts *Plague in an Ancient City,* from the Cook Collection (at the Los Angeles County Museum) I had forced him to buy at a Christie's sale on July 6, 1984, and, surprisingly, his beloved little Rembrandt. The sale took place at Sotheby's in New York on January 30, 1997, and the Rembrandt brought a total price of $2,972,500, more than twice what he had paid, but less than I had previously been offered privately by another client, a friend of Saul's.

Back at Wye Plantation that sunny spring day in March 1975, I made my case to Arthur Houghton, without suggesting for a moment that he was wrong to have dismantled it in the first place, that the *Shahnameh* ought to be reunited; that as a national treasure of Iran, it should be returned; that if a sale to the Iranian government were consummated, it would be seen as a significant goodwill gesture not only on Arthur

Houghton's part but on our government's as well, and that this would be in our national interest; and, finally, that the manuscript would bring a very great deal of money. I was surprised at how quickly Arthur warmed to my idea, and by the end of the afternoon he had made me his agent in the sale. He also agreed with the balance of my project: that once a deal with Iran was consummated, he would give his blessing, as the donor, to an exchange by the Metropolitan of their seventy-eight miniatures for important Persian objects in Iran's possession, so that the *Shahnameh* could be reunited. I had a sense that Arthur regretted having dismantled the manuscript and would have liked to see his deed undone. He agreed with me that the whole project was to be kept secret, but most particularly the part involving the Metropolitan Museum swap. Not only was the then director, Thomas Hoving, acquisitive, but he loved controversy and the limelight, and was politically volatile. Hoving was not one to be counted on to honor the integrity of a work of art, to honor a donor's wishes, or to be involved in delicate diplomacy. We were in agreement on all points. Arthur said he would have a contract drafted, and true to his word, the draft arrived in a few days.

As for the price Arthur had set, $28,500,000, which included a $3,500,000 commission for me, I didn't flinch. The Iranians could afford it. It wasn't even the price of a single one of the armada of F-16s we were flogging them. My attitude about great art has always been that the printing press is closed, but for paper money it isn't, they just keep printing away, so however many pieces of green paper it takes to get a great object, it's cheap. Arthur asked me to meet him in New York to sign the contract the following week at the Corning Glass building at 715 Fifth Avenue, where his office was located, and where the ninety-seven miniatures that were not hanging at Wye Plantation and the text and binding were held in safekeeping.

I phoned Hoveyda to tell him the news, that not only could I now make amends for embarrassing him with the *Gulistan,* but I was able to offer to return to Iran its greatest treasure. He asked me to put the proposal in written form so he could forward it in a diplomatic pouch to his government in Tehran. I sent Houghton a draft, and he replied with a note suggesting a slight change in my reference to stubbing my toe on the Goelet manuscript, and making more tacit my idea of ultimately effecting a swap with the Metropolitan.

Arthur and I convened for our meeting at the Corning Glass building on April 11 and signed the contract. In it, he stated that the remaining miniatures were his "greatest treasures," that he had "no plans to part with them during [his] lifetime," that he had "long intended to bequeath them in [his] will to The Metropolitan and other American Museums." He went on: "I have thought about this and can clearly understand why this masterpiece of Iranian art should again be a national treasure of Iran, returned to the country of its origin as a supreme example of its great heritage, accomplishments and traditions. . . . [A]fter deep considera- tion of the entire situation, I am prepared to give you—and you alone— the exclusive right to offer all that I continue to own of my 'Shah-nameh' to the Government of Iran or one of its national institutions during the next sixty days. . . . I have decided, after most careful consideration, to place a price of 28,500,000 dollars (net to me after commissions and any expenses of the transaction) for all of the manuscript that I continue to own—the 180 miniatures, text, and binding. That is the lowest price at which you may offer on my behalf, under the circumstances previously noted." The asking price was later changed in the contract to the $28,500,000 figure, with net proceeds of $25,000,000 to Houghton and the balance of $3,500,000 as my commission. The contract was duly signed by Arthur Houghton and myself.

Houghton had asked to meet Iran's ambassador to the United Nations, Fereydoun Hoveyda, after the contract signing. We went over from the Corning Glass building to the Iranian Mission at 622 Third Avenue. Houghton and Hoveyda both seemed impressed with each other and the seriousness of the project. All along, I presented Arthur as someone interested in seeing the manuscript go where he thought it should go, pointing out that he had little interest in the money and cer- tainly no need for it.

I look back on all this now with some surprise at my obliviousness to the politics of Iran and the nature of our government's interests there. By the spring of 1975, I had been militant for twelve years about our involvement in Southeast Asia. I had clear ideas about our support, in the name of democracy, of antidemocratic dictators everywhere—in Central America, South America, Africa—regardless of what crimes they committed against their people in the name of anti-Communism. I was aware not only of our sponsorship of these gangsters, and of our efforts to eliminate their opponents, like Allende, but of how this sponsorship promoted the revolutions and regimes we most desperately feared. Yet about Iran and the CIA's antics there, I knew little. Even had I known more, I still would have wanted the Houghton manuscript to return home.

My formal proposal was delivered to Hoveyda on April 15, in time to be included in a pouch to Tehran. It gave the Iranian government an option on the manuscript at a price of $28,500,000 until June 11. The proposal carried a stipulation insisted on by Houghton, that should the Iranian government acquire the manuscript, they would allow to proceed its forthcoming publication in two volumes by Harvard University; and two stipulations of mine, that in any news release our firm be named as intermediary in a transaction of which I would have been inordinately proud, and that we be the exclusive agent in any future deal with the Metropolitan for the miniatures in its possession. I frankly couldn't see how, with all the money the Iranians were spending on art, they could turn this manuscript down. I thought sixty days was more than enough to see us through the deal.

A month passed with no word from Iran. I had expected celebration in Tehran, and a prompt and jubilant reply. Instead, my masterstroke seemed to disappear down a black hole. Notwithstanding the fact that his brother was prime minister, Hoveyda knew no more than I did about what had happened to my proposal after it dropped into the pouch. I had a queasy feeling that Fereydoun was really out of it, and a hideous suspicion that I may have done this all wrong. My panic mounted each day that went by without word. Houghton granted me a thirty-day extension on the contract, until July 11.

Finally, the news hit the press of a state visit to Washington by the Empress and Shah of Iran in the third week of May. I also learned that two friends of mine were going to see the empress. Barbara Walters was interviewing her on television, and Robin Duke was meeting with her to discuss Iran's program to control population as well as the world population crisis in general, with which they were both concerned, at Blair House, where the shah and empress were staying. By now in extremis, I decided to breach the secrecy in which I had shrouded the project and recruit Barbara and Robin to my flagging cause.

Barbara Walters agreed to mention the Houghton *Shahnameh* to the empress, but asked me to put the details on paper so she could remember them. I then phoned Robin Duke, and she also agreed to mention the subject. I warned her that I had asked Barbara to do the same thing. I then sent over to the Metropolitan Museum bookstore for several copies of the sumptuous coffee-table book the museum had published on the manuscript, *A King's Book of Kings.* I had the books delivered to Barbara and Robin, along with confidential letters explaining the project. The day of Robin's meeting, I was going to Washington on another mission and found myself on the shuttle with her. We went over the scenario and I dropped her off at Blair House, with gratitude for her help. I phoned Barbara and Robin a few days later, and they both confirmed that they had mentioned the project to the empress. Barbara told me that Ardeshir Zahedi, the Iranian ambassador to the United States, who was present at her interview, would contact me.

More than a week passed with no word from Zahedi. The clock on my contract was ticking loudly. Finally, on May 21, I decided to write Zahedi and the empress herself, who was still in the United States. My letters were addressed to the Iranian embassy, and with them I enclosed copies of the book. When another week passed with no word from Zahedi, I phoned him, and when I couldn't get through to him but was passed to an assistant, I became seriously worried. The assistant told me to contact Karim Pasha Bahadori, the empress's chamberlain, at the New York Hilton.

On June 4 I phoned Richard Herner, a colleague who at that time ran Colnaghi's, the venerable London art-dealing firm owned by Jacob Rothschild, a cousin of Edmond de Rothschild, to find out about Bahadori. Richard had done business with the Iranians. He explained that Bahadori was head of the empress's secretariat; that he was arrogant and insecure; that he knew nothing about art; that he was very influential; that he was close to a dealer named Mahboubian, with whom I had no doubt he would discuss the Houghton *Shahnameh;* and, finally, that he, Richard, did not know whether Bahadori was "on the take." I hung up the phone more confused than before.

I phoned the Hilton the same day and was put through to Bahadori. I assumed he had been briefed about the *Shahnameh* by Zahedi, but he seemed not to recognize my name or know anything about the manuscript. "Your Excellency," I said, "I'm calling at the suggestion of Ambassador Zahedi about the Houghton *Shahnameh.*" "Is this something you are offering for sale?" "Yes, in a sense it is." "Well then, perhaps this should be taken up with our Commercial Office." I said, "Well, it's not exactly a commercial transaction. Mr. Houghton's concerns are not primarily commercial. He wants to see this treasure return to its country of origin. You may know of Mr. Houghton." "Ah," said Bahadori, "I see a letter here about this matter. Mr. Houghton wishes to make a gift of this object to my country." From what he said, it was apparent that Barbara Walters must have handed to the empress, and she to Zahedi or Bahadori, my very private letter of information and instruction. I panicked and waved for my file. Did I in any way infer, in my effusiveness about Houghton's lofty motives, that this was a gift? My assistant handed me the file, I found the letter, and there it was: "offer for sale to the Government of Iran," and the line was underlined. I was obviously the mouse and Bahadori the cat, and he was playing with me before he leapt. "Well, Your Excellency," I said, "you'll notice that the letter does say that Mr. Houghton is offering the manuscript for sale. I hardly think your great country, with its vast wealth, has need of charity from a private American citizen."

Then the cat leapt. "Tell me, Mr. Feigen, if I wished to offer an object to your National Gallery, would you think it appropriate for me to mention it to President Ford?" That was it. My deal had hit the wall. "Well, Your Excellency, I take your point. But there is a difference. Our National Gallery is a private foundation. Despite its name. And I believe your museum is a national institution. But, Your Excellency, I am unsophisticated in these matters. I would be most grateful for your guidance if you could spare me a few minutes." Was it too late to pay him off? Bahadori said he would review the proposal and contact me.

I spoke with Houghton on the fourth and wrote him on the fifth, bringing him up to date; asking him to confirm my commission arrangement, particularly since I might have to make a payoff; and asking for an understanding in the event of a sale to Iran resulting from my efforts but consummated after the expiration of our contract. I said I would phone the following week if I needed an extension of the time limit. On Monday afternoon, June 9, Bahadori phoned. He said that the price I had quoted was "ridiculous," that the tax appraisal for the Metropolitan gift was $4 million, and that any purchase for Iran would be by a private foundation. Clearly he had spoken to his friend Mahboubian, the "connected" New York dealer who, not having a piece of the deal, had spiked it. He asked me to send him a letter outlining the terms, specifically not a photocopy of the Hoveyda letter, and I sent the letter the same day. In a letter also dated the ninth, Houghton formally extended my contract until July 11 and confirmed our understanding about the $28.5 million price and $3.5 million commission. I heard nothing more from Bahadori. A letter, dated July 17, finally arrived from the Iranian embassy, signed by Fatola Samly, counselor for educational affairs. "Dear Mr. Feigen," it said, "The Chief of Her Majesty's Secretariat advises us that purchase of the miniatures, and other parts of the *Shah-nameh* of Shah Tahmasp may not be considered at the present time."

In later months, when discretion had become academic, Iranian friends laughed when I told them my story. What an idiot I was! How naïve! Didn't I know that Bahadori had to be paid off, that not a single object entered the empress's collection or the national museum on which he did not collect? $1 million "baksheesh" of my $3.5 million would have sealed the deal. It also would have preserved a masterpiece intact.

The only happy part of the otherwise sad epilogue is that even before the revolution toppled the shah, Bahadori fled into exile in Switzerland in disgrace, and, as far as we know, is still hiding there. My ill-fated project having planted in Arthur Houghton's mind the alternative of selling the miniatures rather than bequeathing them to the Metropolitan, he consigned seven of them to an auction at Christie's on November 17, 1976. The seven were cross-sectional in quality. They brought a total of £863,500, or $1,416,140. One of the miniatures, the first lot, brought $505,000. Using the total price of the seven miniatures as an average, the value of the 180 miniatures covered by my contract would have been $36.4 million, plus the considerable value of the 1,006 pages of text and the binding. The $28.5 million price was a bargain.

On November 17 I phoned the Iranian embassy in Washington and was referred to the assistant to Dr. G. Kazemian, minister counselor for cultural affairs, who in turn suggested I write Kazemian, which I did the same day. I asked whether his government, its original rejection having been based on price, might, in light of the prices realized at Christie's, be interested in acquiring the remaining 173 miniatures, the text and the binding. Kazemian replied on the twenty-fourth: "We have received instructions from Tehran to inform Mr. Houghton that [the] Iranian Government will not be in position to buy the Shahnameh."

The full *Shahnameh* was lavishly published in two volumes by Harvard in 1981. The door having finally been slammed shut by Iran, Houghton had proceeded to sell privately through dealers a further 40 miniatures, leaving him with 133 as of November 27, 1985, when an appraisal was made that totaled $19,865,000. In 1987 Houghton asked me to appraise a Guardi, Stubbs, and Cranach and advise him on prospects for sale, so I visited Wye Plantation again in August 1987. In his letter of August 4, Arthur wrote, "If there is action on the Persian miniatures please get in touch with Jim Nelson. He is fully authorized to negotiate for me. . . . [A]t the present time we are dealing with no one but you." A week later, I made offers of the remaining miniatures to contacts I had established in Kuwait, Dubai, and Abu Dhabi during a two-week stay in the Gulf in 1978. Nothing happened. Arthur wrote me again on August 14, just before leaving on an Alaskan cruise, offering a set of the Harvard books to any purchaser I might find for the remaining miniatures.

Early in October, I met in New York with Donna Stein, former curator of the Museum of Contemporary Art in Tehran. I wanted to find out if she knew what had become of the modern European paintings in the collection since the revolution. I wondered if some kind of swap could be engineered for what remained of the Houghton manuscript. Stein had no links with the present regime or information about the current status of the collection. She wanted, however, to collaborate with me in the sale of the remaining Houghton miniatures, though she did not seem optimistic about prospects. By her count, 51 of the miniatures had been sold up to that point, leaving Houghton with 129. Stein wrote me on July 21, 1988, saying that a client of hers was interested in buying the binding of the *Shahnameh* if I could get a price from Houghton. I didn't have the stomach to even mention to Arthur this obscene dismemberment. Stein wrote me again on this subject on September 14.

The sales continued. Fourteen more of the Houghton miniatures were sold at Christie's in London on October 11, 1988, for a total of $1.7 million. Arthur Houghton died on April 3, 1990, at the age of eighty-three. At his death, his estate still held 120 of the miniatures, the text and the binding. Houghton's executors asked Oliver Hoare, a London dealer, to sell what was left of the cannibalized manuscript. A value of $20 million was placed on the package. Then somehow the idea of a swap materialized. Though I had often tried, as a citizen of an enemy country I had never been able to find a contact in Tehran. As Souren Melikian reported in the April 27, 1996, *International Herald Tribune:* "Complex discussions took place, often interrupted. Eventually, an improbable agreement was struck. The Shah-Nameh in its reduced state with an arbitrary valuation of $20 million would go to the Museum of Contemporary Art in Tehran, which would part with a de Kooning, *Woman III,* on which an equally arbitrary valuation of $20 million had been pinned. The exchange took place in the international zone of the Vienna airport in a cloak-and-dagger atmosphere. Mehdi Hojjat, an architect who founded the Iranian Cultural Heritage Organization, without whom the transaction would not have been possible, stepped off an unmarked jet sent by Tehran. The van in which the cardboard boxes enclosing the Shah-Nameh folios were stashed was attached with chains to the aircraft. While the de Kooning was taken out of the jet and checked by a Swiss dealer and expert, Hojjat sat in the van supervising the unloading and reloading of the boxes into the aircraft. . . . The Shah-Nameh is on view, in its mutilated state, in the Museum of Contemporary Art in Tehran, and the de Kooning is now the property of David Geffen."

An epilogue, perhaps not even the last one, to the Iranians' 1975 valuation, took place on Tuesday, April 23, 1996. Four of the miniatures came up for sale at Sotheby's in London. These four had been sold by Houghton through Agnew's to the British Rail Pension Fund after the first auction at Christie's in 1976. The four miniatures now realized a total of $3 million. I had offered the Iranians all 180, the text and the binding, for $28.5 million, and Bahadori, presumably advised by his expert friend Mahboubian, said the whole thing was worth only $4 million.

This is a story that could have had a happy ending instead of a tragic one. It's true that my plan for the Houghton *Shahnameh* started out as just a business deal. But if it had succeeded, not only would I have turned a profit, but the great manuscript would now almost certainly be reunited in Tehran instead of scattered all over the world. In this dismemberment I was an accomplice—an unwitting one, but an accomplice nonetheless.

Had Stuart Cary Welch acted more like the academic I imagined him to be than a dealer, deliberately derailing my sale of the Goelet *Gulistan,* I would

Willem de Kooning,
Woman III, 1952

Collection of David
Geffen, Los Angeles

never have approached Arthur Houghton for his *Shahnameh,* and he would probably have bequeathed the rest of it to the Metropolitan. Had Bahadori cared more about his country's cultural patrimony than lining his own saddlebags, the deal would have been done and the manuscript would be where it belongs. . . . Or if I had been street-smart about baksheesh and paid Bahadori off . . .

THE POWER OF THE PRESS

When the "Power Moves" issue of *Art & Auction* (December 1996) arrived, I was surprised to find myself mentioned in it. I had made an effort the past few years to stay clear of the press. I had learned two lessons, in succession. First, that appearing in the press in a purely social context may get you up front at Le Cirque but does nothing for business, at least my business.

Second, getting your name out there, even in a more serious vein, for purely business reasons, like making art "discoveries," may indeed give a modest boost to business—free advertising—but seems to irritate everyone else so much that in the long run it's not worth it. In any case, I firmly believe in the power of the press, and in using it, to get certain things done. I find that sometimes it's the only way. Politicians, for instance, rarely pay attention to anything else.

Well aware of the press's power, I was nonetheless astonished at the effects of all the coverage of Ray Johnson's suicide on Friday the thirteenth, January 1995. This of course was not a case of the press being used, unless it was used by Ray himself. Ray Johnson was an artist of the first rank in his generation, the generation of Johns, Rosenquist, Oldenburg, Warhol, Rauschenberg, and Lichtenstein. The artists all so considered him, and it was they themselves who were the main collectors of his work. To the public at large he remained unknown. This was partly his own fault, partly luck. During the years until 1967, when he fled to Locust Valley, Long Island, after his friend Andy Warhol was shot, Ray was more or less accessible. But he was so strange, tenacious, and demanding in his rela-

The author and Ray Johnson installing *A Lot of Shirley Temple Postcards* exhibition at Richard L. Feigen & Company, New York, 1968

Photograph: William S. Wilson

tionships, and at the same time distant, that he remained a shadowy, "beat" figure. The bad luck part of it was that during those years when the sixties stars soared into the firmament and Ray reluctantly submitted to gallery representation, he was not with the right gallery at the right time. There were politics involved in those years, as there are still, and Ray Johnson was no politician.

The 1960s saw the unfortunate birth, like *Rosemary's Baby*, of the artist superstar. In those days there was a lot of socializing and communication between the artists. They almost all lived around Coenties Slip and Front Street at the tip of Manhattan, and, later in the decade, between Houston and Canal streets. They had not yet achieved the affluence that would later scatter them from the Hamptons and upstate New York to the Caribbean and the west coast of Florida.

The Vietnam War boom began to heat up in the early sixties. The resulting fortunes spawned power and glamour and hangers-on. Ethel and Robert Scull were the first of these to discover that, even with nothing more than Ethel's father's taxi fleet, "Scull's Angels," power could be garnered from an art collection, particularly if the artists came with the art. So the chosen artists, those represented by the right dealers—generally those who, like their predecessors Betty Parsons and Charles Egan, most resembled artists themselves and showed no interest in money, notably Richard Bellamy, Leo Castelli, and Eleanor Ward—were scooped up, invited to wildly publicized parties, and lionized into superstars. By not only buying their paintings but dragging the artists into their social milieu, climbers like the Sculls acquired power and the artists acquired fame. The artists wanted a market for their work, which was almost nonexistent at the outset, and people like the Sculls provided one.

Ray Johnson, although very much a charter member of this vanguard scene, didn't really fit into the social and commercial part of it. He never wanted a real gallery affiliation. Nobody, no dealer and certainly no socially ambitious collector, could hold on to this strange, mercurial personality. So, with all the credentials in the world, he never became a superstar, though he undoubtedly would have liked to have been one.

For twenty-eight years, starting in 1967, Ray lived in what he called "the Pink House" out in Locust Valley, recruiting members all over the world for his "Correspondance [*sic*] School," arriving from time to time in Manhattan, shaven-headed in studded leather and jeans, with his sidekick, Toby Spieselman. No one knew what work he was doing, if any. No one was invited to his house. Exhibition proposals were deflected rather than refused outright. The closest he came with us was to phone my colleague Frances Beatty with an offer of a show with nothing at all in it, what Ray called "a nothing." He had become even stranger than he had been on September 28, 1969, when he asked me to pay for sixty-foot-long linked hot dogs and an airplane to drop them on Ward's Island. The bill arrived. At least in those days a plane was only $100 an hour.

Over the years, with Ray some twenty-seven miles away in Locust Valley, unwilling to receive visitors or show his work, his telephone conversations becoming more protracted and bizarre, contact with him dwindled. So it was odd indeed when, on January 6, 1995, I was told Ray

Johnson was on the phone. Ray said in his high monotone, "Richard, would you like to buy the *James Dean* collage?" This was one of his most important works, a seminal piece of Pop art, executed in 1957, one of the first works by any artist to employ the image of a popular movie star. This from an artist who refused to exhibit, let alone sell, even his most recent work. I said, "Of course I would, Ray." "How much would you pay for it?" I was baffled. Over the thirty-odd years I had known Ray Johnson, I had never heard questions remotely like these. I was afraid to insult him with a price lower than what he considered to be the *James Dean*'s value—whatever that was—or frankly higher than I would have to pay if he really was willing to sell it. There was no established market for Johnson's work, just a few aficionados who would discover one from time to time in some small auction, much to the others' jealousy. I said, "Ray, I would really like to have it. Let me give it some thought. I'll try to figure out what it's worth and call you." Still not knowing quite what to say, I left for London on Thursday, January 12. On Saturday my assistant, Sam Trower, phoned me in London to tell me that Ray had killed himself the day before by jumping off the low Sag Harbor bridge into the icy water. Two teenage girls had spotted a figure in black, backstroking out to sea. They looked for a policeman but hadn't been able to find one and went off to the movies.

The *James Dean* call was only one of many Ray made that day. He phoned Frances Beatty and said, "Well, I think you'll really be able to do your show now, Frances. . . . I'm finished with the *nothings* I've been doing for years and I think I'm going to do *something*." For my part, I was plagued by my failure to get right back to Ray with a price for *James Dean*. Did the delay further depress him? When the shock of his death subsided a bit, though, I realized that he had done what he intended, to execute the ultimate performance piece. I can only suppose that Ray resented the obscurity in which he had lived all those years while his contemporaries soared into stardom like Ray's own movie heroes. Yet he had prevented anyone from helping to make him known by showing his work.

When Ray's body was fished out of the icy water the afternoon of the fourteenth, the police found that he had rented a car in Locust Valley, driven out to Sag Harbor, and checked into the Baron's Cove Inn. Over the weeks that followed, there was an avalanche of newspaper and magazine articles about Ray, his work and his death. They all referred to him as "enigmatic," "a famous unknown artist," an "engaging recluse"; his death a "riddle," his "final work of art." As Harry Hurt III titled his *New York* magazine article on March 6, "A Performance-Art Death," and described how "Legendary (and legendarily unknown) artist Ray Johnson plotted his apparent suicide like one of his practical jokes. Now he's a celebrity." Like the celebrities Ray celebrated in his work.

When finally, accompanied by the lawyer hired to represent the eleven cousins unearthed as his heirs, I gained the access to Ray's house which I had never had during his lifetime, I was shocked by the plastic bags on the table, into which the police had put his belongings from the motel, and amazed by the parallels with Joseph Cornell's little house on Utopia Parkway in Queens. The only differences seemed to be Mrs. Cornell's touches. It occurred to me that if Joseph had lived alone, or even with his brother Robert, his house might have been just like Ray's, or if Ray's mother had lived there, "the Pink House" might have been just like Utopia Parkway. In any event, I resolved then that I would not let happen to Ray's environment what had happened to Joseph's: to go unrecorded, at the expense of all the doctoral dissertations and biographies that were sure to come. So in the weeks that followed, we had every inch of the place, outside and in, videotaped and photographed, and every item in the house methodically inventoried. In the process, all kinds of hidden messages for people turned up, as if part of a macabre treasure hunt.

The print coverage of Ray's death and of the subsequent memorial exhibition (Richard L. Feigen & Company, New York, April 27–June 16, 1996) fills a thick loose-leaf binder. There was a radio program on which his friends were interviewed. A documentary film is being produced. Crowds like none I had known in forty years in the business poured in throughout the exhibition. A major touring museum retrospective began in 1999.

The press spawned another celebrity in August 1995. My Chicago gallery, Feigen Inc., whose cutting-edge program, although enthusiastically subscribed to by me, was determined by the young codirectors, Lance Kinz and Susan Reynolds, had opened a summer group exhibition on June 23. Among the twenty-four artists in the show, there was a

Gregory Green, *10,000 Doses,* 1995

young Brooklyn conceptual sculptor, Gregory Green. Green, a pacifist, makes sculptures and performances *about* violence. His works are not themselves violent, and although they resemble tools of violence, like pipe, letter, and suitcase bombs, an atomic bomb, a pirate radio station, they contain no explosives and are in no way dangerous. On July 21 an article about Green appeared in *The Reader,* a weekly newspaper, and one of his *Suitcase Bomb* pieces was reproduced. On July 25 two bomb and arson squad detectives came into the gallery, followed the next day by Commander Grubisic of the bomb and arson squad and a colleague. Kinz explained Green's work and thought he had satisfied the police on the explosives score.

In the same exhibition, however, was another piece of Gregory Green's, *10,000 Doses.* This sculpture was *about* LSD and radical 1960s "counterculture empowerment strategies." It consisted of twelve permanently sealed laboratory bottles, filled with an amber-colored fluid, set in two rows on an industrial table. The piece was placed in the front of the gallery, and on the gallery's storefront window was printed a four-foot-high enlarged and altered recipe for LSD from *The Anarchist Cookbook.* You could see the sculpture through the recipe on the window.

On Thursday morning, August 10, the phone rang in my country house in Katonah, New York. It was Susan Reynolds, in a panic. "The gallery is being raided. The place is full of police. The street is full of police cars. They've arrested Lance and confiscated *10,000 Doses.*" This was Chicago's Organized Crime and Narcotics Division, armed with a search warrant.

"Susan," I said, "calm down. Just get the phone numbers of the *Sun Times,* the *Tribune,* and the four network television stations and call me back. I'll take care of it." I knew the power of the press. I also knew Chicago. The thing could boomerang and infuriate the police and the mayor's office. Susan phoned back with the numbers and I made the calls. "A drug bust is on at an art gallery, but there are no drugs." Within half an hour, Wells Street was crawling with reporters and network television trucks.

Even in his own panic, when Lance asked Susan to phone me, he had also asked her for a camera to photograph the sculpture being confiscated. One of the cops warned him. Lance asked, "Are you denying me my right to photograph this?" The cop said, "Usually we just kick the door down, push guys like you up against the wall, and tear the place apart." That, handcuffs, and a fast trip to the slammer for Lance. The message was clear. In her phone call, Susan asked me what lawyer to call, and I gave her the name of Scott Hodes, a politically connected lawyer known for his involvement in art matters, as was his late father, Barnet Hodes, former corporation counsel for the city, well-known surrealist collector, and old family friend. Scott got the police laboratory to hold off breaking open the bottles over the weekend.

From the perspective of one who has spent a lifetime in Chicago, I reflected on all this. First, there was the ideological war abroad in the country, instigated by Jesse Helms's crew, identifying art with radicalism, pornography, homosexuality, and blasphemy. Then there undoubtedly remained on the Chicago police force disgruntled redneck veterans of

6   CHICAGO SUN-TIMES, FRIDAY, AUGUST 11, 1995

Metro

Cops Raid Gallery, Seize 'LSD' Art

Artist Denies His Work Contains Illegal Drugs

BY ADRIENNE DRELL
STAFF WRITER

Chicago police raided a River North art gallery Thursday and confiscated a valuable piece of contemporary art: 12 sealed bottles of liquid that they said may contain LSD.

Gallery owner Richard Feigen called the seizure "censorship and a serious assault on the arts" and retribution for his letter of complaint about closing Wells Street for a festival. City and police officials deny the charge.

The artist, Gregory Green of New York, is consulting lawyers about retrieving his 1994 work, "10,000 Doses," which he said is worth $6,000 and has been shown without problems in Los Angeles and New York.

Feigen gallery attorney Scott Hodes said late Thursday that the police crime lab had agreed not to damage or tamper with the bottles.

"This incident shows a lack of concern for what is art in a constantly evolving art market," Hodes said.

Green said the bottles "do not contain LSD or anything illegal" but rather components of lysergic acid (including ground-up morning glory seed), as well as a substance that induces vomiting and starter fluid, which renders the entire liquid inert.

The bottles were on a metal table in the window of the gallery at 742 N. Wells. On the window was another artwork—the text of a revised recipe from the *Anarchist's Cookbook* on how to make LSD in a kitchen.

Green, who received a master of fine arts degree in 1985 from the Art Institute of Chicago, compared Thursday's raid to the 1988 seizure by aldermen of a painting of the late Mayor Harold Washington wearing women's underwear, and the uproar over an exhibit of the U.S. flag on the Art Institute floor.

"I think it reflects the general aggressive trend the Chicago police tend to have," Green said. "My work

"10,000 Doses," by Gregory Green, does not contain any illegal substances, the artist says.

is about potential and possibilities, not reality." Other works by the artist include inert suitcase bombs, suspicious-looking packages, and an atomic bomb—without radioactive materials.

Chicago Police spokesman Patrick Camden said the seizure by the department's organized crime and narcotics unit resulted from a tip from bomb and arson unit officers. They had gone to see the exhibit last month after seeing a newspaper article about it.

Feigen said it was "highly suspicious" that police acted Thursday, one day before the show containing "10,000 Doses" is to close and just days after gallery director Lance Kinz wrote letters to Ald. Burton F. Natarus (42nd) and City Special Events Director James Sheahan protesting the closing of the street in front of the gallery for this weekend's Taste of River North festival.

"That's an absolute lie," Natarus said. "I had no knowledge what was in those bottles till you told me." He called Kinz "a complainer who has known about this festival for months and then comes in a week before the event and asks us to cancel it when people have made commitments."

Sheahan has been on vacation "and probably hasn't even seen the letter," said his spokeswoman, Margaret Jones DeNard.

PABLO MARTINEZ MONSIVAIS-SUN-TIMES PHOTOS

Lance Kinz and Susan Reynolds of the Feigen gallery, 742 N. Wells, stand next to the empty table that held "10,000 Doses" before the artwork was seized by police Thursday.

Article from the *Chicago Sun-Times,* August 11, 1995

the 1968 convention riots, or their progeny. And finally, there was Lance's role as an organizer of the gallery and artists' community against the commercialization of the River North area. On August 8 he had written a letter to the Forty-second Ward alderman, Burton Natarus, and to the director of the Mayor's Special Events Office, protesting the closing of the 700 block of Wells Street for a street fair on August 12 and 13 without discussion with residents, largely for the benefit of a huge, glitzy new tourist trap, the Crab Shack, across the street from our gallery. I originally connected the raid to this letter, though Lance tended not to, and my suspicions were quoted in one of the papers. I was told through mutual acquaintances that my remark had infuriated Natarus, whom I had never met. I thought it was too coincidental that the raid had not taken place until two and a half months after the show opened, three weeks after the

Reader review, more than two weeks after the arson and bomb squad raid, and just the day before our show closed. Lance suspected the president and board members of the River North Association, who would profit from commercializing the neighborhood, and one of the arson and bomb squad detectives. He is probably right.

Gregory faxed the police crime lab a complete list of the contents of his sculpture and pleaded with them not to break any of the sealed bottles. He could no longer find these bottles to repair his piece if they damaged it. Nothing in those bottles had anything to do with LSD. Notwithstanding Gregory's pleas, the lab cut open two of the bottles, and on August 14 Lance was informed that "test results were positive," that the bottles contained 230,000 "doses" of LSD with a "street value" of $1,200,000. The *Chicago Tribune* announced all this in a headlined article. Lance was arrested on a charge of "manufacturing and unlawful possession of a controlled substance," and a warrant was issued for the arrest of Gregory Green in Brooklyn. Notwithstanding the fact that it would be difficult to access, let alone sell, a "controlled substance" from permanently sealed bottles. Mandatory minimum sentence: ten years in prison. Lance and Gregory were terrified. Lance was ordered to appear for arraignment on August 15, $10,000 bail was arranged, and he was told he would be released on his own recognizance. But the cops kept him in jail all day, hassling him about getting his fingerprints wrong, and we only just succeeded, with legal intervention, in getting him released late that night, so that he barely avoided a night in a jail cell with serious felons.

The lawyers moved swiftly for an injunction to prevent destruction of the evidence. I suspected that after completion of their "tests," the crime lab would be told to destroy the rest of the sculpture and we could never prove the absence of LSD. The press coverage was intensive, headlines and television segments every day. The story was picked up on the wire services and published all over the country. There were several editorials, including one by Richard Roeper in the August 17 *Chicago Sun-Times*—"Drug Police Could Use Dose of Reality"—that described a street corner in the nether regions of Chicago's ghetto which served as a drug dealers' supermarket—drug dealing so blatant you could watch the buying and selling as you drove by. The police could not have cared less. Yet this little art gallery was busted by the full force of the narcotics squad over some young artist's sculpture, filling the street with squad cars, blue roof lights flashing away, brandishing search warrants.

On August 18 the *Sun-Times* reporter who had been covering the case phoned and said, "Have you seen the press release?" "What press release?" "The police department's." "No, I've seen nothing." "I'll fax it to you." And through my fax machine came the Chicago Police Department release, signed by the superintendent of police and the director of news affairs. " 'Police Drop Charges Against Artist and Gallery Owner' . . . The apparent results of that test were misinterpreted by a laboratory technician. . . . [S]ubsequent technical review . . . determined that the data did not support the earlier conclusion. . . . The artwork will be returned to the gallery." At a subsequent hearing on August 22, the state attorney's office said that a second test had "proved negative," and charges against Lance (the gallery's director, not "owner," as the release had stated— maybe I was the one they really wanted) and Gregory were dropped. The sculpture was returned, the necks of the two bottles cut, along with amusing notes from some sympathetic cops, all of which Gregory incorporated into the reconstituted conceptual piece. Gregory's lawsuit against the city is still pending at this writing. I have the uneasy feeling that, but for the power of the press, Lance and Gregory might well be moldering in jail. Few people, let alone a little cutting-edge art gallery, can marshal power equal to that of the press. But all this had carried a risk. The conscious use of the press in this case had nothing to do with generating publicity for Gregory Green. That was a side effect. The purpose was to make the police and politicians look ridiculous and intimidate them into dropping the charges. It might have done the opposite and goaded them into throwing the book at Lance and Gregory.

The Gregory Green episode brought back to vivid memory an event that had taken place in the same city, for much the same reasons, twenty-seven years before. This was another case where art used the press to make a political point, when all else had failed. The event took place in the wake of the infamous 1968 Democratic National Convention.

This was a time when I was politically active, Lyndon Johnson was being nominated for his second term after breaking his promise to get us out of Vietnam in his first term, Hubert Humphrey had thus far stuck with his boss on the issue—and the convention was taking place in my hometown. I went out there with my wife, three stepdaughters, our two-year-old daughter, and two sets of convention credentials.

Mayor Daley reigned supreme, dictator of all that lay within the vast city limits to the north, south, and west. He had succeeded in balkanizing Chicago into the biggest Italian city after Genoa, the biggest German city after Bremen, the biggest Polish city after Cracow. Unfortunately, he had also bottled up almost half the city's population in an African ghetto on the South Side. Each of these fiefdoms was granted its own measure of patronage. There was no intercommunication between them. The Polish neighborhood spoke Polish, the Italian Italian, and so on. Each alderman took care of his own, and Mayor Daley took care of them all. The black ghetto had its Uncle Tom aldermen, and a congressman in Washington. In return for the city jobs each alderman was allotted, he delivered the votes the mayor required. If he didn't, he was out, or the city jobs stopped. All this gave the mayor his legendary political power. He delivered Illinois, happily, as it turned out, to Kennedy in 1960, it swung the election, and he was the first invitee to the White House after the inauguration. The Cook County Republican party in those days was a farce. All the powerful Republicans—the old Chicago families who lived in Lake Forest and on the Near North Side, the money that really owned the town, that controlled the great companies that gave Chicago its muscle, like Sears Roebuck, Standard Oil of Indiana, and Inland Steel, and that ran the cultural institutions, the Art Institute, the Chicago Symphony, and the University of Chicago—supported Daley.

Because of Chicago's particular geography, strung out along the lake, north, south, and west, the proprietors of the city, who by then lived to the north, never needed, throughout their lives, to venture into the ghetto to the south or the ethnic neighborhoods to the west. They never had to worry about strikes or the mob or unpaved highways or property taxes. The mayor had all that in hand for them. Everybody minded his own business. Nobody supported candidates who opposed the mayor. Nobody supported the Republican party. Nobody minded the graft to the aldermen for even such things as a permit for a driveway. I remember when, in 1959, I wanted an indentation in the curb and a canopy in front of an apartment building I owned with my parents. Months went by and the architect simply could not get these routine plans approved by the

Building Department. I asked him what the problem was. He just didn't know. So I phoned the alderman, whom I knew and who knew my parents. He said $5,000 would take care of it. I blew up and said that my next call would be to the *Chicago Sun-Times*. And that was the end of the driveway.

Now all this efficiency and tranquillity carried a price. This was a dictatorship. At the time, it fit the mood of the old Chicago aristocracy. The "trains ran on time," as in Mussolini's Italy. There is a strong strain of Calvinism in our country anyway. We talk about "rugged individualism," but boat-rockers don't get ahead, nor do they find themselves with any power. Unlike the British, with their impregnable and cocky hereditary aristocracy, we do not patiently suffer eccentricity. Least of all in Chicago in the 1950s and 1960s. The dictatorship had a strong ethnic component, and these Irish, Polish, Italian, and German families were not used to insolence from their children. They also didn't like black people, and probably not Jews either, but the old Jewish neighborhood on the West Side had long since dispersed to the middle-class suburbs, and the ethnics probably never even met any Jews. The Chicago police, largely from this ethnic background, were as tough as the Mississippi Highway Patrol.

I had a man working for me in those days, Jerry Chambers, a black man, who among many other chores drove my car. One day he was very late to pick me up. He explained that the police had stopped and hassled him. I asked him why. He said there never was a reason. They always did it when he was driving my fancy car and I wasn't in it. So I bought him a chauffeur's uniform and cap, and it never happened again. That was Chicago. As Martin Luther King said, marching in Skokie—a largely Polish suburb to the west—was more dangerous than the Mississippi Delta.

All this was background for the Democratic convention events of 1968. Daley and the Chicago cops weren't used to insolence, and the Vietnam protestors weren't used to a dictatorship. What unfolded during the convention is one of the city's, and the country's, best-documented political traumas. But there was an art-world aftershock that only after some thirty years has drawn active scholarly attention. At the time, it didn't seem that important, and most of the surviving record is from press accounts.

I had planned a Claes Oldenburg exhibition in my Chicago gallery for October 1968. Oldenburg had grown up in Chicago, and came out to the

1968 convention as a reporter. After he was assaulted by police and called a Communist, he decided to cancel his show, which he had conceived as a celebration of Chicago. The Oldenburg show finally took place the next spring. Meanwhile, a group of older artists living on Long Island announced a ten-year art boycott of Chicago, to which it was their intention to commit artists throughout the country. Faced with these events, potentially catastrophic to Chicago's cultural community, I decided to try to break the boycott, bring artists everywhere into solidarity on the issue of Daley's brutality, enlighten Chicago's financial and social powers as to where the world stood, and hopefully embarrass Daley through the press. The way to do this was certainly not through the Long Island artists' nonstatement, because only those who cared about art would notice art's absence (certainly not Daley), but instead to make a statement. The statement was to be an exhibition, *Richard J. Daley.*

As I wrote in the catalogue of a 1988 reprise of the 1968 exhibition:

The advancing protestors . . . knew not into what they were marching. Nor did the Mayor and his police know what to expect. They had never before been disobeyed. The demonstrators, deeply outraged by the Vietnam war and frustrated by Humphrey's paralysis, arrived at the convention-site of the party of peace and dialogue assuming their statement would be heard. This was, after all, the Democratic convention, not the Republican, and this was not the deep South. They had no clue that they were marching on a tough, disciplined dictatorship, unused to disobedience, disruption and heterogeneous dress and hairstyles, and with a distinct tinge of . . . European anti-semitism. The Mayor certainly had no idea what was coming, nor did he and his police have any experience in dealing with it. Bloodshed was inevitable.

Chicago was appalled at the protestors' disregard for authority. And the world was appalled at the sight of nightsticks cracking heads and Daley shouting anti-semitic epithets at Senator Ribicoff. Even visitors with legitimate convention credentials were shocked to find their seats usurped by Daley's unaccredited soldiers, and infuriated by shouts to "go back where you came from." [The outside world] had no knowledge of Chicago's unique sociopolitical background, and the city became the target of hostility and ridicule.

Barnett Newman, *Lace Curtain for Mayor Daley,* 1968

Art Institute of Chicago. Photograph: Paulus Leeser, courtesy of The Barnett Newman Foundation, New York. © 1999 Barnett Newman Foundation. Artists Rights Society (ARS), New York

In place of exhibition advertisements, we published [Oldenburg's] open letter cancelling his celebration of his home town. The Oldenburg exhibition finally took place in the Spring of 1969, and much of the imagery had to do with Mayor Daley, nightsticks and Chicago fire-plugs. Meanwhile, it was obvious that the Mayor could not have cared less whether artists boycotted Chicago. . . .

So we organized the "Richard J. Daley" exhibition. Every important artist was contacted by telephone, and work or messages of support were received from the famous and the unknown. Only one artist refused to contribute—Josef Albers, who told me he was "not political." We took all the art the gallery could hold. A number of artists set to work on projects specifically for the exhibition. Barney Newman made the sculpture, "Lace Curtain for Mayor Daley," which he gave me, and which I returned to his widow, Annalee, in 1973. [It is now in the Art Institute of Chicago.] Jim Rosenquist made the painting, the lithograph (of which he donated one-third of the edition of 100 to the 1968 Allard Lowenstein congressional campaign), and the exhibition poster, "Daley Portrait." Oldenburg made an edition of 50 Chicago fire-plugs and two "Daley Head Monument" drawings. Tinguely sent "Hello Claes—Mort aux Vaches." . . .

The exhibition got a lot of press and a huge attendance. Daley's people obviously noticed because, despite the burly bodyguard Oldenburg hired to escort our gallery director, Lotte Drew-Bear, to and from her apartment, some goons came into the gallery and trashed the place. But the point was made and the boycott broken.

The exhibition carried its message, in abbreviated form, to venues at the Contemporary Arts Center in Cincinnati and at my gallery at 141 Greene Street in New York. The press coverage was extensive—the national television networks, *Time, Newsweek,* the *Wall Street Journal, New York Times, Los Angeles Times,* newspapers all over the country. If indeed the message got through to Daley, and to the shocked Chicago paladins, and if it had any impact on the future, as it may well have done through Richard J. Daley, Jr., a successor to his father, then it was the press that delivered it.

There are two categories of material things that seem more valuable than anything else: what remains of the natural environment; and, even more precious, works of art. Losses in either category are painful, and I do what I can to prevent them. To these ends, on at least two occasions, the power of the press was turned.

As to the precariousness of the environment, if any evidence were needed, there appeared in the February 17, 1997, *New York Times* an article headlined "Trees for Sale, but Not to Savior." An environmentalist thought he had finally beaten the U.S. Forest Service in its diabolical game of delivering the remaining public forests up to the lumber interests for destruction. He had showed up at a federal timber auction with cash in hand, made the winning bid for the stand of ancient trees, then saw his bid rejected because the sale was restricted to bidders who would cut the trees down. He couldn't save them no matter how much he paid.

I didn't think that little story, buried back on page 12, could unleash the true power of the press to change laws that protect major political interests. The people who drew up our laws in the eighteenth century knew little of the country's natural resources, and even if they had, they could never have imagined the technologies that only three lifetimes later would lay waste to the planet's wonders. And if ever they had suffered such nightmares, these giants of the "Age of Reason" would never have believed their new nation would so soon deliver itself into the hands of selfish political pygmies. Their brilliant structure was inherently flawed: a two-party system instead of a parliamentary one, leaving neither party with a philosophy, leaving us with no choice but to vote for candidates on the basis of "charisma" projected over a device unimaginable in their time, at a cost of hundreds of millions of dollars every two, four, or six years, money raised by mercenaries selling to foreigners beds in a White House built by those Founding Fathers to symbolize to foreign nations the grandeur of our country. Meanwhile, as a tenet of its "philosophy," one of the parties would adopt a slogan of "family values" while depriving families of ancient forests to enjoy, rivers to raft, pure air to breathe, and art to stimulate their children's imaginations. Among the "special interests" that had to be taken care of, of course, were the "fundamentalists" who had promised their votes to George Bush and came now for the payoff.

Of inestimable value to the representatives of this redneck constituency was a program whose advocates were relatively few in number, powerless, and geographically spread out across politically irrelevant jurisdictions. The National Endowment for the Arts cost the government, before the 1996 Republican cuts, only $162.2 million a year. The

French government, with an economy one fifth the size of ours, spends some $3 billion; and the Australians, as Paul Keating, the outgoing prime minister, proudly told me in a meeting in March 1996, $300 million with an economy one twenty-third the size of ours. The Helms wrecking crew has now reduced the funding to $99.5 million, and Congress scheduled the NEA's total elimination by 1998. Opponents of arts funding will of course claim that the tax-deductible status of arts foundations constitutes an indirect federal subsidy. What they ignore is the enormous psychological boost that direct government funding provides—the stamp of approval it lends to the specific cause, and the matching private funds it generates.

This ideological war, the rednecks' proof of commitment to those "family values," has been money in their political bank, a war waged at no cost whatsoever. The San Diego Museum gave $1,700 of NEA money to a conceptual artist and he used it instead for a political statement, handing out ten-dollar bills to illegal aliens and thus depositing millions in Helms's political bank; the Walker Art Center gave $100 of NEA money to an AIDS-stricken artist for a performance; and the Robert Mapplethorpe and Andres Serrano exhibitions took place in museums that happened to have received some NEA money, even though it did not relate to these specific exhibitions. All this was priceless political money in Helms's bank.

The only things we leave behind that matter at all are the beauty that nature created and, even more important, the beauty that we ourselves create. The former we seem determined to see destroyed, and now some of us seem intent on ruining the latter as well. Where every civilized government has a ministry of culture, the only agency we have is this tiny NEA, and the only official its chairman. Yet the American cultural product is perhaps our most credible export commodity. Our president and secretary of commerce do not have to run to Tokyo to sell it; the Japanese come to the States to buy. These exports earn us billions of dollars of foreign currency—not only the foreign revenue for our films, books, paintings, and performances but the money tourists spend here. In 1989, the last year for which there are statistics, the "industry" provided 6 percent of the country's $314.5 billion gross national product. It employed 3.2 million Americans, 2.7 percent of the country's total workforce (agriculture, for instance, employed 2.6 percent; civilian defense, 3.0 percent), and this includes only those directly employed, not all the working stiffs—carpenters and set painters, waiters and bellmen, taxi drivers and electricians, makers of musical instruments and toe shoes, canvas and paint. This figure also does not include all the volunteers. All these workers have no single union, and no lobbyist to golf with the senators. They have no political power. They have only one representative of their interests: the NEA chairman.

I harbored few delusions at the outset of the 1992 campaign that Bill Clinton, fresh from Little Rock, not a city known for its cultural product, would make the NEA appointment a priority on his agenda. Clinton was, after all, a master politician, and anticulture, not culture, commands the political capital. At the same time, I did not envision any active contention for the job which might delay the appointment. However, there were, as it turned out, on all the "transition" teams, hordes of pressure groups—women, blacks, gays, Hispanics—all jockeying for power, and Clinton unable to say no to any of them. The NEA was not exempt from the politics.

The NEA chairmanship was one of the jobs in the new administration that one thought, naïvely, it seems, might be spared. If one values the cultural above all the nation's other products, certainly the tools of war, then this is, for several reasons, a significant appointment. First, the chairman is the only bridge between the creative and governmental communities. Without a ministry of culture, without even a desk at the State Department, she is the only spokesperson for the arts in government. Unlike almost every other country except Germany, Australia, and Israel, the United States has not one capital but two—Washington for government, New York for the arts. In the other national capitals—Paris, London, Rome—the makers of art and the makers of government have some opportunity to get to know one another. In the United States, they inhabit different worlds, hundreds of miles apart. I doubt that Jesse Helms has ever encountered an artist in social circumstances. It seems to me that if he and his confreres had such opportunities, it might be more difficult for them to take such hard positions.

At the same time, the artists feel alienated from their government, beset by fears of censorship. If the chairman of the NEA can indeed serve as a bridge between these two alienated constituencies, then it seems necessary that it be someone whom the artists trust, someone coming from their own group, not from the other side.

After repeated efforts to contact someone in the "transition" apparatus involved in the selection process, and after being told once when I was in Milwaukee giving a speech that I would be called back, then hearing nothing and being shunted from Little Rock to an office in Washington, I finally got the feeling that there were political interests even in this arcane job. The office I was referred to was run by Deborah Sale, an old political crony of the Clintons, and it did not take much stonewalling from that office to make me realize that it was Sale herself who wanted the NEA chairmanship. I soon learned that she had in fact been promised the job for services rendered in the campaign. Trying to get some kind of hearing on the subject, I wrote a letter to the editor that was published in the *New York Times* on New Year's Eve, 1992, hardly an issue of the paper likely to come to the attention of anyone involved in the selection process.

Early in January I heard that Jane Alexander's name had been put forward for the chairmanship. Her work in the theater and films was distinguished and she commanded universal respect in arts circles. She was appearing at that time on Broadway in Wendy Wasserstein's *The Sisters Rosensweig*. Would Jane really leave a hit play and interrupt, perhaps permanently relinquish, a flourishing acting career for a low-paying government job under siege from right-wing ideologues and cost-cutters? I phoned to ask her, and the answer was yes. She felt strongly about government funding for the arts and was challenged by the opportunity.

Fortunately, Jane's talent is not ephemeral. Her opportunities in films and on the stage would not diminish during the years she would spend in government. She had convincingly played roles of all ages, from romantic young women to Eleanor Roosevelt. She was certainly one of the great ladies of the American stage and screen. The legislators whom she would have to lobby, even the likes of Jesse Helms, would have to be flattered and impressed by an NEA chairman of her stature.

Jane's willingness to be considered for the NEA was certainly a patriotic gesture, made at great personal sacrifice, and a signal opportunity for the country. There seemed no one better qualified, combining the credibility of an artist of the first rank, respected by both fellow artists and the legislators, with a serious, low-key, gentle, apolitical history and style.

Inauguration day approached, and although some higher-level appointments were announced, nothing was heard about the NEA. This didn't surprise me. Other matters were more pressing. But then weeks passed into months. There seemed to be jockeying and pushing and shoving over every single job, and the president seemed paralyzed. The appointment of a famous person like Jane Alexander should have been a slam-dunk.

Then, all of a sudden, the dirty tricks started. First the rumor that Jane wouldn't take the job if offered it, reported in the press. Then the rumor that, since Jane and her husband, Ed Sherin, had had their life savings stolen by Jane's business manager, she could not afford to take the job, also duly leaked to the press. The theft was old news. Jane had told me about it weeks before, when I was visiting her dressing room after a performance. She and Ed had been devastated, but she took it in her mature, stoic way and said, "Well, we'll just start over again." If appointed, they could live off the NEA salary and Ed's earnings as a television producer. It did not affect her decision on the potential appointment. The sources of these news leaks intrigued me. Obviously hardball politics.

On Sunday morning, March 6, as I was leaving the tennis court in Bedford, Lou Harris, one of the foursome that followed us onto the court, pulled me aside and told me that the president was going to announce the appointment of Deborah Sale the week of the fourteenth. I had never heard of Sale before her name came up as head of Clinton's NEA transition office. On Monday morning I tried to check up on her. It seemed that she was an old Arkansas high school friend of Hillary Clinton's and that she had helped loyally throughout the campaign. She had taken a leave of absence as chief of staff for Stanley Lundine, Mario Cuomo's New York lieutenant governor, and had been diligently lobbying "arts organizations" all over the country for months. None of this, however, seemed to qualify her for the job, except perhaps her links to the Clintons and her political savvy, which qualifications, although not in my opinion paramount, were not to be totally discounted. But as I checked around among the artists to find out if any of them had ever encountered Sale and to see how they felt about Alexander, it was apparent that in all Sale's lobbying, she had never made contact with any artists. The contacts were with organizations, to which artists, notorious "loners," most definitely do not belong. It was this blatant misunderstanding of the creative process and its practitioners that seemed to make

it imperative, even at the eleventh hour, to upset the impending appointment in favor of Alexander.

I have had a love-hate relationship with politics since the old antiwar
days of the Lowenstein, McCarthy, Robert Kennedy, Howard Samuels,
and McGovern campaigns. I got to rather like the game, but not the
players and usually not the results. I had bought into the convention
delegate reforms of the McGovern commission, then discovered that
the 1972 New York McGovern campaign, run by Richard Wade, was
using the same old exclusionary tactics. I had threatened to run a rene-
gade McGovern slate in Westchester, been told by Wade that if elected,
my slate would be disavowed by the candidate before the credentials
committee at the convention in Miami. Then, with friends like Gloria
Steinem, I had joined a Shirley Chisholm delegate slate in Manhattan,
only to be defeated, derailed as were most of my quixotic political ven-
tures, by the professionals running the McGovern slate. Through
all this, going back to my old days growing up in Cook County under
the Daley machine, I had picked up a journeyman's acquaintance with
politics, and I certainly knew it when I saw it. And I saw it with the
NEA.

With less than a week to go before the expected announcement, the
only thing that seemed to make sense was a petition to the president on
behalf of Jane Alexander, signed by a galaxy of artists so famous as to give
pause even to a provincial politician from Arkansas. The Clintons had,
after all, gone to Yale and he had been a Rhodes Scholar. So a letter was
drafted and the search for phone numbers began. By Thursday afternoon,
the eleventh, twenty-one artists, architects, writers, dancers, actors, and
musicians had been contacted, including Ellsworth Kelly, James Rosenquist, Frank Stella, Robert Rauschenberg, Eric Fischl, April Gornik, and
Jasper Johns; Charles Gwathmey and Richard Meier; Frank Conroy, E. L.
Doctorow, Norman Mailer, George Plimpton, and Brooke Hayward;
Tony Randall, Michael Douglas, Anne Jackson, Eli Wallach, Teresa
Wright, and Lily Tomlin; Itzhak Perlman, Isaac Stern, and Peter Duchin;
Heather Watts, Peter Martins, Darci Kistler, Helgi Tomasson, Maria
Tallchief, and Kevin McKenzie. Joanne Woodward and Paul Newman
were contacted and their names added to the list at the last minute when
it was reported that they had dined with the Clintons at a Washington
restaurant the week before. All of the artists agreed with the idea that the

NEA chairman should come from their own ranks, and either knew Jane Alexander or knew of her and respected her.

I unearthed the White House fax number with some difficulty, and by late Friday afternoon the fax went off. This was a letter to the president from a group of the country's most distinguished artists. Just as the fax went off, I remembered that Bruce Lindsey, Clinton's chief of staff, was an old Arkansas buddy of Sale's, and probably the one responsible for her imminent appointment. The fax, notwithstanding the distinction of its signators, would more likely find its way into the wastebasket than onto the president's desk. The only way the president might see this before the putative Monday announcement was in the newspaper, and the most logical paper was the *Washington Post*. I phoned the *Post* and asked for the arts editor, then the city desk, and I was finally put through to Jacqueline Trescott in the Style section. Trescott was interested and asked to be faxed a copy of the letter. The article appeared in the Saturday, March 13, *Post*, headlined "Artists Back Actress for NEA Post." As it turned out, the press may well have had a key part in saving an indispensable government agency.

The president finally announced Jane Alexander's appointment in a letter to Senator Edward Kennedy, chairman of the Senate Labor and Human Resources Committee, on August 6. The delay may have resulted from infighting after the shelving of Sale. Before Jane's Senate confirmation hearing, she diligently paid courtesy calls to all of the relevant senators. On the morning of the hearing, she had tea with Jesse Helms. When I entered the packed Committee Hearing Room and saw Helms, who was not a member of the committee, conspicuous on the podium with the committee members, I was sure of trouble. But the hearing turned into a coronation. There was no voice raised in opposition, not a single adversarial question. Helms himself delivered an encomium.

There are many who are convinced that but for Jane Alexander, the NEA would not have survived. Was the press integral to her appointment? Probably only the president, or his wife, could answer that. As in the Barnes Foundation emergency, the press was a last resort. But it worked.

MARY AND LEIGH BLOCK

May 20, 1981, was a night for the art world to remember. At a time before the avalanche of Japanese money had transformed auctions into full-scale media events, there was an unusual buzz around the old Parke-Bernet building at 980 Madison Avenue. By seven forty-five the place was packed. Anyone with Chicago connections could see that something odd was happening. Despite the fact that Chicago's great collecting days were almost over, there, mingling nervously in the crowd, was a clutch of Chicago Art Institute trustees. This was the night of the Leigh Block sale, the remnants of a legendary collection, assumed since its inception in the 1940s to be going intact to the Art Institute. Some paintings had indeed been donated; and a number of the masterpieces, like van Gogh's *Self-portrait with Bandaged Ear* and *Town Hall of Auvers,* had been sold off privately. Mary Block had recently died, and a few more pictures were bequeathed; it was this group that was being auctioned, and the few things remaining were being taken by Leigh Block with him to his final retirement in Santa Barbara, California.

In a "democratic" society, anyone can theoretically achieve anything, go anywhere, do anything. But in most American cities, particularly in the middle of the country and particularly in the middle of this century, this worked in theory, not in practice. There are, or at least there were until recently, perquisites—club memberships, tenancy in buildings and even neighborhoods—that were available only by heredity, or at least ethnicity. In most cities, the vast majority went about their lives oblivious to these perquisites, but for some, those beset with their own insecurities, they were irresistible carrots dangling out there, an obsession for such as Mary and Leigh Block.

This was particularly true of an important city like Chicago, which, despite its size, functioned socially and journalistically like a village: every activity of the elite was faithfully reported in the newspapers by popular "society" editors, the leading socialites became celebrities, and the names of their clubs and the addresses of their apartment buildings imprimaturs of rank. Not only did such a system of false democracy misdirect energies, in heightening insecurities it brought out the worst in people. And in the case of Mary and Leigh Block, an insecure Jewish couple, there was much of it to bring out.

Although Mary and Leigh Block were considered great benefactors of the Art Institute of Chicago, measured by the magnitude and splendor of their art holdings, their benefactions in the end proved disappointing. And the damage suffered by the museum during their tenure may well have outstripped their substantial donations. Yet in a real sense the Blocks were more victims than villains. Though the conditions in Chicago that drove them to their destructive behavior have largely disappeared over the past quarter century, the lessons are there to be learned by other cities and other museums.

Leigh Block was a scion of one of the great Jewish families of Chicago, controlling shareholders of Inland Steel. The Blocks had arrived in Chicago in 1893 from Cincinnati, a cradle of the German Jewish community in America. Joseph Block, his grandfather, was an original investor that year in Inland, which by 1933, the year it acquired Ryerson Steel, had become one of the great American steel companies, the most conservative, most stable, and least volatile in a cyclical industry, and one of the cornerstone companies of the Chicago economy. With the 1933 merger, the Ryersons became the other family with a major share of Inland. In Chicago's Christian hierarchy, the Ryersons were a counterpart of the Blocks. The Ryerson family mausoleum in Graceland Cemetery is a famous Louis Sullivan masterpiece. Their painting donations to the Art Institute of Chicago constitute one of the cores of the museum collection. Both families had been important in Chicago since the nineteenth century. Chicago, it will be remembered, had been a fort, a defense against Indians, as late as the 1830s, was incorporated as a village in 1833, as a city not until 1837, and was almost entirely consumed by the Chicago Fire thirty-four years later, in 1871. So its aristocracy only began to evolve in the post–Civil War industrial revolution, after the fire. By

Vincent van Gogh,
*Self-portrait with
Bandaged Ear and Pipe,*
1889

Private collection

the time the Blocks arrived, a number of the city's pioneer families, Christian and Jewish, had been in place since before the Civil War. The Blocks were already, or soon became, related to most of the other leading families in their world, as were the Ryersons in theirs. But in Chicago, these were very different worlds, worlds that overlapped only in business, never socially. In that world of old Chicago, upper-class Jews went about their lives barely aware of, or oblivious to, this prejudice. And so all the Blocks did—except Mary and Leigh.

Leopold E. Block, Leigh's father, had been brought to Chicago from Cincinnati in 1893 by his father, Joseph, to work for Inland Steel. His brother, Phillip D. Block, had also joined the company in 1893. L. E. Block became chairman in 1919. He had two sons, Joseph and Leigh, and they both joined Inland. Joseph later became president, then chairman in 1959, and Leigh was shunted off to the relatively insignificant post of vice president for purchasing. Joseph married Lucille Eichengreen in 1924. They lived quietly, without ostentation, leaders in the city's civic and charitable life, respected by everyone in Chicago. Joseph Block went on, as chairman of Inland Steel, to be the de facto leader of the American steel industry, an industry notably devoid of Jews. In his seminal book *The Protestant Establishment: Aristocracy & Caste in America*, E. Digby Baltzell made the interesting observation that since each of the Pittsburgh steel companies had a luncheon table at the Duquesne Club, since all the upper management lunched together there, since important business decisions were made there, and since no Jews were permitted in the club, there could be no Jews in the upper management of any of the Pittsburgh steel companies. Inland, headquartered in Chicago, was the industry exception.

President Kennedy's fierce campaign in February and March 1962 to control inflation led to the signing on April 6 of a "non-inflationary" wage contract, containing what amounted to a minimal ten-cent hourly increase, between the steel union, whose concern was job security in the face of

Vincent van Gogh, *The Town Hall of Auvers on Bastille Day,* 1890

Private collection

accelerating automation, and management, led by U.S. Steel and Bethlehem. Both sides agreed to the president's strictures against further wage and price increases. Then, suddenly, on April 10, U.S. Steel announced price increases averaging six dollars a ton, effective that midnight. The next day, five major companies—Bethlehem, Republic, Jones & Laughlin, Youngstown, and Wheeling—followed U.S. Steel's lead. The president was enraged, and took it as a deliberate affront to his administration. He summoned Roger Blough, chairman of U.S. Steel, to the Oval Office and read him the riot act. The president, in a white rage, attacked the companies for "irresponsible defiance of the public interest" and "ruthless disregard" of their duty to the nation. He spoke in tones of cold anger about the "utter contempt" for the American people of a "tiny handful" of steel executives. He determined to break their backs.

The union immediately threatened further wage demands. Time was of the essence. The price increase had to be rolled back before it clicked into the economy and triggered an inflationary spiral. The only solution was to find one of the remaining steel companies, one large enough to force a rollback, to hold the line. Arthur Goldberg, the secretary of labor, had a suggestion. Goldberg came from Chicago and knew the Blocks and Inland Steel, their character and sense of public responsibility. He may have taken into account that the Blocks, although they controlled Inland jointly with the Ryerson family, would not necessarily feel compelled to act as members of the steel industry club, into whose ranks they had never been fully accepted, notwithstanding that the chairman, Joseph L. Block, was perhaps the most respected man in the industry. And if it held the price line, as eighth-largest company it had the markets and the power to force the rollback.

Another member of the administration, Edward Gudeman, undersecretary of the Treasury, was a close Chicago friend of the Blocks. Gudeman had been executive vice president of Sears Roebuck, in line for the presidency, but had been passed over by the anti-Semitic chairman, General Robert E. Wood. Wood, it seemed, had never gotten over the fact that he had been given his job at Sears by Julius Rosenwald, founder of the modern-day company and its principal shareholder. At Goldberg's suggestion, the president asked Gudeman to intercede. Gudeman phoned an old friend, Phillip D. Block, Inland's executive vice president.

"P.D." Block located his cousin, Joe Block, Inland's chairman, in Kyoto. Joe's reaction was as might have been expected from a man of his stature: he decided on the spot that Inland would act in the country's interest and hold the price line, despite the flak it would take as an industry pariah. Embarrassingly, the story leaked to the *Chicago Daily News* through a reporter friend of Joe and Lucille Block, Keyes Beech, who was in Japan at the time, before the Inland board could meet and give formal approval to Joe Block's patriotic decision. But the deed had been done. The six major companies, furious at the maverick for breaking ranks, had no choice but to roll prices back. President Kennedy phoned Joe Block to express his, and the nation's, gratitude.

Culture, embodied in Chicago in the Art Institute and the Chicago Symphony Orchestra, had been established almost immediately after the 1871 fire as the domain of Chicago society. Membership on either of those two boards was the ultimate insignia of social power. Art objects themselves were the only tangible attribute a Jew could own that might connect him to the establishment in general or the Art Institute in particular. Indeed, proprietorship of the city's premier art collection might even crack open the door to the Art Institute board.

Leigh Block, who lacked his brother's business ability as well as his character, had married Mary Lasker, daughter of the advertising genius Albert D. Lasker, in 1942. Mary had herself been a successful copywriter at her father's firm, Lord & Thomas, during her first marriage to Gerhard Foreman, another of Chicago's "Our Crowd." Mary and Leigh have always been included in the handful of great American collectors, and in a sense they were. No one has ever disputed the extraordinary quality of the paintings they owned. But their commitment to the objects was always tenuous, and from the outset the collection seemed to have been formed to serve as a ladder out of Chicago's Jewish world into Christian society. Finally, by 1949, Mary and Leigh's meticulous collecting had accomplished its purpose and landed Leigh a trusteeship of the Art Institute. Mary followed him onto the board in 1955. Leigh had also been elected to the Chicago Symphony Orchestra board, along with the Art Institute the ultimate bastion of Chicago social power.

But none of this seemed to work. Mary and Leigh's names appeared regularly in the social columns, but they were never welcomed into Chicago society. They were not invited to join the clubs, nor were they

Leigh Block, circa 1955

able to move to Lake Forest. They were spoken of derisively, and in the process embarrassed and earned the disrespect of their own Jewish circle, which they had largely abandoned and in which they had few close friends.

Chicago's segregation prevailed even in the summer, in Charlevoix, Michigan, the resort of choice of both the Christian and Jewish groups. This notwithstanding, there was an implicit respect by Christian society for their Jewish counterparts, particularly for those who had controlled major Chicago companies like Inland and Sears Roebuck since the nineteenth century, and most particularly since these Jewish families carried themselves with considerable dignity, made no effort to penetrate Christian society, had erected snobbish barriers of their own, and lived lives indistinguishable from their Christian peers'. Neither group paid much attention to the main thing that separated them: religion. It was a point of some pride that in those days, if you walked out onto the terrace of the Jewish country club, Lake Shore, in Glencoe, you might for an instant think you were at Shoreacres or Onwentsia in Lake Forest. There was perhaps only one thing these Brahmin Jews detested more than their less affluent, more recently immigrated Eastern European coreligionists, and that was Jews who tried to pass into Christian society.

Because their paths never crossed except in the realm of business, where they both conducted their affairs with equal propriety, the anti-Semitism was relatively invisible. There were some exceptions. All of the grand apartment buildings along Lake Shore Drive, except for 1540 North Lake Shore Drive, which was a "Jewish" building, and 209 East Lake Shore Drive, in which one Jewish family lived, were barred to Jews. I remember my grandfather, then well into his nineties, recalling with ire that in the midst of the depression, when the buildings along the drive were virtually empty and threatened with foreclosure, he was still refused an apartment at 1430 North Lake Shore Drive. Lake Forest, some forty miles along Lake Michigan to the north, was the other enclave of Chicago society. No Jews lived there either. Their domain was the suburbs immediately to Lake Forest's south: Highland Park and Glencoe. All of the students at the Chicago Latin School, which my sister attended, were invited to subscription dances at the Fortnightly Club and a New Year's Eve dance at the Casino Club—all, that is, except the two or three Jewish children. Visible, and vocal, in his anti-Semitism was General Robert E. Wood, who became chairman of Sears Roebuck in 1939. His comrade-in-arms and fellow "America Firster" was Dr. Loyal Davis, the city's dean of neurosurgery and Nancy Reagan's father. This anti-Semitism, common in the Midwest of the time—overt in rural areas like Charlevoix, covert in big cities like Chicago—ultimately took its toll on cultural institutions.

The best example of this Chicago syndrome I can summon up is the story of my Yale sophomore roommate. He came from a pioneer Chicago Jewish family. His grandfather and father were the city's most distinguished obstetricians. Each had held a monopoly on Brahmin baby deliveries. Almost every social pooh-bah had been pulled into the world by one or the other of them. His grandfather had married a Christian, and his father had been baptized in the Episcopal Church and married the daughter of the Episcopal bishop of Illinois. He himself had been baptized. By the time we got to Yale, Chicago's peculiar ground

rules seemed to have left him a basket case. His anger used to erupt intermittently at his father's exclusion, on the basis of his Jewish ancestry,
from Chicago's rather bourgeois University Club. He had no roots. He
had a home in neither world. Although back in 1948 I knew nothing
about the Nazi system of a scant few years earlier, I did at the time
wonder how many generations of purity Chicago society demanded. I
suppose one of his family's generations might have accelerated the purifi-
cation by changing their name and obliterating almost a century of
distinction.

The country's older museums had been established in the 1870s, at the
start of the post–Civil War industrial revolution, as a pivotal step in the
aristocratization of the new moneyed class. The Art Institute of Chicago
was founded in 1879. In 1942, the year Mary Lasker Foreman and Leigh
Block were married, the founding families were still represented on
the Art Institute board. Although ostensibly a public institution, the
museum was run by and for the city's oldest families, but of these the
Jews were conspicuous by their absence, just as they were from the city's
clubs. The Art Institute, like its sisters in Boston, New York, and Philadelphia, had, after all, been conceived not only as a cultural institution
but as a club, membership in which was a hallmark of social rank.

In the museum's early years, this made little difference, and the bulk
of the holdings of the early collectors, active in the days when their own
social aspirations took them abroad in an effort to emulate the European
aristocracy, had by the 1940s long since found their way into the Art
Institute, endowing it with one of the world's great museum collections.
By the time Leigh and Mary Block started collecting, the families that
still dominated the Art Institute board had collected nothing for at least
a generation. The great Chicago art collectors were now, or soon would
be, Florene and Samuel Marx, Claire Zeisler, Muriel Kallis Newman,
Jory and Joseph Shapiro, Nathan Cummings, Adele and Arnold Maremont, Rose and Morton Neumann, Lindy and Edwin Bergman, Niesen
Harris—all Jews. Even James Alsdorf, whose scholarship and catholicity
of taste, along with that of his wife, Marilyn, placed him in the first rank
of the world's collectors, although not nominally a Jew, was of Dutch
Jewish background.

Ivan Albright,
*Portrait of Mary
Block,* 1955–57

The Art Institute of
Chicago, gift of Mr. and
Mrs. Leigh Block, 1959.
Photograph © 1999 The
Art Institute of Chicago

It seems to have been with a certain rage, erupting perhaps out of Chicago's anti-Semitism, out of all the slights the Blocks suffered from being so long excluded from what they considered their rightful world, that Leigh, after six years of collecting, finally in 1949 claimed his Art Institute board seat. Mary joined him on the board in 1955, the year the Blocks commissioned Ivan Albright to paint Mary's infamous portrait.

By mid-century, the art-collecting founders of the Art Institute had long since died off, and their progeny, who still controlled the board, no longer had much interest in art. They regarded their seats as inherited fiefdoms. The Blocks, as internationally known collectors, slipped comfortably into the vacuum and began to take control of the museum. Their fellow trustees, unwilling to accept the Blocks socially, deferred to them as art experts, as they would to a Jewish lawyer or doctor.

By the time I returned to Chicago in 1957, the Blocks' collection was already world-famous. Not long afterward, during a visit to their apart-

Henri Rousseau,
*Tropical Landscape:
An American Indian
Struggling with an
Ape,* 1910

Virginia Museum of Fine Arts,
Richmond. Collection of Mr.
and Mrs. Paul Mellon.
© Virginia Museum of Fine
Arts

ment, I stood before the white couch in their living room admiring their splendid Henri Rousseau (*Tropical Landscape: An American Indian Struggling with an Ape,* 1910). Leigh came up behind me and said they wanted to sell it. I asked him why they would sell such an irreplaceable picture. He explained that they needed the wall for a Monet *Nymphéas,* by no means a rarity even after the Japanese carted most of them off some thirty years later. The Blocks wanted $90,000 for the Rousseau. I had only recently begun my business, and had no clients for such a painting. They eventually sold it to Paul Mellon. The Rousseau sale turned out to be a harbinger of events to come. I got the feeling, through all the years I knew them, that Mary and Leigh were not at all attached to any of the paintings, only to the status they conveyed.

Simple Art Institute trusteeships didn't seem to help Mary and Leigh storm the gates. They still charged around in social Siberia. They tried to buy a country house in Lake Forest, but Jews weren't welcome there and they moved to Lake Bluff instead, on Lake Forest's northern border. From the onset of Mary and Leigh's collecting, it was assumed by all the world that their collection, as well as that of Florene and Samuel Marx, the other premier Chicago collection of twentieth-century masterpieces, would end up in the Art Institute. But after the death of Sam Marx, a noted architect of the Art Deco period and Leigh Block's fellow token Jew on the museum board, Florene, who had come from St. Louis with her May Department Stores fortune, moved to New York with her great collection, where on her death in 1997 it was divided between the Museum of Modern Art, where she was a trustee, and the Metropolitan, whose curator of twentieth-century art, William Lieberman, formerly at the Modern, was an old friend.

Leigh set his sights on the Art Institute chairmanship. The chairman in 1949, when Leigh was elected to the board, was the august old guardsman, William McCormick Blair. When Blair stepped down in 1966 and Frank Woods, much respected but not an art collector, was elected instead of Leigh, the Blocks, in a rage, decided to put the fear of God in their fellow trustees. They proceeded to sell their premier masterpiece, van Gogh's *The Town Hall of Auvers on Bastille Day,* to the infamous Frank Lloyd of the Marlborough Gallery, later to be convicted, in 1977, of a felony in the Mark Rothko case, and to flee to the Bahamas, where he spent several years as a fugitive before a high-powered legal team arranged for him to return and be sentenced to what amounted to a wrist slap. The Blocks went on to further decimate the collection by selling Lloyd two other famous paintings, Matisse's *The Young Sailor (II)* and van Gogh's *Self-portrait with Bandaged Ear and Pipe.* Marlborough sold the van Gogh self-portrait to Stavros Niarchos and the Matisse to Jacques Gelman, whose widow, Natasha, bequeathed it to the Metropolitan Museum in 1998. With the rest of the collection at risk, Leigh was elected president in 1970, and finally chairman in 1972.

Meanwhile, through all this, the Art Institute administration was in turmoil. Daniel Catton Rich had been director since 1938. He and his wife had befriended Katherine Kuh, who, after several years of teaching art classes in her pupils' homes in the early 1930s, had opened a gallery in the Diana Court building in 1935 at the age of thirty-one. She showed the work of some serious photographers, Ansel Adams in 1936 and Edward Weston in 1939. In 1937 she met Laszlo Moholy-Nagy, one of the refugees, along with Mies van der Rohe, from the Weimar Bauhaus, and with whom he founded the "New Bauhaus" at the Illinois Institute of

Technology. Kuh gave Moholy-Nagy a show in her gallery in 1937 and fell under his influence, which led to her involvement with the work of such old Bauhaus colleagues of his as Klee and Kandinsky. The remnants of the Arthur Jerome Eddy collection were auctioned in Chicago in 1937, and Kuh made some prescient purchases, including a fine 1910 Kandinsky for James Eppenstein, an architect, and his wife Louise, and another Kandinsky Kuh held on to. It must be said that although there wasn't much of an art market in the 1930s and the Kandinskys went for only a few dollars, the artist was already in his seventies, famous in the world of culture, and Kuh's submission to Moholy-Nagy's advice was not, after all, that risky.

Kuh brought to her gallery her links to Chicago's old-line German Jewish community and became an artistic doyenne to several of the early collectors, like Claire Florsheim Zeisler, who became one of the country's important fiber sculptors, and who bequeathed to the Art Institute, which had given her a full-scale show in 1979, four major Klee paintings and Miró's *Le Gendarme.* She had already given to the Whitney Museum Rauschenberg's *Satellite,* one of the artist's most famous "combine paintings," which Claire bought for $900 in 1955, the year it was painted. The Whitney had recognized Claire's importance in her field when it gave her an exhibition in 1984.

When Kuh closed her gallery in 1941, her friend Dan Rich invited her to join the Art Institute as head of public relations. While in that job, she started a Gallery of Art Interpretation in the museum, and then became curator of twentieth-century art. Somewhere along the way, there began the long affair with Dan Rich. He left the museum in 1958, under a cloud after some ill-advised sales of Monets to a controversial New York dealer by the name of Abris Silbermann, and Kuh kicked up a public storm when she was not named director. She tendered her resignation after a year, and to her shock it was accepted. She then resumed commercial activity as an art advisor, primarily to the First National Bank, and when she moved to New York in the 1960s, one of her clients, Arnold Maremont, got her a job as art critic on the *Saturday Review.*

The embarrassment associated with Dan Rich's mismanagement and indiscretions led the trustees to inaugurate the first of the country's unfortunate dual directorships. On Rich's departure in 1958, the board hired John Maxon, who had been director of the museum of the Rhode Island School of Design, but named him director of fine arts, coequal with Allan McNab, director of administration. Both reported to the board. This step turned out to be critical, and calamitous, in the history of the great museum.

Maxon came loaded with baggage. Although he had a commitment to art and was a man of considerable taste, Maxon was a loner, an underdog, petulant and self-pitying, and it was the underdog artist that Maxon's artistic program championed. His weak personality was certainly no match for the ambitious Scotsman McNab, nor indeed for his fellow victim, Leigh Block, who, although he was not to win the presidency for another twelve years, by the time of Maxon's arrival in 1958 was already the real power at the museum. Maxon fell completely under Block's spell—to what extent could only be guessed at—and Block acted as his protector until Maxon tragically choked to death at a dinner at the Tavern Club in 1977.

The damage suffered by the museum during Maxon's tenure, and continuing thereafter, was not, alas, entirely remediable. It was not damage merely to the morale of the staff, which was considerable. Although Maxon often came to dinner at my house on Division Street in the early sixties to cry on my shoulder and I did feel sorry for him, I also brushed off my shoulder the tears of another, far more distinguished man, Harold Joachim, curator of prints and drawings. Joachim, who carried on the work of his eminent predecessor, Carl Schniewind, in building one of the world's great drawings collections, could not stand Maxon and his secretive, meddling administration, nor Block and his megalomaniacal control, and it was almost weekly that I had to plead with Harold not to leave for the Cleveland Museum, with his great work unfinished.

There were other significant human casualties at the Art Institute during the Leigh Block era. A promising young museum man, Allen Wardwell, came to work at the museum in 1960, during the period when William McCormick Blair was still president but Leigh Block had already taken control. Wardwell was fresh out of NYU's Institute of Fine Arts, with no previous museum experience, and he was hired by Maxon as assistant curator of primitive art. Allen and his wife, Sally, brought much more to Chicago than a master's degree in art history, at least from Mary and Leigh Block's standpoint. They came connected. Allen's father, one of the country's eminent lawyers and a pillar of the WASP establishment, was senior partner of Davis, Polk & Wardwell. Sally was a Tilgh-

man. They were attractive and intelligent, and they were gathered immediately into the bosom of the Chicago society to which Mary and Leigh
had long aspired and from which they were excluded.

These were the Camelot days, and the young bloods of Chicago society, at least the ones who had come in from Lake Forest to live in the city,
on the Near North Side, were of liberal bent, militant on civil rights,
soon to oppose the Vietnam War. The Wardwells fitted right in. Leigh
took to calling Allen a "hippie" and carping about the length of his hair.
They had some confrontations on the Art Institute's steps, mainly about
Leigh's interference in curatorial affairs. It did not help Allen's case that
on one occasion he infuriated Block by permitting an art school student
to photograph a nude girl in the decorative arts galleries. It was clear to
Allen that if you weren't with Leigh Block, you were against him.

The Blocks seemed to tolerate the Wardwells for a few years, until the
late sixties. It was at that point, after the Blocks had been rebuffed by
Lake Forest and moved to Lake Bluff, that things suddenly soured and
Mary and Leigh took a palpable dislike to Allen. It occurred to me at the
time that there may have been a reason more sinister than the opposition
of the young "Astor Street crowd" to the war—the old saw about love
and hate being related emotions—why Leigh at this point went after
Allen like a terrier.

John Maxon had been protected, despite his obvious deficiencies, first
by Blair during his tenure, which ended in 1966, and then by Block,
both for reasons that are obscure. In 1965 Charles Cunningham was
appointed director and Maxon, whose title had been director of fine arts,
was demoted to vice president and associate director. Cunningham, formerly director of the Wadsworth Atheneum in Hartford, had been the
first fully qualified director in Chicago since the 1930s. He knew and
cared about art, and, because of his family connections, enjoyed the confidence of his Lake Forest board. Though Cunningham himself never
spelled it out for me, Leigh Block's increasing power, his interference in
curatorial affairs, and his continued protectiveness of Maxon certainly
spurred Cunningham's retirement in 1972. It was said that finally, when
Leigh told Cunningham about an exhibition he, Leigh, was planning for
the museum, Cunningham knew it was time to go. It was the end of the
hands-off era of his old patrician friend William McCormick Blair, and
the beginning of the new era of hands-on board chairman-directors,
which has since spread like the pox to museums throughout the country.

Cunningham was smart enough to spot it early and get out before Leigh Block had a chance to spill any of his blood. Block had essentially been the de facto director of the museum for at least the preceding six years.

Maxon was now named acting director. Wardwell was at that point assistant director, heir apparent, it was thought, to the directorship, one of the museum world's golden boys. Soon after Cunningham's retirement, Wardwell, wary of Maxon's meddling, wrote a memo to Maxon, with copies to the personnel who had been reporting to Wardwell, requesting a written definition of his areas of authority. Maxon apparently had a passkey to Wardwell's office, and one day Allen found a note on his desk from Maxon announcing dissolution of the position of assistant director and demoting Wardwell to curator of primitive art.

Hoping that an effective administration could end the years of chaos, the trustees in 1972 appointed Lawrence Chalmers president. Chalmers, who had been chancellor at the University of Kansas, had no museum experience and no knowledge of art. It was yet another humiliation for Maxon to be demoted to vice president for collections, reporting to Chalmers. Cunningham had at least been a respected senior museum director, an art man. As for Wardwell, he still had two implacably jealous enemies crouching in the wings, Block and Maxon. Fed up with the politics, which had nothing to do with his commitment to art, and seeing the handwriting writ large upon the wall, Wardwell resigned a few months later, in 1973. A number of trustees were aware of what they were losing in Allen Wardwell. Another faction was either in the Blocks' thrall or considered Allen a "pinko." The board was split. But then Allen did something that pulled the rug out from under his trustee supporters, like the Alsdorfs, unified the board, and sealed his fate, not only at the Art Institute but effectively throughout the museum world, which, true to American form, dislikes whistle-blowers: he published an article the following autumn in *Chicago* magazine describing in detail the chaos at the Art Institute. Sally and Allen moved to New York, where Allen closed out his museum career as director of Asia House and consultant to Christie's. He died of a heart attack in the spring of 1999, a casualty, in the end, of Chicago's byzantine social structure.

After three decades of strife, the great museum still had no director, only Chalmers, a putative administrator, as president. The museum drifted along through the next five years under Block's and Maxon's curatorial control, with erratic acquisitions and exhibitions policies. As usual in these situations in which the curatorial and administrative functions are split, the administrator increasingly began to interfere in curatorial matters, and tension mounted between Chalmers and Maxon. The same had happened from 1959 to 1966 between Allan McNab and Maxon. The strife between Chalmers and Maxon had made it apparent to the board for some time that Chalmers had to go, but he simply refused to leave. After Maxon died in 1977, a search committee of the board started to look for a replacement. Meanwhile, word of tension between Chalmers and the board, and of Leigh Block's infamous interference, continued to spread among museum professionals, and the job, whatever it was to be called, and whatever its responsibilities, with the many shifts through the years, became increasingly difficult to fill.

In 1978 a willing candidate was finally found in Alan Shestack, director of the Yale Art Gallery. James Alsdorf, who had succeeded Leigh Block as Art Institute board chairman in 1975, invited Shestack to Chicago to talk about the job. Shestack met with several members of the search committee, and Jim Alsdorf then made him an offer he found difficult to refuse: double his Yale salary and a lot of perks. Shestack phoned back in a week and accepted the offer. He made two more visits to the Art Institute, and it was on the second of these that he first encountered Leigh Block, who was visiting Chicago from his retirement home in Santa Barbara.

It was on this second visit that the job description was defined as vice president, reporting to Chalmers, who as president objected to anyone carrying the title of "director." Chalmers still had enough board clout at this point to get his way. Leigh Block, despite having moved away to Santa Barbara, had by no means removed his talons from the Art Institute, and was offended that Shestack was demanding a title more august than Maxon's had been. It was on this visit that Leigh took Shestack on a stroll through the galleries, pointing out all the paintings he and Mary had donated, making no bones to Shestack about who was in charge—geography notwithstanding—and when Shestack indicated his intention to change some of Maxon's idiosyncratic installations, Block told him that in deference to Maxon's memory, and for an undefined length of time, nothing should be rehung.

Meanwhile, one of the trustees, not realizing Shestack was Jewish, took him aside and told him that if it bothered him to deal with Block and Alsdorf, he should relax and not worry, because when Alsdorf's term was over, there would never again be a Jew in charge. Another local lady, not realizing Shestack was Jewish, was dealing with Jim Alsdorf, and said she knew how difficult it was dealing with Jews. Shestack, unused to Middle Western social mores, and realizing that it was not, after all, a real directorship he was being offered, decided it was not the job for him. But the museum had already leaked the story of his appointment, and Shestack, who had never given Yale a clue that he was leaving, was in an embarrassing situation. The Chicago trustees therefore decided to cast blame on Shestack's wife, labeling her an East Coast snob. Stories supporting that theory appeared in the press. Embarrassed by the whole episode, Shestack returned to his Yale directorship, and Chicago continued its search for a director.

It was a public relations fiasco in 1978 that enabled the board to finally relieve itself of Chalmers's services. Though Chalmers was president, nominally at this point director, of the Art Institute, so ignorant was he of the collection that he was unable to identify in a television interview a Cézanne painting that had been stolen from the museum. For the first time in some forty years, peace finally settled on the Art Institute in 1980, when James Wood, director of the St. Louis Museum, was hired as full director.

It was in the years of turmoil at the Art Institute, the years during which Leigh Block, and through him his protégé Maxon, controlled its destiny, the 1960s and 1970s, that grave damage was inflicted on the museum's collection. It is with this that the trustees, and the public, must continue to live, long after the departure of Block and Maxon. In 1961 Maxon hired a forty-five-year-old conservator by the name of Alfred Jackstas. He was named chief conservator in 1971, in which position he remained until 1979.

Painting conservation had, until the 1930s, been treated as a craft, not a science. Art history itself was not recognized as an academic discipline in the European universities until late in the nineteenth century, or in the ancient English institutions until our own time, and connoisseurship—the identification of objects by their aesthetic qualities—was born at Harvard under Paul Sachs, the transplanted banker, only in the second decade of this century. So it was logical that the study of conservation, its transformation from craft into science, should also commence at Harvard, in 1928. This was a necessary transformation, but as with the inauguration of any science, there had to be an initial period of experimentation, and it is in these periods of initiation that mistakes are made. In medicine, inaugural experiments are done on animals, and mistakes are supposed to do no harm. Only after much time and proof are humans exposed to new technologies. So it is with all the sciences. Few risks are taken, whether under the sea, on earth, in space, or anywhere else—except with art, which, to those who care, is a product of the human spirit, as precious as life itself.

Out of the conservation courses at Harvard's Fogg Museum came the new technology's best-known practitioners, Caroline and Sheldon Keck, and they came to personify the science of conservation. The Kecks became conservators at the Brooklyn Museum before setting up a conservation center in Cooperstown, New York. Their theories seemed to make the first sense in a field in which much damage had been done to paintings in the past, mainly in the late nineteenth century, and then during Lord Duveen's huckstering in the 1920s and 1930s. One has only to visit the painting collection at Harvard's own postdoctoral center, the Villa I Tatti in Florence, to see how oblivious even the great connoisseur Bernard Berenson had been to the condition of paintings and their conservation, and to realize how the study of art conservation was a logical product of Paul Sachs's Harvard courses in connoisseurship and museology, and followed the inauguration of art history itself as a discipline in the European universities by less than half a century. For if from history and iconography we can situate a work of art geographically and chronologically; from documents perhaps ascertain its existence and that of its putative author; and through connoisseurship identify the handwriting of its author, then it follows that if that handwriting is obscured, whether through grime, overcleaning, overpainting, or flattening of the artist's brushstrokes, the artist's message is at best muted, at worst obliterated. So it becomes as logical, if not urgent, an academic enterprise for a university's art history department to address the treatment of the illnesses of works of art as it is for its medical school to address the illnesses of people.

At its best, painting conservation had been, in times past, a cure for a problem a painting had suffered; at its worst, in Duveen's time, it had been a tool for gussying up a painting to make it more saleable. If a painting was dirty, it was cleaned, and little care was taken to consider the strength of the solvent used to clean it. If it had a hole or tear in it, another canvas was glued to its back under great pressure, and the restorer hadn't a clue that the impasto being flattened contained the essence of the artist's personality. In those days before connoisseurs informed the restorer about the particular artist's technical habits—the support, the ground, the underpainting, the pigments, glazes, and varnishes he used—the craftsman-restorer had no idea what had been there originally, what visual effect the artist had intended, what to take off, what to leave on. Not only was the study of connoisseurship at Harvard an attempt to systematize all this in light of the artists' emerging personalities, but it turned out a generation of museum director-disciples of the new faith. As it tragically evolved, it would take almost forty years for the powerful influence of the Kecks' scientific bias to be shaken off and for science and aesthetics to be brought into balance.

A conservation department had been established by Edward Waldo Forbes, director of the Fogg Museum, in 1928. The department evolved as handmaiden to the courses of study in connoisseurship, but its initial stimulus was Forbes's lifetime preoccupation with technical components, the artists' materials and techniques. His most famous course at Harvard, "Methods and Processes of Painting," was nicknamed the "egg and plaster" course. Forbes "considered technical studies to be complementary to other methods such as historical research and iconography." While Forbes's colleague Paul Sachs was fathering the study of connoisseurship and training the eyes of two generations of museum directors, Forbes's scientific approach was being used to train the hands of conservators, creating a forum for experiments in conservation, a field more physically dangerous, in its initial stages, to the objects themselves.

The creation of this new science soon generated a debate in the art world as heated as that in the architectural world between the preservationists who would leave old buildings or neighborhoods just as they found them, merely shored up against further deterioration, and those who would "gentrify" them to modern standards. At the very outset, there were those who felt passionately that old paintings should remain as time had weathered them, with yellowed varnish, with only the surface grime removed and any holes and tears repaired, just as there are those who feel that old people should leave their hair gray and unpainted, their pates shiny and unadorned with transplants and hairpieces, their wrinkles—all that reveals experience and character—undisturbed by plastic surgeons.

There were others who approached the problem more scientifically. Paintings consisted of their material components and should be stripped of all changes to the artist's original construction, areas of loss should be restored to what was there when the painting left the artist's hands, and steps should be taken to prevent further deterioration. This was the scientific approach on which the Fogg based its curriculum and which the Kecks, trained at the Fogg, taught at their school of conservation in Cooperstown to scores of painting conservators, later to preside in the 1950s, 1960s and 1970s over laboratories across the country at museums like the Museum of Modern Art, the Nelson-Atkins Gallery in Kansas City, St. Louis, Oberlin, Yale, the Sterling Clark Institute in Williamstown—and the Art Institute of Chicago.

The new science seemed to make all kinds of sense, as sciences are supposed to do. The problem is that science, when applied to subjects like the human mind and the art it dreams up, does not always work as planned. When a conservator, ignorant of an artist's personality and idiosyncratic techniques, attacked a painting to reduce it to the original surface, removing all the dirt, discoloration, and later restoration, he sometimes went too far, because he did not understand the artist's intentions, and also removed original glazes, thinking they were later varnish layers. This is the tragedy that befell the James Jackson Jarves collection at the Yale University Art Gallery.

Jarves was born in Boston in 1818, heir to the New England Glass Company, makers of Sandwich Glass. Uninterested in the family business, Jarves took up residence in Italy, and by 1858 had put together the first collection in the Western Hemisphere, by a generation, of early Italian paintings. Having squandered his glass fortune on the 119 paintings, in 1867 Jarves borrowed $20,000 from Yale University for three years at 6 percent interest, using the collection as collateral. He was unable to repay the loan, and it was declared forfeit in 1871. Yale maintained that the paintings could not be sold piecemeal, no other buyers came forward to acquire the collection as a whole and thus enable Jarves to redeem it, and Yale became its reluctant owner at a cost of the $20,000 loan, plus $2,000 interest. Jarves claimed the collection had cost him $60,000. Over the years, the Jarves collection became the Yale University Art

Gallery's primary claim to fame, for its holdings by such rare artists as Luca di Tommé, Giovanni del Biondo, Lippo Vanni, Gentile da Fabriano, Neroccio dei Landi, the Master of the Osservanza, and, most notable of all, *The Rape of Deianira* by Antonio Pollaiuolo.

The Jarves paintings remained in the condition in which they were acquired, many of them, as with most paintings five or six centuries old, with losses and areas of repaint. I knew them in this state when I graduated from Yale in 1952. But in the early 1950s, the collection's destiny had been placed in the hands of a Yale art history department professor, curator of Renaissance art, and son of a former Yale president, Charles Seymour, Jr. With such holdings as the Jarves collection, the Mabel Brady Garvan collection of early American furniture, Katherine Dreier's Société Anonyme collection of twentieth-century art, and the Stephen Clark bequests of late-nineteenth-century French paintings, the Yale Art Gallery had long since taken its place as much more than a teaching collection, but it was as teaching tools that Seymour viewed the Jarves pictures. And it was in this spirit, and with no oversight from the university administration, his own faculty, or the art gallery governing board, that he charged his friend, a restorer by the name of Andrew Petryn, with an extensive, twenty-year program of cleaning the Jarves paintings to "show the role played by conservation in increasing our understanding of early panel painting." The approach was scientific, not aesthetic. In a medical school, the sort of work that was performed on the Jarves pictures would have been reserved for cadavers in an anatomy class, not living human beings. And after the artists' techniques had been laid bare, even when Jarves's beloved pictures had been scraped down to the panels, Seymour and Petryn found no traces of the spirits that had made them. Nothing was left but the maimed cadavers. As Keith Christiansen writes about one of the masterpieces of the Jarves collection in his definitive catalogue raisonné on Gentile da Fabriano, "The condition is ruinous. The panel, cropped on all sides, was radically over-cleaned in 1950–52. . . . There is nothing left of the final layer of pigment. The deep green and maroon glazes on the gold pillow are almost completely lost, as is the modelling on the Child's pillow and Virgin's dress."

In a chapter devoted to the impact of American social pressures on cultural institutions and ultimately even on the physical condition of objects in museum collections, it seems appropriate to digress here to discuss the culture at Yale in the 1950s. What was it that bred Charles Seymour, Jr.'s arrogance in simply taking over and disposing of as he pleased a collection that had lain undisturbed at Yale for over eighty years? What were the "values" that allowed a charter member of the "Yale family" such license? The stage for this New Haven massacre was certainly set by the Yale culture.

Yale's anthem, "For God, for country, and for Yale"—one wondered from time to time what was the proper order—was taken to heart in New Haven. Yale's, more than any other university's, was always an insular family. The "family" concept fostered a feeling of security among its members, the warmth of belonging, of knowing that the family would take care of you for the rest of your life. From this family came generation after generation of cabinet members and presidents—and generous benefactors. In my day, between 1947 and 1952, the State Department and the CIA, by then themselves branches of the extended family, came on their annual recruiting calls, and to go into the foreign service, even to become a "spook," was considered an honorable calling. I marvel in retrospect at how I so bought into this pervasive and intoxicating Yale culture that I submitted to an interview by the CIA, an agency whose activities, within a dozen short years, I came to revile.

The sanctification of secrecy, of clandestine activity in God's, the country's—and Yale's—service had its origins in Calvinist mysticism and was instilled in generation after generation of Yale's elite—and in awe of this indigenous aristocracy, the vast undergraduate body—through the secret societies. On Thursday nights there was the lockstep march of the fifty black-suited members to the societies' tombs—Skull and Bones's for instance, dated from the 1850s and is one of the glories of Egyptian Revival architecture in America. The annual tap day in the courtyard of Branford College was the biggest day of the university year, the day into which fed the university's elaborate social system of fraternities and extracurricular organizations, all ranked according to their value in securing election to the secret societies, each of the societies in a rigid pecking order. All this was meant not only to strike awe in the hearts of the student body but to define an American elite, the masters of our universe, and the bounty out there awaiting those who chose to ascend loyally, without deviation, the prescribed ladder to power. Yale was, in this sense, a microcosm of the American society the students were to find when they graduated, and to succeed in the Yale incubator would not only assure them for life the support of their predecessors but have trained them to get to the top themselves.

Yale had never, since its founding in 1701, welcomed outsiders or eccentrics into its system, any more than did the country at large. There were of course few non–Anglo-Saxon outsiders for the country to either welcome or reject until after the Civil War, and at Yale, bastion of Calvinist values, few until after World War II. The legions of white Anglo-Saxon males descending annually on New Haven from Andover, Taft, and particularly Hotchkiss, with its heavy Middle Western representation from Grosse Point and Lake Forest, arrived with the baggage of protective anti-Semitism. But their induction into the Yale system, launched at boarding school well before their arrival in New Haven, was quickly, or at least superficially, moderated by Yale's cherished Jeffersonian aristocracy. This was a democracy in which Yale proudly proclaimed that anyone could make it, white or black, Christian or Jew, private or public school alumnus, as long as he did not deviate, in behavior or dress or the activities he pursued, as long as he did not rock any boats or blow any whistles, as long as he became and remained a member of the family. It helped to have been born into the family—more time could therefore be allocated to academics and less to social climbing—but adoptions became more commonplace with the arrival of former servicemen and the return of members of the class of '45W after World War II. There were, in my early years at Yale in the late forties, along with a few vestigial valets and wood-sided wagons, their backboards loaded with martini shakers and wicker picnic baskets at Yale Bowl, a handful of eccentrics, born into the Yale family, tolerated but not accepted, cast out by Skull and Bones and Scroll and Key families for their failure to be tapped, their rooms full of blue china, lilies in their lapels, brandishing Edwardian sword canes, conscientious Wildean eccentrics, practicing or feigning homosexuality, defiantly flouting not only the Yale family but their own as well. Most of these few exceptions became, after graduation, wandering expatriates, living off trust funds bequeathed by trusting ancestors. Of the many who became and remained loyal to the family and its values, so secure had Yale made them and so insecure outside its protective walls, a fair number chose to remain in New Haven for the rest of their lives, working for Yale or in pursuits close by. Charles Seymour, Jr., was one of these, son of a Yale president and charter member of the family. Yale was his home, and its property his own. This included the James Jackson Jarves collection.

It was tragic that the Seymour-Petryn experiments on the Jarves collection could not have waited just a few more years, for by the mid-1970s the flaws in the Kecks' theories had become manifest; their methods were discredited, and modern techniques of painting conservation refined and codified. Basic new tenets had been adopted: that restoration be necessary; that it be the cure for existing problems, not a preventative against future ones; and that it be reversible. Insofar as possible, a painting was to be left alone. Old varnish, surface grime, discolored or unnecessary old restorations were to be removed only when possible without risk. New restorations, when called for, were applied in pigments more soluble than the original paint surface so they could be removed without risk of damage to the materials the artist himself had applied. There is still some debate about whether old paint losses should be concealed by inpainting or revealed, and the decision is usually the owner's in consultation with the conservator, depending on the nature of the painting and its period. If new varnish is applied, the degree of glossiness is calculated to approximate what the artist intended. In no case is the original paint surface to be disturbed.

One of the most destructive of the Kecks' disciples was Alfred Jackstas, the conservator at the Art Institute of Chicago. He subscribed to the theory that a painting should be relined, even if cracks due to age had not developed into surface cleavage, as a reinforcement of the original fabric support to prevent future cleavage and potential paint loss. Since only organic varnishes existed prior to the 1950s, and these tended to yellow with age, the Kecks initiated the use of nonorganic varnishes that did not yellow and were supposed to remain clear. As for relining pictures, older techniques had involved the binding together of the old and new canvases with glue by applying great pressure, and in the days when conservation was a craft rather than a science, this often resulted in the squashing of the painting's impasto, essentially the artist's handwriting. The Kecks' technique used wax, and the two canvases were bound together not with pressure but with heat that melted the wax.

These theories led Jackstas, in a frenzy of prevention, to run rampant through the museum's collection, apparently concentrating on the most important paintings rather than just the ones that were in an acute state of deterioration. If the commitment is to prevention, why not spend one's time on the masterpieces rather than dealing with deteriorating inconsequentia? The traditional organic varnishes did indeed yellow over the years. So science dictated, for instance, that nonorganic varnishes (in this case methacrylates) be used; these would not yellow, it was thought, and the painting's original colors would be visible beneath them. All this made sense, except that as time passed from the fifties, sixties, and seventies into the eighties and nineties, although those clear, nonorganic varnishes, applied to hundreds of important paintings throughout the country, indeed did not yellow and remained white, they became opaque and milky instead. The wax that had been melted to bind together the original canvas and the lining canvas, replacing the application of glue and pressure, was often found to permeate the canvas, bleed into the painting's surface, and alter the aesthetics. Sometimes, when the canvas was porous, such as burlap, the wax could not be removed. Irreversible damage was done in those experimental years. So it was that Jackstas relined and damaged the great Manet *The Mocking of Christ* and overcleaned the Botticelli *Madonna and Child with an Angel,* painted on wood panel. Neither painting had needed restoration at all. If treatments so experimental were applied to humans, the law would intervene. There are no laws to protect works of art.

This then was the legacy of the Blocks, mutant spawn of a provincial social system: the cream of their own paintings sold off, whole collections lost to the city through anti-Semitism, masterpieces mutilated, a great young museum director sacrificed. The conditions that warped the Blocks no longer prevail in the city's social structure or at the Art Institute. Suburbs and apartment buildings do not ban Jews. Even the clubs have cracked open their doors. Leigh and Mary Block did not of course damage the paintings themselves. But their exercise of power kept competent management away from the Art Institute and protected two incompetents, Maxon and Jackstas, and it was Chicago's social order that inspired the Blocks' grab for power.

This is the saga of how a great international city—its cultural institutions second to none in the world—developed at a pace with which its provincial Middle Western social structure could not keep up; architectural monuments demolished, lakefront defiled, collections dispersed, masterpieces desecrated. The Art Institute's violated paintings stand as tombstones of an unlamented era, a warning for the future, as do the corpses of the Jarves paintings at Yale. Manet's flayed masterpiece, *The Mocking of Christ*, towers ironically as the greatest among them, for Christ was indeed mocked and crowned with thorns by Chicago's legions of the night.

GERTRUDE STEIN: THE INHERITANCE

There are volumes about Gertrude Stein and Alice Toklas, many of them by contemporaries who knew them. There is, however, a chapter that has not yet been written, concerning events that transpired after they both had died.

Gertrude Stein's fame and power was, I think, more the result of fortuitous timing and her American origins than her literary accomplishments. She arrived in Paris from Baltimore in 1903, and Toklas from San Francisco in 1907, where they were both born to affluent Jewish families, Stein in 1874 and Toklas in 1877. Stein and Toklas met at the home of Gertrude's brother and sister-in-law, Michael and Sarah Stein, the great Matisse collectors, in 1907, moved in together, and launched their salon just in time to see out the nineteenth century and usher in the twentieth.

The French had, since the Paris days of Benjamin Franklin, romanticized the rough-hewn, plainly dressed and plainspoken American. They had come in contact only with the occasional robber baron's daughter on the prowl for a title, Brahmins on the grand tour, or the cultivated expatriate, not yet the hordes of artists, writers, and tourists that within five years would be overrunning the streets and brasseries. Stein and Toklas were the vanguard of the vanguard, eccentric of dress and lifestyle just before bohemianism became commonplace. By the time their compatriots arrived, they were already famous, their art collection and Friday salon a legend.

Stein seems to have been a rather unlikable character, Toklas less so only after Stein was no longer around. Before that, Toklas played the artist's wife, keeping everyone at bay. Stein's arrogance and snobbishness were part of a theatrical show. In 1996 I saw the first American performance in sixty years, with costumes and sets, of *Four Saints in Three Acts,* the opera Stein wrote with Virgil Thomson, and even with Robert Wilson's costumes and sets it seemed like a dated piece of conscientious vanguardism. I came away with the feeling that most of the excitement at the famous 1934 premiere performance in Hartford must have been supplied by Florine Stettheimer's designs, which Robert Wilson told me had not survived, and by the audience itself.

In barely over a century and a quarter, America had produced only a handful of real geniuses like Walt Whitman and Winslow Homer. By and large, the country was still in awe of European culture; the American posture exemplified by Nathaniel Hawthorne, Thomas Cole, and Henry James, and much later by Joseph Cornell, was one of peering at Europe from the outside. There were more artists like Mary Cassatt and Gertrude Stein than Whitman and Homer. Both Cassatt and Stein were more catalytic than creative, yet both were seminal in bringing European culture to the Americans.

Still, Stein and Toklas loomed large in my imagination as icons of an age, a city, and a neighborhood, the neighborhood I lived in for half a year in 1950. The streets around the Jardin du Luxembourg and the Boulevard Saint-Michel were hallowed ground, and so was the legend of the Stein-Toklas salon, which saw in modernism and the twentieth century.

I always stop and read historic plaques on buildings, and on several occasions in 1950 I set out to find the storied 27 rue de Fleurus, from which Gertrude and Alice had been forced by their landlord to move in 1938 (they relocated to 5 rue Christine, where Alice lived for eighteen years after Gertrude's death in 1946). On my walks, looking for something older, with charm and certainly bearing a plaque, I had passed by a nondescript apartment building, with the date "1894" on the wall, built only nine years before Stein and her brother Leo had moved in. I had seen photographs of the building's interior courtyard garden, with the Stein pavilion diagonally bisecting the northeast corner, and of the famous studio with all the Picassos. As far as I knew, no one had ever photographed the building's exterior. Toklas was a great cook, so I took my search to the local grocers, asking if anyone remembered the pair by name, or at least a stout lady with cropped hair who dressed like a man and a thin lady with a black mustache. Twenty-two years later, no one remembered the odd couple.

Each time I saw "27" on the wall of that dreary building, I thought I had gotten the number wrong. I finally confirmed it in a Stein biography, knocked on the concierge's window, and asked if Gertrude Stein had lived there. She shrugged her shoulders. I went through the passage into the courtyard. It was depressing, paved now, with no vegetation at all, not even a single tree, and a mechanic working in a garage against the north wall. There, to the right against the wall, was the pavilion in which Stein and Toklas had held their salon, and the glass passage they had built to connect it to the little two-story house on the east wall, with the second-story bedroom window Stein is seen leaning out of in the famous photograph.

I knocked on the door. A young working-class family was at lunch, but the man who answered the door said, yes, this had been Stein's studio, he graciously invited me in, introduced me to his wife and small children, and offered me a coffee. Then he took me through the glass-walled passage into the studio. The wallpaper had not been changed since Stein's day. The nailholes from the paintings were still there. I said to my host, "I'm terribly sorry to disturb your lunch. You must have pilgrims bothering you all the time." "Not at all," he said, "you're only the third person in the last year."

It was easy to imagine, in 1950, Gertrude Stein's salon in full flower. Most of the cast was still around, although I didn't meet any of them until 1958, and then my friends were mainly the surrealists, a generation younger than Stein and Toklas, not sympathetic with her aesthetic and not members of her circle. Many of them, like Ernst, Magritte, Miró, Dalí, Brauner, and Matta, had not even arrived in Paris from their far-flung countries until the 1920s and 1930s, by which time Stein's taste in artists had deteriorated. Her favorites then were a mediocre English painter, Francis Rose, of whose works she ultimately bought almost one hundred; Francis Picabia, a minor dadaist who joined her circle years after his brief moment in the vanguard sun between 1911 and 1917; and Pavel Tchelitchew, a representational Romantic. Notwithstanding Stein's early sighting of Picasso and Juan Gris, her taste seems to have been based more on which artists curried her favor than on hard-eyed connoisseurship.

Georges Hugnet and Man Ray, both of whom in the 1950s lived in penury nearby, were the surrealist exceptions, *anciens combattants* of the Stein-Toklas salon. By 1960 Hugnet badly needed money and wanted to sell me Max Ernst's huge *Paysage aux germes de blé* (now at the Kunstsammlung Nordrhein-Westfalen), and I wanted to buy it. Of course I had to see the painting before I paid Hugnet. I had no idea what condition it was in. But he had hocked it years before at the municipal pawnshop, the Crédit Municipal, and there was no way to get access, even for purposes of inspection, without paying off the loan. I knew that if I paid off Georges's debt and didn't buy the Ernst, he could never refund my money. So, with no alternative, I took the gamble. Hugnet repossessed his painting, it turned out to be splendid and in fine condition, and I paid him the balance.

Another of that generation, Kiki of Montparnasse, who, although still only in her forties, was well over the hill and in a sad state, did a little dance nightly at a bar off the Boulevard Saint-Michel, lifting her skirts and passing the hat. In any event, even in 1958, when again I found myself passing 27 rue de Fleurus, the romantic scent of the old salon was still fresh in the street.

There, on the outside wall of the building, was a big sign, ATELIER D'ARTISTE A VENDRE, with an agent's telephone number. I knocked for the concierge. It was indeed Stein's old studio. I phoned the agent as soon as I got back to the hotel. The price came to $12,000. Notwithstanding the lack of light, the gloomy courtyard, the concrete paving, and the active auto repairman, I had visions of a Paris branch of my gallery housed in that famous space, an opening exhibition with the Stein pictures borrowed back, nails in their old holes, salon veterans invited to the grand soirée, undoubtedly to be covered by *Life* magazine. My imagination took flight. All for $12,000.

The agent brought me down: "Of course the studio is occupied." "What does that mean?" "A family lives there." The family that had given me coffee. The agent referred me to a lawyer. There was no way to get possession from a family with two children who had occupied the place for years. In their economic bracket and at their age, it wasn't likely they would be moving anytime soon.

The *New York Times* carried the story of Alice Toklas's death on March 7, 1967, at the age of eighty-nine. Gertrude had predeceased her on July 31, 1946. The era had ended, but not without a final flourish, provided by the great Picasso collection and the peculiarity of Gertrude's will.

Stein, of course childless, as was her estranged brother Leo, had left everything to her nephew Allen, Michael and Sarah's son. Upon Allen's death, the estate was to be divided between his three children—Daniel, by Allen's first marriage, living in California; and Michael and Gabrielle, by his second, living at the time in Pittsburgh. The other bequests were her famous 1906 portrait by Picasso, left to the Metropolitan Museum, and her papers and memorabilia—50 manuscript notebooks and 142 presentation volumes—to the Yale University library, undoubtedly because of her old friendship with Thornton Wilder, who was intimately connected with Yale.

The estate, however, could not be distributed until the death of Toklas, because she was to have the use of it for her lifetime. This meant custody of the paintings and the right to sell what she needed to live on. The will gave express authority to the executors to "reduce to cash any paintings or other personal property insofar as it may become necessary for [Toklas's] proper maintenance and support."

In her old age and frail health, Alice exercised that right by selling two small Picasso paintings and some Picasso drawings to Daniel-Henri Kahnweiler, Picasso's old dealer. Clearly this is what Gertrude would have wanted Alice to do. But not Rubina Stein, Allen Stein's second wife and mother of Michael and Gabrielle. Allen himself had died in 1951 at the age of fifty-six. As soon as Rubina and her lawyer, Bernard Dupré, learned of the missing Picassos, they went to court and had the entire collection sequestered on the grounds that it was neglected and unprotected. The paintings were taken away from Alice and put in a vault at the Chase Manhattan Bank in Paris.

To add to the old lady's misery, having been born a Jew and converted to Catholicism in 1957, she had left her apartment on the rue Christine in 1960 for a lengthy retreat in an Italian monastery. While she was gone, her landlord launched eviction proceedings under France's arcane and often draconian rent control laws, and finally had her evicted in 1964. She lived out her remaining three years in an apartment on the rue de la Convention, arthritic and bedridden, almost blind and deaf, prohibited by the landlord from hanging on the thin walls her only remaining Picasso, a portrait of Dora Maar, a gift from her old friend Picasso.

Defying Gertrude's wishes for her inseparable companion of forty years, Rubina and Dupré had given lip service, with a small allowance for Alice, to Gertrude's instructions. The literary and artistic worlds were shocked by this maltreatment of Alice in her frailty and poor health, and about $10,000 was raised through friends like Janet Flanner, Virgil

Thomson, Doda Conrad, and primarily Thornton Wilder. But all this was barely adequate to cover housing costs, and with no paintings to sell, Alice was left destitute. All this while the collection rested comfortably in its vault, accumulating value for Rubina's offspring.

Apart from the specific bequests, Stein's estate on her own death in 1946 was inventoried at twenty-nine Picassos, seven Juan Gris, and one Matisse drawing. On Alice's death twenty-one years later, and even without the Picassos Alice had sold, there were thirty-eight Picassos, thirteen Juan Gris, and six Picabias. Clearly Rubina Stein and Maître Dupré were more meticulous in their inventorying than was Gertrude's administrator.

There wasn't much of an art market in 1946 when Gertrude Stein died, and as the years passed, the famous art collection was forgotten—except by Rubina and Bernard, who never took their eyes off it, and who had had it seized and sequestered during Alice's infirmity in the mid-1960s.

Alice's *Times* obituary was a long one. She had died at age eighty-nine, having outlived Gertrude by twenty-one years, and was buried beside her companion in Père-Lachaise Cemetery. The second paragraph revealed the forgotten secret, "With Miss Toklas' death, an important art collection—27 Picassos, 7 Juan Gris and a Matisse—will pass into the possession of Miss Stein's relatives in the United States." In 1997 this news would have caused an art dealers' and auctioneers' traffic jam, but not in 1967.

I found the name of Gertrude Stein's Baltimore administrator, Edgar Allan Poe, Jr., in John Malcolm Brinnin's *The Third Rose,* and telephoned him. Mr. Poe's august ancestry made me wary of an icy reception, but he turned out to be an easy man to talk to. He asked me to write him, which I did on March 8. In another conversation on the tenth, Poe dictated a letter for me to write, to be passed on to the Paris lawyers handling disposition of the estate, and my letter was sent the same day. Poe wrote me on the fourteenth reporting that he had referred my inquiry to the Paris lawyers and that I would be hearing directly from them.

A month went by with no word from Paris, and I phoned Poe again. On April 11 he wrote Russell Porter in Paris stressing his urgent desire that I be contacted, and on the same day Poe wrote me giving me Porter's address and suggesting I see him on my forthcoming trip to Paris. Poe wrote me another friendly letter on the eighteenth, and on the same day I wrote Porter saying that I would be in Paris on the twenty-fourth and suggesting we meet. Finally, Porter wrote Poe on the nineteenth explaining that there were three heirs to whom the paintings now belonged, that he had spoken to Mrs. Stein and "Mr. Dupré," that they had already been contacted by Sotheby's, Wildenstein, and "a variety of other people," and that "for the moment [they] are making no move, the paintings are still in the Chase Bank." This was the first mention of the paintings' actual whereabouts. I wrote Mr. Poe again on the twenty-ninth, the day after my return from Paris. I reported that I had spoken to Porter on the phone, and that since Stein and Dupré, representing the two French heirs, did not yet want to meet with me, I had asked Porter if I should make contact with Daniel Stein, the California heir. He said he thought that would be a good idea, and that I could get his address from Poe. Poe did not have Stein's address, but tried to contact him on my behalf.

Poe wrote me on June 15 saying that he had been unable to locate Daniel Stein, whom I had meanwhile heard was a peripatetic West Coast gambler, much in debt. Poe said his Stein family files were no help, since "the larger part of them were destroyed several years ago." Then, on June 21, through a chance encounter with a friend in San Francisco, I learned the name of Daniel Stein's lawyer: Tevis Jacobs.

I telephoned Jacobs, who turned out to be much respected, an art collector and chairman of the University Art Museum Council at Berkeley. We became friendly and almost immediately were on a first-name basis. Jacobs told me that he and Maître Dupré did not get along and that they had little contact. They disagreed about the disposition of the Stein paintings. Jacobs cared how they were sold and where they went, and Dupré was interested only in the money. Jacobs definitely did not want them to go to auction, and did not want them shopped around, and Dupré for some reason was insisting on Sotheby's. Since Dupré represented the heirs to two thirds of the paintings, the majority interest, Jacobs suggested I contact Dupré directly. Over the next eighteen months I acted as intermediary between the two lawyers, trying to effect a mutually acceptable disposition of the collection.

As the standoff between the lawyers dragged on, I became convinced that if Picasso died before they got the paintings out of France, there would be trouble. Under French law, if the work of a dead artist has been in France for more than fifty years, it may be called a national treasure and prevented from leaving. Picasso was already eighty-six in 1967. Almost everything in the collection had been painted more than fifty years before, and had been in France all that time, and there was no collection on which the spotlight could possibly shine so brightly. There were at least seven masterpieces, of which two, *Femme sur fond rose* and *Jeune fille aux fleurs,* were already famous in the days of the Stein-Toklas salon.

I telephoned Dupré on July 19, and at his suggestion wrote him the same day, stressing my interest in the collection, either as agent or as principal, and offering to come over to see it at any time. I heard nothing, and when I phoned he said perhaps it would be possible after September 15, when he was to return to Paris from the summer holidays. But the delaying tactics went on, to Tevis Jacobs's frustration, into the New Year. Jacobs agreed with me about the looming export problem, and with my general plan for the collection. Furthermore, his client, Daniel Stein, had huge gambling debts and needed the money. I went out to San Francisco, where I spent a pleasant evening with Jacobs and his wife at Trader Vic's. On August 29 I wrote Dupré again, saying that I had blocked off time for a trip to Paris right after September 15 and asking if this would be convenient.

My plan was to act as agent either for the Stein heirs or for a collector with deep pockets—they were scarce in 1968—who would buy the collection outright, have the paintings cleaned and carefully restored, framed, photographed, and catalogued, and see to it that a book was written about the history of the collection and a major touring museum exhibition mounted. All this would take at least three years, probably more. But if done well, the buyer would score a historic coup. Meanwhile, the Stein heirs would have the money they wanted.

In 1968 the auction market was not the retail forum it is today; these paintings would, I was sure, bring more as a collection than individually at auction. Tevis Jacobs agreed. But Dupré was obstinately holding out for Sotheby's, whose chairman, Peter Wilson, was as shrewd and ruthless as he was polished. Jacobs suspected a conflict of interest.

I finally convinced Dupré of the urgency of getting the paintings out of France. The logical place to send them would have been New York. The market for the pictures was in the United States, and conservation techniques there were more advanced than in Europe. But since Dupré's destination of choice was Sotheby's, and London was still Sotheby's primary venue, London was as far as I could bring him. He authorized me to search for a private London bank vault with enough space for potential buyers to inspect the paintings.

Finding a London vault large enough to hold the collection and permit viewing proved a formidable task. I enlisted the help of J. Henry Schroder Wagg & Company, with which I was connected through two directors, Lord Ogilvy (now the Earl of Airlie), whom I had known since my days at Lehman Brothers fourteen years before, and Bruno Schroder. Schroder cabled me on February 23, 1968, and wrote me on the twenty-ninth, saying that he had tried everything, from four of the largest banks to safe-deposit companies, even furniture-storage facilities. He could find nothing secure and private enough, with sufficient viewing space. The only suitable bank he knew of was in Amsterdam.

With the explosion of the art market, and with painting prices pushing $100 million, facilities of the sort we were seeking then are commonplace now. But this was the sixties. No painting had sold for even $2 million until Rembrandt's *Aristotle* startled the world when it sold in New York in 1961 to the Metropolitan Museum for $2.3 million.

The Japanese did not enter and transform the art market overnight until late 1971. In 1968 the war had not yet taken its toll in inflation and on art prices. The auctioneers had not yet advanced on the retail market. Sotheby's had not yet launched itself as a "financial services" behemoth, lending money to buyers and offering guarantees to sellers. These were the days when my room at the Connaught cost £8 11s. 6d. a night.

An article had appeared on January 31 in the *New York Times:* "Sale of Stein Art Planned by Heirs." Neither Tevis Jacobs nor I knew what Dupré was up to. The article went on to say that "negotiations are under way for the sale of all or part of the Gertrude Stein art collection." The reporter had then contacted Jacobs, who said that "we had considered selling the collection at auction, possibly at Sotheby's in London, but we decided against it." Jacobs had been quoted as saying that there "might be a private sale" within the next month in Paris. The article also quoted Jacobs as saying that Dupré was handling the sale, and that he, Jacobs, did not know where the paintings were. He did not, in fact, know where they were, but Sotheby's was by no means out of the picture.

The article panicked me. I still had not found a London repository. Had Dupré found one, shipped the paintings out of France, and started negotiating with a buyer without telling me, let alone Tevis Jacobs? Why else would he talk to the press, generate all this publicity, alert the French cultural authorities, and endanger the whole project? Jacobs was upset, but still unable to communicate with Dupré.

Finally, on February 17, Jacobs informed me that he had heard from Dupré who had succeeded in getting the Picassos out of France. I wrote Dupré the same day, congratulating him on getting the export documents and trying to set a date at the end of February or beginning of March to come to London to see the collection. Dupré informed me that the paintings had not left France and were still at the Chase Bank in Paris.

I was in London again in March, and on the eleventh finally succeeded in finding a vault at the National Provincial Bank which, if not ideal for viewing, would suffice. I gave Dupré the contact at the bank, as well as the names of a Paris photographer and Paris and London shipping agents. I did not get the feeling he trusted me enough, or anyone for that matter, to handle the whole project. Perhaps it had to do with my relationship with Tevis Jacobs. I wrote Dupré again on March 27, asking if I could see the paintings in Paris and offering to catalogue the collection for him. A meeting was finally arranged for late April.

I flew from London to Paris in April and met with Dupré a few days later at his office at 15 Quai aux Fleurs. We discussed the values of the Stein paintings, and I offered to send him photocopies of recent auction catalogues and price records. We made a date for dinner the next evening with Rubina Stein and my wife Sandra. They joined us at our hotel, the Meurice, and Dupré took us out to a Chinese restaurant. It was obvious almost immediately that Bernard and Rubina were not merely lawyer and client. I threw a glance at Sandra. The big encounter, the viewing of the Stein collection, was set for the next morning, May 1, at eleven-fifteen at the Chase Bank on the rue Cambon.

The vault doors were opened, and there, on the floor, propped against the walls, were the paintings, famous from the photographs of the Stein-Toklas salon. And as I stood looking at them, notebook in hand, Dupré nuzzled Rubina's neck. I looked at Sandra. Meanwhile, I took careful notes and measurements and copied everything off the painting stretchers. I had thought of bringing a camera, but decided that might put off Dupré.

Standing there for the first time before the legendary collection, only momentarily distracted by what was going on between Rubina and Dupré, I was struck by something else. There was a consistency to this part of the collection which Gertrude had formed with her brother Leo, and which she had retained after they split up in 1915. The muscular Cézannes and wild Matisses had gone, and what remained was rational and rather feminine.

The public image of Gertrude had been, throughout the century, that of a powerful, masculine revolutionary, straddling the artistic barricades. Yet the major Picassos she had held on to were the lyrical *Young Girl with a Basket of Flowers* of 1905, the *Standing Female Nude* of 1906, both of the "rose period" and pastel in palette, and of Picasso's major analytical cubist pictures, one of the least explosive, *The Architect's Table* of 1912. The wild *Nude with Drapery,* painted in the summer of 1907, which Leo and Gertrude had bought from Picasso that same autumn, had already been sold to Sergei Shchukin by 1913 (it is now at the Hermitage, St. Petersburg), and all that remained with Gertrude as a souvenir of this great painting was a study of the sleeping head.

Already intimates of Picasso by 1907, Gertrude and Leo presumably could have acquired powerful paintings like *Les Demoiselles d'Avignon,* 1907 (now at the Museum of Modern Art, New York), which Jacques Doucet finally bought in 1922, and *The Dryad* and *Composition with Skull,* 1908 (now at the Hermitage, St. Petersburg), both of which were grabbed by Shchukin. The contrast is apparent. Shchukin cleaved to Picasso's emotional side, Gertrude to his intellectual side.

The only Picassos Gertrude acquired after 1914 were a watercolor he inscribed and gave to her in 1918 and a pastel-colored, neocubist painting, *Calligraphic Still Life* of 1922, which was not dissimilar to Gris's work of the period. Perhaps Picassos had gotten too expensive for Gertrude by 1914, but Gris's personality seems more in tune with Gertrude's own. Juan Gris was, despite a falling-out during World War I, a personal and aesthetic passion of Gertrude's. His rational, formal paintings, all still lifes, were acquired between 1914 and 1926, the year before Gris died.

We left Rubina and Bernard at the bank and drove to the airport, spent the night in London, and returned to New York the next day. I posted a letter to Dupré as we left the Connaught, thanking him for the look at the collection and the Chinese dinner and promising him the auction information. Meanwhile, Tevis Jacobs had not even been supplied with a list of the paintings in the collection, and I had promised to put one together.

After I mailed the auction price information to Dupré, he sent me a typed list of the sixty works in the collection: forty Picassos, of which seven were works on paper, including the watercolor apple Picasso gave to Gertrude to console her for the loss of the Cézanne apple Leo took with him when he quit the ménage; thirteen Juan Gris, of which one was a watercolor and one a drawing; and seven Picabias, including a drawing. The nucleus of the collection was seven Picasso masterpieces, as well as four major Juan Gris.

There was no doubt in my mind that the collection should be kept together, for both historical and economic reasons. The minor works would not bring much if sold separately, but would have value as part of the collection. Several of them were gifts to Stein from the various artists and bore inscriptions. Jacobs also wanted the collection sold as a unit. I wrote him on August 13 telling him that I would be sending Dupré's list, which amazingly Jacobs had never seen. I asked him how he felt about commissioning me as agent for sixty days to catalogue the collection and try to sell it intact to a museum. Jacobs was a fellow Democrat, and I closed by saying, "Sandra and I are going out to Chicago for the convention. It ought to be pretty wild. At least in the area around the Amphitheater." Wild indeed.

Tevis replied on the fourteenth that he had heard little from Dupré, who had gone off to South America and then on vacation to Spain until August 20. He added, "I have had no cooperation from [Dupré] whatever." And then he revealed that there had been an offer of $6 million for the collection, which he thought might be raised "somewhat." He wrote, "I will write to him immediately and tell him of your suggestion, but to try to get information out of him is practically impossible. I haven't even got a list of the paintings. I would appreciate it if you would send me a copy of what you have. With this offer confronting us, I do not know why I cannot get word out of him. The offer won't stay open forever. Whether Dupré is trying to get a firm guaranty out of Sotheby's . . . I don't know. I doubt whether he will get it, but I am opposed to that course because we will never get a firm offer if people can think he is going to peddle it elsewhere. . . . I can't seem to get any final program out of Dupré." The offer had apparently come from Marlborough Fine Art, the London dealers.

The offer of $6 million had to be acted upon, Jacobs's client, Daniel Stein, was in dire need of money, Jacobs did not even have a precise itemization of his client's inheritance, and Dupré had gone off on holiday to South America and Spain. Jacobs feared Dupré was stalling, in order to get a guarantee from Sotheby's, and I feared the return in September of Peter Wilson, Sotheby's chairman, from his house in the south of France. With Wilson in Dupré's corner, it would be difficult to keep the Stein collection intact.

Jacobs's frustration was obvious in his letter of August 14, and he asked me for suggestions. I sent him a copy of Dupré's onionskin list of the works in the collection, which had finally arrived. But the titles and sizes were imprecise, the signatures and inscriptions had not been transcribed, and since the collection had never been catalogued, without photographs it was impossible to identify most of the works or collate them with the existing literature. After the difficulty I had had in getting a look at the collection—not wanting to spook Dupré while he was nuzzling Rubina Stein's neck that morning in the Chase vault—and with limited time, I had been afraid to ask if I could take snapshots and measurements and copy inscriptions. So no serious work could be done with respect to cataloguing or offering the collection to a museum until Dupré deigned to cooperate. I commiserated with Jacobs that Dupré seemed in no rush to have this done. I stressed that Dupré should in some way be compelled to put a price on the collection, no matter how high. Otherwise the stalemate could go on forever.

Strange as it may seem in today's buoyant art market thirty years later, there were not many prospective buyers for the Gertrude Stein collection in 1968. In the course of my efforts in 1967, I had what seemed to me an obvious idea, a plan that could produce results quicker, if necessary, than any museum could act, and at the same time hold the collection together, perhaps permanently, but at least long enough to restore the paintings, catalogue and exhibit them. On November 18, 1967, I had drawn up a prospectus to offer the collection to Nathan Cummings, either as agent or coventurer.

Cummings, living at that time between the Drake Tower in Chicago and the Waldorf-Astoria Towers in New York, had been collecting since the 1940s, throughout Chicago's "golden age." Nate had known me since my youth in Chicago, and in fact I had met my wife, Sandra, in 1964 at one of his birthday dances at the Drake Hotel.

Despite his years of collecting, Nate's collection was undistinguished. He had some well-known names and a few good pictures, the best of which was a Berthe Morisot he had picked up from a member of her family (*Le Jardin,* 1883). Nate always bought on price, or by pursuing some artist's importunate descendant up the back staircase. I remember running over to his Chicago apartment in 1961 with a fine 1913 synthetic cubist Picasso that happened to have once belonged to Gertrude Stein, but Nate didn't find $55,000 enough of a bargain, certainly not from "Dick" Feigen, whom he had known as a child. I sold the painting to David Lloyd Kreeger, whose problem was not in recognizing quality or wanting bargains but rather in a $200,000-per-painting psychological limit: two paintings for $200,000 each, but never $400,000 for one. I have, incidentally, encountered few collectors without some such idiosyncrasy.

I had learned early that there are rarely such things as the "bargains" in art that Nate Cummings persistently pursued, and those few are not worth the hunt: you stumble on them or you don't. The real bargains are the masterpieces that also come along but rarely, whether the art market is hot or cold, and always cost too much.

I had, for instance, asked Stephan Lackner, Max Beckmann's friend and patron, to please let me know if ever he decided to part with a truly important Beckmann, the twentieth-century artist I cherish most. One day in 1959 he phoned and offered me a landscape, good but not great. I said, "Stephan, I want a great Beckmann." "All right then, what about *Die Barke?*" Beckmann's *The Bark* is not only one of Beckmann's great pictures, it is one of the landmarks of the twentieth century. It had hung in Berlin in the National Gallery from 1928, when it was donated in honor of the sixtieth birthday of the art historian Julius Meier-Graefe, until Hitler sold it as a "degenerate" painting in 1937. "But," said Lackner, "I want a lot of money, and no offers." I was afraid even to ask. "How much is a lot of money?" "$35,000." I didn't have $35,000, and no idea where to get it. I would never have a chance at a painting like that again, and it was certainly worth a hell of a lot more than 35,000 little pieces of green paper, wherever they came from. "OK, Stephan, it's a deal." Of course I had to buy *The Bark.* My phone rang almost immedi-

Nathan Cummings in his apartment at the Waldorf-Astoria Towers, New York, circa 1980

Photograph courtesy of Mrs. Robert B. Mayer

ately. It was "Buster" May, the greatest Beckmann collector in history and my old adversary in Beckmann collecting, calling from St. Louis. "Dick, you're crazy! You've ruined the Beckmann market! That painting isn't even worth $20,000. I offered $25,000, and that was too much!" "Buster," I said, "you're right. I paid too much. But I couldn't get it for less. You're sitting there with all those May Department Stores and I don't even know where I'm going to get the $35,000. Buster, old friend, it's you I think are crazy!" Fortunately, I learned early enough what Nate Cummings never learned—what a real bargain is. *The Bark* will never be for sale, but if it were right now, I suppose it's worth six hundred times what I overpaid for it.

Nathan Cummings had the two attributes I thought necessary for quick action on the Stein collection: money, and the need for some world-class paintings in his overrated collection. But my real dream was to have time to catalogue, restore, and exhibit the collection, and then sell it intact to the institution where it clearly belonged, the Museum of

Modern Art. I had no clue that Bates Lowry, their director at the time, had gotten the same idea from his colleague William Lieberman and by September 1968 was already chasing the collection.

In late September 1968, while I was still waiting for a chance to catalogue and photograph the collection, Tevis Jacobs phoned me. "Richard," he said, "we've now had an offer of $6,250,000, and Dupré has agreed to accept it. The offer comes from a syndicate of Museum of Modern Art trustees—David Rockefeller, Nelson Rockefeller, André Meyer, Bill Paley, and Jock Whitney. We have twenty-four hours to give them an answer. You've helped me communicate with Dupré, you've worked hard, so I want you to have an option on the collection at the same price for those twenty-four hours." I have rarely met anyone in forty years in the art business as correct and gentlemanly as Tevis Jacobs.

The syndicate was awesome, but it did not seem that its intention was to keep the collection together. This was like going up against the Yankees' old murderers' row, but after almost two years of work I couldn't surrender without at least a shot at my one fallback. I phoned Nate Cummings at the Waldorf. He told me to come over for breakfast at eight the next morning. That gave me until six o'clock the same evening to produce an offer.

The more I thought about it, the more sense it made for Nate to buy the collection. He was by that time in his seventies. He was a man of enormous wealth. He had come down to Chicago from Montreal as a young man and founded Consolidated Foods, which he still controlled, and $6 million meant, or should have meant, nothing to him. Of course Nate could be odd about money. I remember walking out onto Fifth Avenue after a Metropolitan Museum meeting, and there was Nate, by then in his eighties, drenched and almost blind behind his thick glasses streaming with water, trying vainly to hail a taxi in a driving rainstorm. I said, "Nate, what the hell are you doing out here? Why don't you have a car?" "Oh," he said, "I only have to go to the Waldorf."

Nate liked a bargain, and at $6,250,000 the Gertrude Stein collection seemed to me one of the bargains of art history. Nate liked the intrigue of the chase, and what could be more intriguing than outflanking five of the panjandrums of the business and social worlds? Nate liked publicity, and what could command more attention than acquiring the Gertrude Stein collection?

Several years before, Nate had bought, apparently for a song, the Wasserman–San Blas Collection, the outstanding pre-Columbian collection, painstakingly amassed over several generations. He promptly rebaptized it the Nathan Cummings Collection, though he hadn't added a single piece, and put it on loan at the Jeu de Paume in Paris, where banners with Nate's name flew all over the city. When the Art Institute of Chicago refused to give the collection a separate gallery, Nate donated it instead to the Metropolitan Museum, which made him an "honorary trustee," a useful category for donors whose collections it wants but whose presence on the board it could do without.

Not long before the Stein collection was offered to me, it was announced that Nate's art collection was to be exhibited at the National Gallery and the Metropolitan Museum. In my view, the collection was embarrassingly thin. So as I made my way down to the Waldorf that morning, everything fit into place. The Stein paintings, or the major ones that could be cleaned in time, would add extraordinary muscle to Nate's collection and justify the exhibition as more than an exercise in vanity.

I told Nate about the great Picassos and Grises, what this would add to his collection, how in short order they would be worth many times their current price, the names of the grandees he would be outmaneuvering, how hard and how long I had worked for this option that had but ten hours to run, and that I would exercise it in his behalf for a 10 percent commission and the right, when the paintings were cleaned and framed, to exhibit the collection. I offered to arrange all this and catalogue the collection. And how, if he decided later to sell any of it, which I hoped and thought he would not, I would advise him and handle it all at no further cost to him.

Nate said he didn't want to buy the collection for himself, but that he would do a joint venture with me. His plan was that we each put up half the money and share the profits. I said, "Nate, I don't have $3 million or I wouldn't be here." He countered with an offer to secure me financing from the Chase Manhattan Bank for my share. I thought that was amusing, since Chase was the Rockefellers' bank—we would be using their own money to screw them out of the Gertrude Stein collection. All Nate wanted me to do was put up 10 percent, of my own money. I was really uncomfortable with the idea of borrowing the balance of my share. I had no idea how long it would take to carefully restore the paintings and sell them. And I didn't think the deal was fair. I told Nate that I was contributing my option, my professional advice, and my services and clients in selling the paintings. He wouldn't budge, and time was running out. Better an unfair deal than no deal at all. So I agreed.

Then Nate dropped his bomb. "And of course I'll select what I want to keep." "Nate," I said, "don't put two hats on my head. Make me your agent, or make me your partner. Don't make me both. How will we allocate costs between the paintings? I know what I'm doing in this business and you don't. I'll outguess you. We'll end up not being friends. What if we do make a profit? I need it and you don't. What are you going to do with a few extra million dollars anyway? Why don't you listen to me and just buy the collection and keep it?" All to no avail. So I left the breakfast table and six o'clock came and went and the syndicate bought the collection and the rest is history. Until the last surviving member of the group, David Rockefeller, reads this, he won't know how close he came, but for the shortsightedness of one of his own customers, to losing the Gertrude Stein collection.

It was only recently that I learned why and how the syndicate had been organized, and how the price had been arrived at. During the summer of 1968, there had indeed apparently been an offer from Marlborough Fine Art, of London, of $6 million for the collection. This was during the period when Jacobs was having difficulty reaching Dupré. I could not understand at the time how anyone could produce an offer for a collection that had never been catalogued or photographed, nor, as far as I knew, viewed by anyone. Even the simple list Dupré had promised had not been forthcoming.

I had been understandably unenthusiastic about Marlborough's offer. I wanted to handle the collection myself. I was hoping it would remain intact, preferably in a museum, ideally the Museum of Modern Art. Marlborough, notwithstanding its power at the time, was the last gallery in the world to which I wanted it relinquished. Their principal, Frank Lloyd, had, after all, declared in an interview, to no one's surprise, that he was interested not in art but in money.

The offer, however, had served its purpose. It had given me the idea, which I passed on to Jacobs, of bluffing Dupré out of offering the collection to Sotheby's. I had suggested to Jacobs that he tell Dupré that he,

Jacobs, wanted to accept the Marlborough offer. If Dupré persisted with his plan to auction the collection, then he could buy out Jacobs's client's one-third share for $2 million. I had been sure that Dupré could or would not come up with the money. The bluff worked, and Dupré seemed to finally give up on the auction scheme.

It was at that point in the summer of 1968 that Rubina Stein suggested to Dupré that he contact William Lieberman, director of paintings and sculpture at the Museum of Modern Art. Lieberman took the idea to Bates Lowry, director of the museum, who in turn presented it to David Rockefeller, chairman of the museum's board of trustees.

Lowry's and Lieberman's enthusiasm galvanized Rockefeller into action. He knew that the museum itself did not have anything like the $7.5 million that, to the best of everyone's recollection, was Dupré's original asking price. Rockefeller undertook to arrange the financing, and to this end he organized a syndicate of trustees to make the purchase, into which he invited five other trustees—his brother Nelson, John Hay Whitney, William Paley, William A. M. Burden, and Gardner Cowles— and one friend, André Meyer, a trustee of the Metropolitan Museum. Cowles declined, but the others agreed to participate. Burden then changed his mind, and David Rockefeller decided to take Burden's one-sixth share in addition to his own. With this battery of heavyweights, the financing was in place. Two tasks remained: to negotiate a price with Dupré, and to figure out a formula to distribute the collection among the participants.

A firm price could not be established until someone familiar with Picasso and Juan Gris could view the collection. Dupré had by this time followed my suggestion and gotten the Picassos out of France and into the vault I had secured at the National Provincial Bank in London. There was no such rush to get the Juan Gris paintings out of the country, so they had remained in the Chase Bank vault in Paris.

In September 1968 Bill Lieberman, an authority on the work of both artists, was dispatched, first to Paris, then to London, to give his opinion on the collection. Lieberman was joined in London by Walter Bareiss, a scholarly and knowledgeable Modern trustee. They viewed the Picassos and went on together to Paris.

With no photographs, only his notes, Lieberman reported back enthusiastically to Bates Lowry. Lowry went to David Rockefeller with the recommendation that the Stein collection be acquired. Rockefeller agreed to proceed, and undertook to complete the financing. Lowry then walked into the office of Richard Koch, the museum's general counsel, and announced, "We're going to buy the Gertrude Stein collection!" The job of negotiating with Dupré was delegated to Koch.

Dupré was informed of the museum's serious interest, and in short order flew to New York and went straight to Koch's office. The $7.5 million asking price was quickly reduced to $7 million. Koch offered $5 million, which Dupré, having already turned down $6 million, refused. Dupré stayed in New York for several days as the negotiations continued. He then came down to $6.5 million, Koch countered with $6 million, Dupré refused, and Koch then offered $6.25 million on behalf of the syndicate. He stipulated that the offer was good for only twenty-four hours. It was at this point that Jacobs phoned and gave me, in light of all my efforts, the twenty-four-hour option to meet that price. My breakfast proposal to Nathan Cummings failed, and at six o'clock Jacobs phoned Bates Lowry to accept the $6.25 million offer. John Lockwood, the Rockefeller lawyer at Milbank, Tweed & Hadley, was assigned the job of drawing up the contract, which was duly signed for the syndicate by Richard Koch as agent, and by Dupré and Jacobs for the Stein heirs.

Nelson Rockefeller, Paley, Whitney, and Meyer each delivered a check for $1,042,167 to Koch. David Rockefeller's was for double the amount for his two shares. Koch opened a special checking account for the deposit, and the funds were remitted to the Stein lawyers.

The paintings were then shipped to New York. They had never been cleaned and, although in a basically good state, were probably too dirty to arouse the enthusiasm of four excited but busy amateurs. So they were given to Jean Volkmer, the Museum of Modern Art's conservator, for a rush cleaning job. Perhaps it is just as well that Volkmer, who used the wax lining and nonorganic varnishing techniques subsequently discredited, had little time to do more.

When the cleaning had been completed, the paintings were placed on the floor against the walls of the storeroom of the wing that had formerly housed the old Whitney Museum. Finally, on the afternoon of December 14, 1968, the syndicate members convened to view and divide up their prize. Everybody was present except for Bill Paley, who was sick and was represented by his wife Babe, and Jock Whitney, who was represented by Walter Thayer, another Modern trustee. The group was delighted with the Picassos and Grises, as well they should have been. They had just scored one of the great coups in art-market history.

It remained to figure out a way to divide up the paintings. David Rockefeller suggested a formula that had been used in the distribution of the estates of his parents and his aunt Lucy. Slips of paper bearing the numbers 1 to 6, representing the shares in the syndicate, would be placed in Richard Koch's hat. Each member would draw one slip, except for David Rockefeller, who would draw two. The numbers represented the rotating order of choice. Eugene Thaw, a dealer who had done business with David Rockefeller, had been recruited to allocate values among the paintings, to the total of the purchase price. The syndicate members were seated around a table in the clockwise order of their numbers. As they chose, their financial contribution was debited. Also present in addition to the syndicate members and their representatives were Bates Lowry; Irene Gordon, assistant to Richard Koch; and Alfred Barr, the éminence grise of the museum, never very enthusiastic about the project, sitting behind Nelson Rockefeller and coaching him. Bill Lieberman, who was not present, claims he provided Bates Lowry with tonsorial and sartorial counsel for the historic event. David Rockefeller provided the distribution plan, but he made one stipulation: since it was through the Modern that the collection had been procured and evaluated, Rockefeller insisted that six of the paintings be eventually donated or bequeathed to the museum. These paintings, deemed important to the museum collection by Bill Lieberman, had been predesignated before the meeting. The only member who balked at this provision was André Meyer, the only non-trustee, but he eventually fell into line. It was also stipulated that all purchasers agree to lend their acquisitions to the exhibition that was ultimately called *Four Americans in Paris,* the exhibition I had once dreamed of doing, and that opened in December 1970 to wide acclaim. To this there was no opposition at all from the syndicate members.

The financial arrangement proposed by David Rockefeller and accepted by the others was for each member to select works in the rotating order of the number, or, in the case of David Rockefeller, numbers, he had pulled out of Richard Koch's hat, up to the total amount, at the assigned values, of his contribution. After all the members had made their selections, the remaining works selected by no one were to be consigned to Eugene Thaw for private sale at prevailing market values. The proceeds of these sales, after deduction of Thaw's commissions, were to be credited to the syndicate members who had not used up their allocations, and after each had been compensated, either in art or in money, for his total contribution, the remaining proceeds were to be distributed to the members pro rata, reducing the amount of their commitment.

At the conclusion of the lottery, of the nine most important Picassos, David Rockefeller had snared three; Babe Paley, two; André Meyer, two; and Jock Whitney and Nelson Rockefeller, one each. The two most famous pictures, Picasso's *Young Girl with a Basket of Flowers,* 1905, and *Standing Female Nude,* 1906, went to the David Rockefellers and the William Paleys, respectively. It is interesting to note that each of these masterpieces would bring, in the marketplace thirty years later, some $100 million. When Babe Paley succeeded in nailing the *Standing Female Nude,* which was her first choice, she let out a whoop of joy and ran to the phone to tell Bill.

Of the six paintings that had been predesignated for the museum's collection, three belonged to the David Rockefellers, who had secured a total of eight of the Stein Picassos. The historic 1970 exhibition at the Modern, *Four Americans in Paris,* included all the works that could be found and borrowed not only from Gertrude Stein's collection but from those of the other three members of the expatriate family of modernist pioneers, Leo, Sarah, and Michael.

Although my role had been peripheral, most of what I had hoped for had come to pass. The collection was not kept entirely intact, but most of the major works will eventually end up in the Museum of Modern Art. The collection was beautifully catalogued and exhibited in its entirety, along with works owned by Gertrude with her brother Leo before they quarreled and split; works owned by both of them which had been sold over the years, and by her other brother, Michael, and his wife Sarah, mostly Matisses, which had long since been dispersed. The exhibition evoked the excitement of the dawn of the century.

The Gertrude Stein story was not quite over. Tevis Jacobs phoned me in February 1969 and placed in my hands an interesting project. Gertrude had died on July 27, 1946. Alice Toklas, the life tenant in her property, had lived on until March 7, 1967. The lawyers, Tevis Jacobs for

Daniel Stein and Herbert B. Sachs of Pittsburgh for Michael and Gabrielle, now needed an appraisal of the paintings in the estate, as of the date of Gertrude's death in 1946, to determine the tax liability on the differential between the value in 1946 and the price realized in 1968. I agreed to do the appraisal.

I was in school in 1946 and had no knowledge of the art market in those days. I had to find someone who was dealing in Picassos and Juan Grises in 1946. I thought of my old friend Justin Thannhauser, who was living in retirement in Palm Springs, California, and I went down to see him. Justin gave me the information I needed. Interestingly, in 1946 cubist Picassos were apparently unsalable, but the "blue" and "rose" periods were relatively expensive. Jacobs and Sachs insisted on receiving a bill for the appraisal, so I charged them $1,500, including the cost of my trip to Palm Springs, and they split the fee between the beneficiaries.

As my souvenir of the Gertrude Stein saga, I keep in my file a copy of her will and tax return, filed in Baltimore on December 24, 1947. It lists her as "residing at Paris, France"; the date her last domicile was established, "many years ago"; the place of death, "American Hospital, Paris, France"; the cause of death and length of last illness, "death following operation, after short illness"; the names and addresses of decedent's physicians, "Dr. Jean Patel, 6 Avenue de Messine, Paris VIII, France," and "Dr. Jean Ravina, 58 boulevard Lannes, Paris 16, France"; date of birth, "February 3, 1874," and place of birth, "Allegheny, Pennsylvania"; occupation, "authoress"; business address, "5 rue Christine, Paris, France"; marital status, "single"; and as heirs, next of kin, devisees, and legatees, "Allen Daniel Stein, legatee," relationship, "nephew," address, "34 Boulevard Hausman [sic], Paris, France," and "Alice B. Toklas," "intimate friend," "5 rue Christine, Paris, France." "Edgar Allan Poe," "Administrator."

In memoriam,
Allen Wardwell,
ancien combattant, blessé de guerre

and for Francis Haskell,
beloved chronicler of what went before

Index

Page numbers in italics refer to illustrations.

abstract expressionism, 99, *168*
Albers, Josef, 239
Albright, Ivan, 49–56, 92, 192; *The Picture of Dorian Gray,* 49–50, 92; *Portrait of Mary Block,* 52–3, 256, *256; Self-portrait in Georgia, 53; That Which I Should Have Done I Did Not Do (The Door),* 55
Alexander, Jane, 243–6
Alsdorf, Marilyn and James, 56, 187, 255, 262–4
Amos, Benjamin F., 74, 78
Anderson, Bernard, 82, 85, 86
Anderson, Maxwell, 140
Andre, Carl, 195
Annenberg, Walter, 84, 87
architecture: Chicago, 39–40, *40,* 41–2, *42,* 43–5, *45, 46,* 150–1; museum, 142–51; New York, 41–5, 54, 62–3, *63,* 64, 116
Arp, Jean, and Marguerite Hagenbach, 186–7
Arp, Marguerite Hagenbach, 186–7
Art Institute of Chicago, 40, 43, 49, 51, 53, 55–7, 92, 105, 106, 108, 111, 126, 138, 154, 156–60, 163–5, 170–1, 177, 192, 235, 239, 247, 248, 252, 290; Block era, 252–73
Arts Club, 52, 60, 102
Austin, A. Everett, Jr., 140–1, *142*

Bacon, Francis, 56–7, 102; *Figure with Meat,* 57; *Study for Portrait VI,* 57, *59*
Bahadori, Karim Pasha, 218–24
Baldessari, John, 63
Barnes, Albert, 3, 70–91; collection and foundation, 70–91, 246; and Argyrol, 71; Ker-Feal, 71, 81, 84
Barr, Alfred, 95, 99, 191, 294
Basquiat, Jean-Michel, 120
Bauhaus, 258–9

Beatty, Frances, 227, 228
Beckmann, Max, 102, 131–6, 144, 156, 194, 287; *The Argonauts,* 194; *The Bark,* 287–8; *The Beginning,* 135–6; *Self-portrait with Cigarette,* 133 and *n., 134; Max Beckmann in Exile* (exhibition), 144
Beckmann, Mathilde "Quappi," 194
Bellamy, Richard, 99, 127, 227
Bellmer, Hans, 181
Berenson, Bernard, 27, 67, 127, 160, 265
Berggruen, Heinz, 98, 122
Bergman, Lindy and Edwin, 255
Bergot, François, 15
Bernhard, Dorothy and Richard, 134
Beuys, Joseph, 63
Blair, William McCormick, 258, 260, 261
Block, Joseph and Lucille, 249, 252
Block, Mary and Leigh, 4, 40, 52–3, 56, 97, 105, 138, 158, 172, 192, 193, 247–53, *253,* 254–73; collection, 247–73
Blunt, Sir Anthony, 67–9
Bontecou, Lee, 62
Brancusi, Constantin, 102, 140, 191
Braque, Georges, 5, 102, 191, 193
Brauner, Jacqueline, 179–83
Brauner, Victor and Jacqueline, 6, 57, 179, *179,* 180–3, 276; *The Door, 7, 180; Victor Victorach Throws Away the Heart of Guilt, 6*
Brausen, Erica, 57
Breton, André, 6, 101, 190
Brooklyn Museum, 109, 265; *Sensation* exhibition (1999), 109–10
Brown, J. Carter, 87–8, 154–8, 164
Bute, John, collection of, 196–204

Calder, Alexander, 168
Canning, Sandra, 283, 285

Caravaggio, III, II2, 140
Carracci, Annibale, 14, 24
Carracci, Lodovico, 14, 18, 48
Cassatt, Mary, 127, 175, 275
Castelli, Leo, 54–5, 62–3, 99, 227
Cézanne, Paul, 71, 73, 81, 284, 285
Chagall, Marc, 104, 188
Chalmers, Lawrence, 157–8, 262–4
Charles I, King of England, II8–20, 128, 164
Chicago, 36, 39–65, 92–3, 127, 157–60,
    168–74, 180, 188, 192, 286–7; architecture,
    39–40, *40,* 41–2, *42,* 43–5, *45, 46,* 150–1;
    Block collection, 247–73; Neumann
    collection, 92–106; 1968 Democratic
    National Convention, 234–9; press,
    229–39; School, 48–62; *see also specific
    museums*
Chicago Sun Times, 231, *232,* 233–6
Chicago Tribune, 231, 233
Christiansen, Keith, 10, 25–6, 268
Christie's, 63, 104, IIO, II8, 125, 141, 196, 204,
    214, 220–2
Clark, Timothy, 129
Cleveland Museum, 108, 153, 160, 163, 170,
    260
Clifford, Timothy, 122, 153, *153, 154*
Clinton, Hillary and President Bill, 242–6
Cohen, George, 51, 56, 60; *Anybody's Self-
    portrait,* 60
Conger, Clement, 32, 202–3
Connaught Hotel, 282, 285
contemporary art, II4–17, 142
Cooper, Paula, 62
Cordier, Daniel, 104
Cornell, Joseph, 55, 57–8, 134–6, 140, 170,
    180, 194, 229, 275; *L'Égypte de Mlle. Cléo
    de Mérode...,* 58, *60*
Cosway, Maria, 31–2
Crichton-Stuart, Anthony, 196, 204
Cruikshank, Isaac, *The Meat Market
    Evacuated, or The Sans-culottes in
    Possession,* 47–8, *51*
Culberg, Maurice, 52
Cummings, Nathan, 56, 178, 255, 286–8, *288,*
    289–93; collection, 286–93
Cunningham, Charles, 157, 261–2
Curtis, Tony, 194

Daley, Richard J., 235–9
Dalí, Salvador and Gala, 173, 190, 194,
    276; *The Accomodations of Desire,* 173,
    173
Dallas Museum, 140

d'Angeli, Filippo (Filippo Napolitano), 12
da Vinci, Leonardo, 25; Leicester Codex, 125,
    213
Davis, Richard, 156–7
de Chavannes, Puvis, 48
de Chirico, Giorgio, 5, 6
Degas, Edgar, 70
de Groot, Adelaide Milton, collection, 131–6,
    165
de Gunzbourg, Alain, 192–3
de Kooning, Elaine, 189
de Kooning, Willem, 98, 206; *Woman III,*
    222, *223*
Delacroix, Eugène, 128
De Maria, Walter, 141, 146
de Mazia, Violette, 74–7, 83
Democratic National Convention (1968),
    234–9
Dennison, Lisa, 144, 145–6
Des Moines Art Museum, 139–40
Detroit Institute of Arts, 109, 161
d'Harnoncourt, Anne, 75
Dillon, Douglas, 131
Domenichino, 21–30; *Landscape with Shrine
    and Figures,* 21–6, *26,* 27–30
Domínguez, Oscar, 5–6, 18, 180
Drew-Bear, Lotte, 170, 174, 239
Driskell, David, 76, 83
Dubuffet, Jean, 52, 60–1, 98, 101–4; *The
    Automobile, Flower of Industry,* 104;
    Beards, 103, 104; *The Fiat with Bumpers,*
    103–4; *Paris Circus,* 103, 104
Dughet, Gaspard, 66, 69
Duke, Robin, 217–18
Dupré, Bernard, 278–93
Duquesne Club, 250
Duveen, Lord, 35, II7, 127, 265

Eddy, Arthur Jerome, 259
Effront, Nadine, 5–6
Egan, Charles, 99, 227
Elgin, Eleventh Earl of, II8, 121–2
Ernst, Max, 6, 102, 140, *169,* 177, 180, 187,
    189, 194, 276; *Henry IV, la lionne de Belfort
    . . . ,* 177; *Paysage aux germes de blé,* 276–7;
    Vox Angelica, 170–2, *172*

Falk, Toby, 206–10
fashion, 109–10, 146
Feigen, Richard, *226*
Feigen, Richard L. & Co., 47; *Masterpieces of
    20th Century German Art,* 47; Ray
    Johnson memorial exhibition, 229

Feigen (Richard) Gallery, 141 Greene Street, New York, 62–3, 63, 64, 239
Feigen Inc., Chicago, 1995 Gregory Green episode, 229–31, 232, 233–4
Findlay, Michael, 63
Fogg Museum, Cambridge, 127–9, 158, 207, 265–7
Forbes, Edward Waldo, 266
Ford, Gerald, 34, 198, 219
Forlani Tempesta, Anna, 17
Fra Angelico, 10; *Joseph*, 10, 11
Freedberg, Sydney, 128, 129, 130, 158, 160
Freudenheim, Tom, 75, 84
Frick, Henry Clay, 163
Frick, Sidney, 78
Frick Collection, New York, 162–3
Fried, Michael, 129
Frumkin, Allan, 57, 133
Fuller, Buckminster, 150

Gardner, Isabella Stewart, 127
Geffen, David, 222
Gehry, Frank, Guggenheim Bilbao, 142–8, 148, 149–51
Geldzahler, Henry, 133–6
Genga, Girolamo, 25–8; *Adoration of the Child*, 25–7, 28
Gentile da Fabriano, 268; Strozzi altarpiece, 10; Jarves *Madonna and Child*, 268
Gentileschi, Artemisia, 111–13, 175
Gentileschi, Orazio, 111–13, 119–21, 140, 165–6, 175; *The Finding of Moses*, 119–20, 120, 121, 165, 166; *The Penitent Magdalene*, 118–19, 119, 120, 122
German expressionism, 47–52, 56, 168
Getty (J. Paul) Museum, Los Angeles, 69, 125, 139, 165
Giacometti, Alberto, 95, 96, 98, 102
Glackens, William, 71
Glanton, Richard, 78–80, 80, 81–91
Glueck, Grace, 64, 65, 85, 86
Goelet, John, 207–10
Goelet *Gulistan*, 207–10, 215, 222
Goldberg, Arthur, 251
Golub, Leon, 56, 61
Gordon, Eleanore and Milton, 135–6
Gorky, Arshile, 58, 168, 170, 171, 177; *Days, Etc.*, 170; *Love of a New Gun*, 170, 171; *The Plough and the Song*, 135–6
Grassi, Marco, 29, 203
Green, Gregory, 230–4; *10,000 Doses*, 230, 230, 231–4
Greenberg, Clement, 129
Green Gallery, New York, 99

Gris, Juan, 191, 193; in Stein collection, 276–96
Grosz, George, 47; *The Love-sick One*, 47, 49
Guercino, 14, 18
Gudeman, Eduard, 251
Guggenheim Museum, 142–51; Berlin, 143–6; Bilbao, 142–8, 148, 149–51; New York, 95, 142–6, 148, 149, 184; SoHo, 144
Gunzbourg, Alain de, 192–3

Hammer, Armand, 125
Harris, Niesen, 255
Harvard University, 108, 127–8, 129–31, 207–9, 217, 221, 264–6
Haskell, Francis, 128
Helms, Jesse, 155, 231, 241–6
Hill, Walter, 48
Hollein, Hans, 54, 64, 148, 150
Homer, Winslow, 108, 175, 275
Hôtel Pont-Royal, 98, 101, 185–9
Houghton, Arthur A. and Nina, 207–24
Houghton *Shahnameh*, 207–8, 208, 209–24
Hoveyda, Fereydoun, 207–8, 216–17, 220
Hoving, Thomas, 131–2, 132, 133–6, 137, 215
Hughes, Robert, 144
Hugnet, Georges, 276–7

impressionism, 35–8, 108, 114, 117, 127, 137, 165–6
Indiana, Robert, 44
Iran, Empress and Shah of, 206, 217, 220
Iroquois war club, 121, 121, 122
Israel Museum, Jerusalem, 11
I Tatti, villa, 265

Jabach, Evrard, 21, 29
Jackstas, Alfred, 264, 271–2
Jacobs, Richard, 143
Jacobs, Tevis, 280–96
Jaffe, Irma, 203, 204
Japan, 114, 125, 165, 205–6, 241, 247, 283
Jarves, James Jackson, collection of, 267–73
Jefferson, Thomas, 20, 31–4, 201
Joachim, Harold, 138, 158, 260
Johns, Jasper, 44, 59, 60, 62, 225, 245; *Target with Plaster Casts*, 99
Johnson, Ray, 180, 225–6, 226, 227–30; *James Dean*, 228

Kahn, Louis, 147
Kahnweiler, Daniel-Henri, 191–3, 278
Kandinsky, Nina, 183
Kandinsky, Wassily, 148, 183, 259
Kantor, Lawrence, 10

Karp, Ivan, 62–3, 99
Keck, Caroline and Sheldon, 23, 265–7, 271
Kelly, Ellsworth, 44, 245
Kennedy, John F., 250–2
Kiefer, Anselm, 52
Kienholz, Edward, 59–60
Kimbell Art Museum, Fort Worth, 14, 88, 89,
    140, 147, 153, 166–7
Kinz, Lance, 229–34
Kirchner, Ernst Ludwig, 47; *Dancing
    Woman,* 47, *50*; *Masked Ball,* 47, *48*
Klee, Paul, 148, 259
Kleihues, Josef, 151
Kline, Franz, 51
Koch, Richard, 293, 294
Kramarsky, Werner, 125
Krasner, Lee, 176, 189, 190
Kreeger, Carmen and David Lloyd, 41, 287
Krens, Thomas, 141–3, *143,* 144–6
Krugier, Jan, 100
Kuh, Katherine, 157, 258–9
Kupka, Eugénie, 183–6
Kupka, Frantisek, 183–6; *Localisation de
    mobiles graphiques,* 184, 186; *Planes by
    Colors, Large Nude,* 184, *185,* 186

Lackner, Stephen, 287
Lambert, Phyllis Bronfman, 41
Lane, Jack, 140
Lee, Katherine, 160
Lefebvre-Foinet, Maurice, 181–6, 191
Léger, Fernand, 102, 191, 193
Levin, Jack, 132
Levin, Janice and Phillip, 35–8
Levy, Julien, 4, 58, 168–9, *169,* 170–4, 189,
    190; *Memoir of an Art Gallery,* 174
Levy, Richard and Susan, 70, 72
Lichtenstein, Roy, 225; *Girl with a Hair
    Ribbon,* 205; *Live Ammo,* 99
Lieberman, William, 61, 258, 289, 292–4
Lincoln University, 70–91
Lindsay, John, 44, 45, 64, 65
Lloyd, Frank, 131, 133, 258, 291
Loeb (Pierre) Gallery, Paris, 94–5
Los Angeles County Museum, 76, 77, 82,
    104, 161, 180, 214
Louvre, Paris, 14, 16, 20, 21, 29, 30, 163, 164
Lowry, Bates, 289, 292–4
Lowry, Glenn, 111, 146
Ludington, Wright, 168, 173

MacNab, Alan, 157
Magritte, René, 205, 276
Mahboubian, 218, 219–20, 222

Mahon, Sir Denis, 11, 17, 24, 29–30
Mandle, Roger, 75, 84–8, 161–2
Manet, Edouard, *The Mocking of Christ,* 272,
    273
Mantegna, Andrea, *Adoration of the Magi,*
    125
Mapplethorpe, Robert, 241
Maremont, Adele and Arnold, 56, 255
Marlborough Fine Art, London, 131, 286,
    291–2
Marx, Florene and Samuel, 56, 255, 258
Massachusetts Museum of Contemporary
    Art, North Adams, 142
Masson, André, 181; *Antilles,* 177
Matthaei, Konrad, 36–8
Matisse, Henri, 71, 73, 76, 81, 102, 274, 279,
    284, 295; *La Danse,* 89; *Femme au
    Chapeau,* 89; *The Young Sailor (II),* 258
Matta, 57, 58, 177–82, 194, 276; *The Earth Is
    a Man,* 177, *178*
Max Beckmann in Exile (1996, SoHo
    Guggenheim), 144
Maxon, John, 138, 157–9, *159,* 259–64, 272
May, Morton D. "Buster," 288
Meidner, Ludwig, 56, *58*
Melikian, Souren, 205, 222
Mellon, Paul, 154–6, 164, 213, 257
Mendieta, Ana, 195
Menil Collection, Houston, 147
Metropolitan Museum of Art, New York, 10,
    17–19, 26, 56, 75–7, 84, 109–10, *110,* 111–13,
    124, 126, 137, 138, 154, 159, 160, 163–5, 207,
    210–11, 215–20, 224, 255, 258, 278, 282, 289,
    290, 292; Gentileschi exhibition (2002),
    111–13; Hoving regime, 131–6, 137, 215
Meyer, André, 289, 292–5
Michelangelo, 145
Mies van der Rohe, 40, 41, 148, 258; Seagram
    Building, 148, 149
Millken, Michael, 116, 122–4
Minneapolis Institute of Arts, 57, 156–7
Miró, Joan, 23, *93,* 98, 100–102, 168, 172, 187,
    259, 276
Moholy-Nagy, Laszlo, 258, 259
Monaco, Lorenzo, 10
Mondrian, Piet, 140
Monet, Claude, 35–8, 56, 157, 165, 257; *The
    Artist's Garden at Argenteuil,* 35–6, *36,*
    37–8; *Matinée sur la Seine,* 157
Montebello, Philippe de, 112, 159, 160
Mosby, Dewey, 75
Muller, Robert, after John Trumbull, *General
    George Washington at the Battle of Trenton,*
    196–8, *198,* 199–204

Museum of Contemporary Art, Chicago,
40–2, *42*, 57, 150–1
Museum of Contemporary Art, Tehran, 221,
222
Museum of Fine Arts, Boston, 107–8, 126,
141, 154, 163–5, 255
Museum of Modern Art, New York, 60, 61,
64, 75, 95, 98, 99, 100, 104, 111, 143, 186,
258, 267, 284, 291–2; *Four Americans in
Paris* (1970), 294, 295; Stein collection
and, 188–95
museums, 107–67; administration, 113,
129–46, 151–67; architecture, 142–51;
"blockbusters," 137, 158; corporatization
of, 136–51; entertainment industry and,
109–13, 146; Europe emulated by, 126–8;
old masters and, 117–26, 127; *see also
specific museums*

National Endowment for the Arts (NEA),
240–6; Alexander chairmanship, 243–6
National Gallery, London, 119–20, 122, 155,
163, 164
National Gallery, Washington, D.C., 35, 75,
84, 87–9, 105, 134, 153, 154–6, 158, 164, 170,
194, 219, 290
National Museums of Scotland, 122, 153, 163,
164
National Portrait Gallery, Washington, D.C.,
197, 202–3
neoexpressionism, 52, 55
Neumann, Hubert, 93, 95–100, 105, 106
Neumann, Rose and Mort, 4, 56, 92–3, *93,
94, 94*, 95–106, 188, 255; collection, 92–106
Newman, Barnett, 44; *Lace Curtain for
Mayor Daley,* 238, 239
Newman, Muriel Kallis, 255
New Orleans Museum, 140
New York, 39–65, 113; architecture, 41–5, 54,
62–3, *63*, 64, 116; art market, 113–15;
SoHo, 39, 62–4, 116, 144; *see also specific
museums*
New York Times, 64, 65, 84, 87, 111, 136, 150,
210, 239, 240, 243, 277, 282
Nochlin, Linda, "Why Have There Been No
Great Women Artists?," 175
Nolde, Emil, 56, 172; *Three Russians,* 56
Norton, Charles Eliot, 127

O'Keeffe, Georgia, 175
Oldenburg, Claes, 59–61, 62, 98, 99–100,
149, 150, 225, 236–9; Ray Gun Theater, 62;
Gayety, 59; *Soft Shuttlecock,* 146, 149; *The
Street,* 61

old masters, 117–26, 127
Onians collection, 8–11

Paley, William and Barbara "Babe," 289–95
Parke-Bernet, 124, 132
Parsons, Betty, 227
Pennsylvania Academy of the Fine Arts,
197
Penrose, Roland, 105, 190
Persian art, 205–24
Petrioli Tofani, Anna Maria, 27
Petryn, Andrew, 270–1
Philadelphia Museum of Art, 10, 71, 75, 84,
88, 89, 126, 154, 155
Phillips Collection, Washington, D.C., 140
Piano, Renzo, 147
Picabia, Francis, 276, 279, 285
Picasso, Pablo, 3, 71, 73, *94*, 95–99, 102, 191,
193, 206; *The Architect's Table,* 284; *Les
Demoiselles d'Avignon,* 193, 284; *Femme
nue assise (Seated Nude),* 95, *96*, 106; *Nude
with Drapery,* 284; *Standing Female Nude,*
281, 284, 295; in Stein collection, 275–96;
Yo Picasso, 125; *Young Girl with a Basket of
Flowers,* 281, 284, 295
Picón, Carlos, 138
Pillsbury, Edmund P., 153–5, *155*, 166
Poe, Edgar Allan, Jr., 279–80, 296
Pollaiuolo, Antonio, 268
Pollock, Jackson, 190, 206
Pontormo, *Halberdier,* 125
Pop art, 60–1, 228
Pope-Hennessy, Sir John, 25–6, 159–60, *161*
Potts, Timothy, 167
Poussin, Nicolas, 8–20, 66–9, 156; *Capture of
Jerusalem by Titus,* 10–11; *The Death of the
Virgin,* 15, 19; *The Destruction and Sack of
the Temple of Jerusalem,* 9, 10–12;
Landscape with a Calm, 66–7, *67*, 68–9;
Landscape with a Storm, 66, *68*; "Marino"
drawings, 15, 16, 19; *Recumbent Nude, 19;
Saint Denis Crowned by an Angel,* 15–20,
22; *Saint Denis Frightening His
Executioners with His Head,* 12–13, *13*,
14–20, 29
Poussin Before Rome (1994 exhibition), 15–20
Prado, Madrid, 163, 164
press, power of the, 225–46
Pritzker, Jay, 151
Puvis de Chavannes, Pierre, *Euterpe,* 48

Rauschenberg, Robert, 44, 62, 99, 146, 225,
245, 259; *Factum 2,* 99
Ray, Julie, 190, 193–4

Ray, Man and Julie, 170, 179, 183, 190–4, 276; *A l'heure de l'observatoire: Les Amoureux,* 193

Rembrandt van Rijn, 137, 205–6; *Aristotle Contemplating the Bust of Homer,* 124, 125, 282; *Head of an Old Man,* 211–12, *212; Portrait of a Girl,* 125, 212–14; Research Project, 206

Renoir, Pierre-Auguste, 35–8, 71, 73; *Monet Painting in His Garden at Argenteuil,* 35, 37; *Le Moulin de la Galette,* 125; *Young Girls and a Lad in a Landscape,* 36–8

Rewald, John, 35

Reynolds, Susan, 229, 231

Rich, Andrea, 161

Rich, Daniel Catton, 157, 258

Richard J. Daley (1968 exhibition), 63, 237–9

Riley, Bridget, 148

Roché, Henri-Pierre, 95

Rockefeller, David, 289–95

Rockefeller, Nelson, 289–95

Rockwell, Norman, 146

Rogers, Malcolm, 107–8

Rosebery, Earl and Countess of, 197–202

Rosenberg, Harold, 177

Rosenberg, Pierre, 16, 17, 19

Rosenquist, James, 44, 59, 60, 62, 99, 143–6, 149, 176, 225, 245; *F-III,* 143; *The Swimmer in the Economist,* 143–5, *144–5,* 146

Rosenwald, Julius, 78

Ross, David, 140

Rothko, Mark, 133, 258

Rothschild, Edmond de, 207, 210, 218

Rothschild, Lord, 11, 218

Rousseau, Henri, 179, 182, 190–1, 193; *Exotic Landscape,* 132; *Monkeys in the Virgin Forest,* 131–3, *133; Tropical Landscape: An American Indian Struggling with an Ape,* 257, *257*

Rousseau, Theodore, 131–6

Rubin, William, 177

Saatchi, Charles, 110

Sabarsky, Serge, 133

Sachs, Paul, 127–9, *130,* 264–6

Sadek, Marvin, 197, 202

Sage, Kay, 168, 189

Sahlins, Bernard, 43

St. Louis Museum, 109, 112, 264, 267

Sale, Deborah, 243–6

Salz, Sam, 4, 35–6, 38

San Diego Museum, 241

San Francisco Museum of Modern Art, 140

Schnabel, Julian, 52

Schniewind, Carl, 138, 158, 260

Scull, Ethel and Robert, 99, 115, 141, 146, 227

Seattle Museum, 140

Second City, 43–4, 104

Serrano, Andres, 241

Seurat, Georges, 71, 73, 76, 77; *Channel of Gravelines, Grand Fort-Philippe,* 122, *123*

Seymour, Charles, Jr., 268–71

Shapiro, Jory and Joseph, 40, 56, 57, 177, 255

Shapiro, Michael, 161

Shchukin, Sergei, 284

Shestack, Alan, 263–4

Simon, Norton, 3, 132

Sizer, Theodore, 201, 203, 204

Skull and Bones, 269–70

Smith, Tony, 150

SoHo, New York, 39, 62–4, 116; Guggenheim, 144

Solinger, David, 64–5

Sotheby's, 8, 9, 10, 66–9, 106, 119, 125, 174, 212, 222, 280–1, 285, 291

Spear, Richard, 24, 27–9

Spero, Nancy, 61

Speyer, James, 172

Stein, Allen, 277–8, 296

Stein, Daniel, 277, 280–1, 286, 296

Stein, Gabrielle, 278, 296

Stein, Gertrude, 3, 141, 274–96; collection and estate, 274–96; *Four Saints in Three Acts,* 274–5; 27 rue de Fleurus, 275–7; 5 rue Christine, 275–8

Stein, Leo, 275, 277, 284, 285, 295

Stein, Michael, 274, 277, 278, 295–6

Stein, Rubina, 278–9, 283–6, 292

Stein, Sarah, 274, 277, 295

Steinberg, Saul and Gayfryd, 212–14

Strehlke, Carl, 10

Stevens, Roger, 41

Stuart, Gilbert, 197–203

Stuckey, Charles, 56

Sudarkasa, Niara, 75, 79, 83–8, 90–1

Sullivan, Louis, 39, 149, 248; Chicago Stock Exchange, 39, *46;* Garrick Theater, 39, 43, 44, *45*

surrealism, 5–6, 56–8, 101, 168–74, 176–82, 188, 189, 276

Sutton, Peter, 141

Sweeney, James Johnson, 95, 191

Sweerts, Michiel, *Plague in an Ancient City,* 214, *214*

Tamayo, Olga, 187–9
Tamayo, Rufino, 187
Tanguy, Yves, 168, 177, 188, 189
Tanning, Dorothea, 176, 189
Tassi, Agostino, 112
Täuber-Arp, Sophie, 176
Tchelitchew, Pavel, 170, 276
Testa, Pietro, 10, 11
Thannhauser, Justin, 296
Thaw, Eugene, 121, 122, 294–5
Thomson, Virgil, 275, 278–9
Thuillier, Jacques, 10–19
Time magazine, 125, 239
Tinguely, Jean, 239
Tinterow, Gary, 75, 76
Toklas, Alice, 2, 274–96
Tokyo Museum of Contemporary Art, 205
Toledo Museum of Art, 108, 161–2, 164
Trumbull, John, 31–4, 201–4; *General George Washington at the Battle of Trenton*, 196, 199, *200*, 201–4; *Portrait of Thomas Jefferson*, 31–3, *33*, 34
Twombly, Cy, 99; *View*, 99

Uffizi, Florence, 14, 17, 27, 163
U.S. Court of Appeals, Chicago, 39–40, *40*, 41

Valentin, Curt, 99
van Bruggen, Coosje, 149
van Gogh, Vincent, 175; *Dr. Gachet*, 125; *Irises*, 125; *The Olive Pickers*, 134, *135*; *Self-Portrait with Bandaged Ear*, 247, *249*, 258; *The Town Hall of Auvers on Bastille Day*, 247, *250*, 258
van Zant, Esther, 76, 77, 80, 81
Varnedoe, Kirk, 75
Velázquez, Diego, *Juan de Pareja*, 125
Versace, Gianni, 109, 110

Vietnam War, 206, 227, 234–7, 261
Volkmer, Jean, 293

Wadsworth Atheneum, Hartford, 35, 131, 140–1, 261
Walker, Cuyler, 79, 83, 90
Walker, John, 158, 164
Walker Art Center, Minneapolis, 241
Walters, Barbara, 217–18
Ward, Eleanor, 227
Wardwell, Allen, 260–2
Warhol, Andy, 98, 120, 208, 225
Washington Post, 246
Weber, Max, 191
Weitzner, Julius, 25
Welch, Stuart Cary, 207–10, 222
White House, 197–9, 203, 235
Whitney, John Hay "Jock," 289, 292–5
Whitney Museum of Art, New York, 64, 140, 147, 259, 293
Wilder, Thornton, 278, 279
Williams, Franklin, 70–4, *74*, 75–91
Wilson, Peter, 281, 286
Wilson, Robert, 275
Winston, Donald, 156, 157
Wittenborn, George, 100–101
women, artists', 175–95
Wood, Grant, 139
Wood, James, 56, 158, 264
Wright, Frank Lloyd, 63, 148, 149
Wye Plantation, 210, 213, 214, 222

Yale Center for British Art, 155
Yale University, 199–201, 245, 254, 267–70, 278; library, 278
Yale University Art Gallery, 170, 199–204, 263–4, 267; Jarves collection, 267–73

Zeisler, Claire, 255, 259